Angela Keane addresses the work of five women writers of the 1790s and its problematic relationship with the canon of Romantic literature. Refining arguments that women's writing has been overlooked, Keane examines the more complex underpinnings and exclusionary effects of the English national literary tradition. The book explores the negotiations of literate, middle-class women such as Hannah More, Mary Wollstonecraft, Charlotte Smith, Helen Maria Williams and Ann Radcliffe with emergent ideas of national literary representation. As women were cast into the feminine, maternal role in Romantic national discourse, women like these who defined themselves in other terms found themselves exiled – sometimes literally – from the nation. These wandering women did not rest easily in the family-romance of Romantic nationalism nor could they be reconciled with the models of literary authorship that emerged in the 1790s.

ANGELA KEANE is Lecturer in English Literature at the University of Sheffield. She is co-editor, with Avril Horner of *Body Matters: Feminism, Textuality, Corporeality* (1999) and the author of many articles on women and Romanticism.

CAMBRIDGE STUDIES IN ROMANTICISM 44

WOMEN WRITERS AND THE ENGLISH
NATION IN THE 1790s

This series aims to foster the best new work in one of the most challenging fields within English literary studies. From the early 1780s to the early 1830s a formidable array of talented men and women took to literary composition, not just in poetry, which some of them famously transformed, but in many modes of writing. The expansion of publishing created new opportunities for writers, and the political stakes of what they wrote were raised again by what Wordsworth called those 'great national events' that were 'almost daily taking place': the French Revolution, the Napoleonic and American wars, urbanisation, industrialisation, religious revival, an expanded empire abroad and the reform movement at home. This was an enormous ambition, even when it pretended otherwise. The relations between science, philosophy, religion and literature were reworked in texts such as *Frankenstein* and *Biographia Literaria*; gender relations in *A Vindication of the Rights of Woman* and *Don Juan*; journalism by Cobbett and Hazlitt; poetic form, content and style by the Lake School and the Cockney School. Outside Shakespeare studies, probably no body of writing has produced such a wealth of response or done so much to shape the responses of modern criticism. This indeed is the period that saw the emergence of those notions of 'literature' and of literary history, especially national literary history, on which modern scholarship in English has been founded.

The categories produced by Romanticism have also been challenged by recent historicist arguments. The task of the series is to engage both with a challenging corpus of Romantic writings and with the changing field of criticism they have helped to shape. As with other literary series published by Cambridge, this one will represent the work of both younger and more established scholars, on either side of the Atlantic and elsewhere.

For a complete list of titles published see end of book.

WOMEN WRITERS AND THE ENGLISH NATION IN THE 1790s

Romantic Belongings

ANGELA KEANE

CAMBRIDGE
UNIVERSITY PRESS

PUBLISHED BY THE PRESS SYNDICATE OF THE UNIVERSITY OF CAMBRIDGE
The Pitt Building, Trumpington Street, Cambridge, United Kingdom

CAMBRIDGE UNIVERSITY PRESS
The Edinburgh Building, Cambridge CB2 2RU, UK   www.cup.cam.ac.uk
40 West 20th Street, New York, NY 10011–4211, USA   www.cup.org
10 Stamford Road, Oakleigh, Melbourne 3166, Australia
Ruiz de Alarcón 13, 28014 Madrid, Spain

© Angela Keane 2000

First published 2000

Printed in the United Kingdom at the University Press, Cambridge

Typeset in Baskerville 11/12.5pt [VN]

A catalogue record for this book is available from the British Library

Library of Congress Cataloguing in Publication data
Keane, Angela.
Women writers and the English nation in the 1790s: romantic belongings / Angela Keane.
p.   cm. – (Cambridge studies in Romanticism)
Includes bibliographical references and index.
ISBN 0 521 77342 3 (hardback)
1. English literature – Women authors – History and criticism.   2. English literature – 18th
century – History and criticism.   3. Women and literature – England – History – 18th
century.   4. Romanticism – England – History – 18th century.   5. Politics and literature –
England – History – 18th century.   6. Nationalism in literature.   I. Title.   II. Series.

PR448.W65 K43 2001
820.9'9287'09033 – dc21   00-028929

ISBN 0 521 77342 3 hardback

Contents

In memory of Katie Keane

Acknowledgements

I would like to thank Marilyn Butler, Josie Dixon and Paul Hamilton for encouraging me to develop this book from my doctoral thesis. Thanks also to those who helped me through my doctoral studies at Leeds University, including Patricia Badir, Danielle Fuller, John McLeod, Andrew Mousley, Mark Robson, Jenny Rogers, Matthew Pateman and Susan Spearey. At Salford University I had the good fortune to work with a group of colleagues whose sense of humour and generosity exceeds the call of duty, and who all provided me with time and with enthusiasm whenever my own lagged. Particular thanks in the latter respect are due to Peter Buse, Kirsten Daly, Scott McCracken, Antony Rowland and Nuria Triana-Toribio. For guiding me through the final stages, thanks to Sara Adhikari and Linda Bree. For distracting me through the final stages, thanks to Eddie Jones. My extensive and under-appreciated family has been looking forward to this book's completion for a long time and I would like to thank them for bearing with me. My biggest debt is to Vivien Jones and John Whale, who have supported me in innumerable ways since I was an undergraduate student and have always gracefully maintained the illusion that they were learning from me too.

Earlier versions of Chapter Two and Chapter Four appeared as 'Resisting Arrest'. The National Constitution of Gothic and Picturesque in Radcliffe's Romances', *News from Nowhere: Theory and Politics of Romanticism*, eds. Tony Pinkney, Keith Hanley and Fred Botting (1995), 96–120 and 'Helen Maria Williams's *Letters From France*: A National Romance', *Prose Studies: History, Theory, Criticism* (December 1992), 271–294.

CHAPTER I

Introduction: Romantic belongings

The subjects of this book, five English women writers of the 1790s, are no longer the unrepresented underside of the English Romantic canon, as they undoubtedly were even ten years ago. Critical studies of Ann Radcliffe and Mary Wollstonecraft, in particular, have proliferated in the last decade. The poetry of Charlotte Smith, if not her prose fiction, is now relatively well known due to the services of Stuart Curran and others who have seen fit to edit and analyse the work which was barely noticed for two hundred years.[1] The prose of Helen Maria Williams and Hannah More has been less researched, although these writers too are coming into focus: the former principally for her poetry, the latter to illustrate that not all women writers of the period were feminists, or that not all women writers who have been appropriated by feminism were republicans or even democrats.

If they are no longer unrepresented, they have not by any means been deemed 'representative': neither of the literary movement we now nervously call Romanticism, nor of the 'Romantic Englishness' which until the late 1970s was largely associated, in the academy as well as popularly, with Wordsworth and Nature. Since then, contributions by cultural historians, postcolonialists and feminists have ensured that to study 'English' anywhere in the world in the 1990s is to be confronted with difference and contestation, not unity and coherence. This book emerges from that contested disciplinary context, and as such embodies its own contradictions (for only some of which I can account). It is in part a work of feminist historical recovery, building on the 'archaeology' of predecessors and peers.[2] I have willingly succumbed to two of the 'new English' axioms: that reading women's writing is an inherently valuable activity, and that literary canons have cultural meaning that is best understood by the recovery of marginal, 'excluded' texts. While I have a reflexive sympathy for both of these positions, the rationale of this study needs a more nuanced explication, so the remainder of this introduction

1

and the chapters that follow will map out the connection between Romanticism, women writers and the English nation in the 1790s that underpins the subsequent readings.

The book is not simply a case for inclusivity, nor a history of exclusion, although my readings do raise questions, as others have, about the relative literary historical fates of, say, Helen Maria Williams and William Wordsworth, or Ann Radcliffe and Walter Scott, and look closely at the exclusionary effects of Romantic nationalism and the organicist metaphors on which it is founded. The exclusions are largely the symptom of nineteenth-century literary and imperial history that is beyond the scope of this book.[3] Rather, it looks at the 'proliferation' of meanings of Englishness and national belonging in the 1790s, aiming to fracture rather than complete the historical map of a literary period.

I have used the term *belongings* to signal, in three principal ways, the economic and affective underpinnings of the imagined community of the English nation, and women's relation to it in the 1790s. In the most literal sense, belongings are owned goods, the property that defines the individual in modern, contractual society. In the light of feminist critiques of the gendered bases of Lockean contract theory and the material effects of eighteenth-century contract law on women's status as property-owners, it goes without saying that women were more often belongings than proprietors.[4] Secondly, the present participle, belonging, evokes a metaphorical form of ownership: having property in common, sharing in the interests of other people. The idea of belonging to a nation holds out the promise of full and equal participation for all nationals. This is a deliberately tautological statement, as one of the things this book addresses is the historical, contested and discursive character of the nation, and how it is shaped in the interest of different groupings competing for hegemony. In the 1790s, radicals, reformers and loyalists all claimed ownership of the sign of English nationhood. Although, as I shall argue, the ascendant model was the Burkean organic nation-state, we should not be blind to the other forms of belonging that preceded it and co-existed with it, and their implications for women's national status.

There is a third term embedded in belongings that is a corollary of the idea of the nation as a discursive event: the participle 'longing' neatly captures the dynamic of desire that, I would argue, is endemic to national discourse. The nation is constituted by longing for community, and for a place of origin and stability. This pastoral fantasy of plenitude and local sustenance is symptomatic of the alienating condition we define as 'modernity' and of the enforced mobility of populations under the burgeoning capitalism of the eighteenth century. It is all the more potent, however, in a decade of radical upheaval such as the 1790s, when, due first to revolution and then to war, European subjects were displaced within and between national boundaries and when those boundaries were being redrawn.

As an object of desire, a longed-for place for mobile populations, the nation is gendered feminine: the *heimlich*, a familiar place. The feminised home is a concept that appears frequently in the texts I address here. It figures not only in the predictable spaces of Ann Radcliffe's and Charlotte Smith's Gothic fictions, whose wandering protagonists dream of home, but in the letters and travel narratives of Helen Maria Williams and Mary Wollstonecraft, and in the more prosaic, but equally compelling didactic tracts by Hannah More. More's work in particular, like that of other counter-revolutionary writers, places much emphasis on the nurturing place as the source of national security.

The interpellation of the woman into the feminine, maternal subject position in national discourse, and its exclusionary effects, is apparent across the range of women's texts I have analysed for the purposes of this book. Of these five only Hannah More, resolutely single and childless, explicitly sanctions the logic of the national family romance, despite the compromise to her own subjectivity. Smith and Wollstonecraft to varying degrees critique the suffocating effects of a symbolic order that destines most women to lives of material and psychic impoverishment, whilst Ann Radcliffe and Helen Maria Williams fantasise about the power of femininity (but not necessarily maternity), and of national affection to effect a transformation in the institutions of state. It is obvious from the work of these writers that the feminised space of the nation does not provide equal rights of access to male and female travellers. The masculine subject is intelligible both inside and outside of this domain, free to define nation/home/woman as object of his desire or his possession; as a national subject he can literally come and go, long and belong at the same time. This mobile condition perhaps accounts for the 'representative' national status of male writers as peripatetic as Shelley and Byron and for the paradoxical elevation of the male traveller/adventurer in the Romantic national tradition. In the Romantic national imaginary, the woman who wanders, who defines herself beyond the home and as a subject whose desires exceed or preclude maternity, divests herself of femininity and erases herself from the familial, heterosexual structure of the nation. Her belonging depends on her belonging to another, desired not desiring, and her romantic attachment to person and place is sanctioned only by her literal and symbolic reproduction of the national family. However, as the work of Mary Wollstonecraft in particular testifies, whilst the archetypal feminine subject of the Romantic nation is the mother, the emerging structures of capitalism that coincide with modern nationhood institutionally misrecognise the mother's status as citizen of the state.[5] As I shall suggest, the tensions between the cultural centrality of the mother and the downgraded position that mothers occupy in the political economy of nations inflects women's relation to the symbolic reproduction of the nation, not least their relation to literary production.

To claim that the nation is a gendered space is to read against the grain of hegemonic analyses that have addressed issues of nationhood as continuous with a 'neutered' political, public sphere.[6] The 'public sphere' is the term coined by Jürgen Habermas to describe the civic space of political participation, debate, and opinion formation. For Habermas, the public sphere mediates between the economic exchanges of modern civil society and the family (which together constitute the private sphere) and the state. It specialises in socialisation and cultural formation, but its critical debates serve an economic function, protecting commercial economy from the incursions of state.[7] Feminist critics have rehearsed the tensions of the universalist rhetoric and the gender blind-spots of Habermas's model of the public sphere, drawing attention to the inadequacy of eighteenth-century public debate to treat subjects deemed as private and particular, and the material exclusion of unpropertied subjects from its domains.[8] Further, as Carole Pateman has shown us, the social contract that organises the relationships of the eighteenth-century civil society is a sexual contract; the public sphere not only mediates between civil society, the family and the state, but reproduces one in the image of the other.[9] Gender is central to the economic language of the civil domain: first, because there are contractual differences in women's and men's relation to material goods, land and capital; second, again in Pateman's terms, because social contracts are underpinned by sexual contracts, the subject of which is 'the property that individuals are held to own in their own persons' (p. 5). The property that subjects hold in their own persons – their sense of belonging – is determined as much by gender as by social rank.

Despite the frequent elision of 'national' and 'public' life in critical commentary, it is impossible to simply map on 'the nation' to 'the public sphere'. Although the interests of the English public sphere may have been presented as the interests of the nation, the matters of the nation are both too particular (non-universal) and too general (explicitly incorporating public and private life, in its civil and domestic forms) to be accommodated by the public sphere. Models of national belonging are premised on a more expansive and amorphous kind of contract that is not, even in its ideal sense, open to rational enquiry. As I have suggested, the affective, organic and often biological discourse that characterises nationalism – particularly Romantic nationalism – has particular repercussions for women, by restricting female subjectivity to maternal reproduction.

Familial and gendered metaphors are of course etymologically embedded in the term 'nation', which, in Romance languages, has its origin in the notion of 'naissance, extraction', whilst its Germanic equivalent – *natie* – refers to a birth and descent group. Romantic nationalism foregrounds these organicist associations, as it cross-breeds Renaissance and Enlightenment ideas of national development and merges the notion of territorial acquisition with historical progress. As Marlon Ross has argued, the Romantic nationalist grafts these ideas on to the notion of 'the folk as an organic unity with a natural relation to the nurturing place, the motherland, or the place of dissemination, the fatherland'.[10]

One of the most significant texts in the canon of Romantic nationalism, Edmund Burke's *Reflections on the Revolution in France*, brings together these images of the land and the constitution in the familial unity of the nation-state.[11] In Burke's text, metaphors of birth, maternity, paternity, generation, nurturing, origin and progress in Britain jostle with images of French social engineering, unnatural graftings, geometrical carving up of community, matricide, patricide, the eating of children and monstrous women marching on Paris. That the sight of women on the streets are, for Burke, a sign of a crisis in public order and of a lost civilisation, demonstrates the extent to which the discourse of citizenship and social contract had become 'biologised', absorbed into the Romantic national idea, by the 1790s. In the middle of the eighteenth century, when for good or ill, citizenship was associated with the temporarily feminised realms of commerce and the performative domain of clubs, coffee-houses and associations (the public sphere), it was, at least rhetorically, available to women. The work of Adam Smith, David Hume and Adam Ferguson, or the Scottish 'feelsophers' as Thomas Paine called them, was instrumental in forging the ideal citizen of the eighteenth-century public sphere. In a range of texts dedicated to redesigning the economic and moral infrastructure of Britain, they effectively deconstructed the classic language and ideals of civic morality, which limited the citizen's expression of virtue and moral autonomy to political life in a legalistic or martial sense.[12] Their investigations led them to consider as citizens, women and men who did not have the means to participate in the political process, but who displayed their moral autonomy in economic, social and intellectual activity. The Scottish Enlightenment imagined a republic in which conversation, friendship but, most importantly, exchange became public virtues. The citizen of this republic – the commercial humanist – could take up a pen, read a newspaper, or make a purchase to fulfil his or her public duty and participate in national life.[13] These Scottish writers and their nervous philosophical enquiries made conceptually possible a balance between subjective will and the greater good, sentiment and sociability, individual desire and consensus in the mobile, historical environment of commercial society. They made a public virtue of private interest, and in the process took the patriotic sting out of antagonism to marketplace citizenship, helping to naturalise the image of the nation and state – the English nation and the British state – as a consensual community. The most visible expressions of this expanded definition of citizenship were the provincial clubs and societies which, as Kathleen Wilson has argued, '[w]hether devoted to philosophical inquiry, politics, or competitive gardening . . . endowed their memberships with the identity of decision-making subjects capable of associating for the public good'.[14] As Wilson also notes, whilst the values of these clubs were indeed homosocial, 'associational life per se was not a male preserve'.

The rationalist discourse of the public sphere, although in practice largely homosocial, is potentially more flexible in terms of gender identity than the affective discourse of nationhood. In the public sphere, gender is constituted performatively, not biologically, and its modes of address are, hypothetically, appropriate to men or women. Rudimentary historicisation problematises this Utopian image of the public sphere, which I am aware echoes Habermas's own optimistic vision of the transformative power of a rational bourgeoisie. In the course of the eighteenth century, the material spaces of the public sphere became less receptive to women's participation, as they reproduced the divided economy of capitalism and were inflected by masculinist models of citizenship. However, as is evident in the life and works of Charlotte Smith, Mary Wollstonecraft, Helen Maria Williams, Hannah More and Ann Radcliffe, all of them at some time 'wandering women', it is the discourse of the public sphere, not of the nation, which allows them to imagine themselves as participating citizens. It is the discourse of nationality not rationality that turns them into exiles, by naturalising a patriarchal social contract and putting it beyond rational enquiry.

Not everyone, however, invested sympathetically in the construction of the nation-state as a public sphere or a consensual community of 'associates', especially a construction which was imported from across the Scottish border and which included women. Patriotism as the language of opposition to the Hanoverian state, intent on exposing corruption, persisted throughout the century, and remained masculinist and xenophobic, perhaps increasingly so in the aftermath of the Seven Years War and the subsequent battle with American 'rebels'.[15] Radical English patriots in the later part of the century rejected the image of commerce as conversation, and reinvented it as a form of military enterprise. Epitomised by the campaigns of John Wilkes in the 1770s and 1780s, radical patriotism revived the image of the ancient constitution and portrayed a variety of alien, corrupting and miscegenating forces, which threatened the liberty and masculinity of the freeborn Englishman.[16]

In debates about public life and citizenship in the 1790s, one does not find a simple opposition between feminised, commercial models of citizenship and a xenophobic, masculine patriotism. The Revolution debate threw light on the figure of the cosmopolitan patriot, exemplified by Richard Price, whose political and intellectual roots were in Enlightenment philosophy and Dissenting traditions. Price had famously called for a new attitude towards France, asking in his *Discourse on the Love of Our Country* for his congregation to lend their patriotic service to the battle for French liberty. In the 1790s, then, the discourse of patriotism itself fragmented, divided between an inward-looking loyalism and an internationalism, as radical dissenters championed universal civil liberties and embraced the intellectual strand of Enlightenment cosmopolitanism.[17] These various languages of citizenship – commercial humanism, loyalist patriotism and cosmopolitan patriotism – depend on different conceptualisations of the origins, progress and wealth of nations. They inflect the work of the women I focus on here, in ways which often compromise their own political agendas and more often their gendered, authorial identities. Mary Wollstonecraft, for instance, betrayed her femininity when she issued a hasty riposte to Burke's *Reflections* (which she caricatures as an extended sentimental apostrophe on the French queen) in her 1790 polemic *A Vindication of the Rights of Men*.[18]

Wollstonecraft's rhetoric draws on an ideal commonwealth of manly, autonomous, independent, rational citizens and old-style patriots. In this vein, she portrays Burke as a corrupt, effeminate, state-ventriloquist, trying to seduce the nation away from the fulfilment of their rights in an enlightened republican future. In later texts, most significantly, her *Letters Written During a Short Residence in Sweden, Norway and Denmark* (1796),[19] Wollstonecraft explicitly turned against the image of the commercial citizen, portraying the deadening effects of trade on the imagination, which she regarded as a vital faculty for social sympathy. The imagination, she suggests, has been appropriated by capitalism. In a similar vein, she demonstrates the degrading impact of capitalism on the nation's most valued asset, the maternal body. As though to illustrate the extent of this public degradation, Wollstonecraft succumbs in her own rhetoric to the downgrading of maternity.

Helen Maria Williams, the poet and *salonnier*, who, like Wollstonecraft, found a public and political voice in the early years of the Revolution, with her *Letters From France*,[20] departed from her contemporary's view on commerce. She attempted to describe French revolutionary patriotism in terms that were commensurate with myths of English constitutional liberty and commercial humanism. Her descriptions of the sublime spectacles of the early French republic, significantly in epistolary 'exchanges' with an unknown recipient, incorporate the familial, the domestic, the beautiful and the feminine. She called herself a citizen of the world, *une patriote universelle*, and embraced the icon of French liberty as though she were a younger sister of the matronly English spirit. When Marianne became the sign of French republic under the rule of Robespierre, however, Williams held on to a sense of liberty that she saw as distinctly English, albeit formulated in the public sphere rather than by the nation. Her faith in universal citizenship turned to fear of French imperial zeal and a newly masculinised French public sphere, and, with the unsolicited help of the republican régime, she exiled herself from her adopted *patrie*. Significantly, she did not return to England, which was even less hospitable than France to her cosmopolitan ideals.

In her 1790s fiction, Charlotte Smith undertook a critique of 'things as they are' in English society, and allied herself tentatively with the radical ideals of cosmopolitan patriots. Never quite a 'Jacobin', however, she represented the internationalism of Godwinian radical philosophy with scepticism, portraying it as little more than a romantic ideal, which is pursued by her ingenuous protagonists at the expense of more quotidian, local concerns.[21] Radical idealism, these fictions suggest, produces its own exiles, principally women. Significantly, against the inherently fallen British nation-state, Smith projects the possibility of primitive New World community. This is figured principally in North America, a republic now dissociated from British rule.

Ann Radcliffe's fiction, like Smith's, provides fantasies of a Rousseauan return to nature, but, like Williams, she more confidently allies primitivism to the values of a civilising commercial world, which she champions explicitly in her 1794 *Journey* through Holland, Germany and the English Lakes.[22] More melodramatic than Smith's romances, Radcliffe presents her glimpses into the feudal lore of a vaguely historicised, Catholic Europe through the lens of that distinctly English, Whig aesthetic, the picturesque. Her fictions forge imagined communities that take pleasure in this restrained aesthetic and its associations with the private property of the 'middling classes'. Implicitly, Radcliffe's readers register the signs of the best of English culture figured by the didactic hand of this dissenting author.

Hannah More picked up on the internationalist turn of patriotism in 1793 when she used the term disparagingly in 'Village Politics', to describe a man 'who loves every country better than his own, and France best of all'.[23] In 1799, however, she unblushingly applied the term patriot to the loyal women who joined the war effort, and who came forward, 'without departing from the refinement of their character, without derogating from the dignity of their rank, without blemishing the delicacy of their sex . . . to raise the depressed tone of public morals, and to awaken the drowsy spirit of religious principle'.[24] In the war years, with the rhetoric of the local in the ascendant, the language of patriotism took a loyalist turn, and was nowhere better exemplified than by More's idea of female patriot who stays firmly in the home.

Attention to the kinds of belonging that these women and their contemporaries advocate demonstrates the multiple ways in which the emergent vision of Romantic nationalism, with its familial subject positions, was contested in the 1790s. However, it is the Romantic national idea, with its emphasis on the organic relationship between nation and state, allied to a localist attention to the folkloric connection between people and place, which becomes hegemonic. It provides the foundation for the political nation-state of the nineteenth century, and its imperialist logic. Although Romantic nationalism, with its emphasis on the local and the indigenous, constructs an image of the nation that is in tension with imperialism, it so effectively naturalises the relationship between nation and state that it prepares the ground for state-sanctioned imperial expansion. In the face of Napoleonic imperialism, the British state could justify its own imperialist activity by claiming to counter the spread of French totalitarianism with the more benign gospel of British civilisation.

Whilst the political and the imperial nation-state of the nineteenth century consolidated its power through aggressive territorial and industrial expansion and explicit cultural élitism, it came to power in the first place through the simultaneous possession and redefinition of 'national' property which was effected through its promises of participatory politics. Burke's Romantic and sentimental construction of the nation-state is the culmination of a cultural revolution, which, in the space of one hundred and fifty years, transformed the relationship between the English nation and British state, at least in representation. Whilst materially, state power remained in the hands of the few, its authority was newly conceptualised. The state, once represented as an aristocratic cabal, which exerted its authority through threat of violence, was reimagined as a professionalised, bureaucratic public sphere in which each individual – or, I want now to argue, each literate individual – was self-governing.

As I have suggested, although the function of the new mythology of state power was disciplinary, the promise of participation was tangible in a mid-eighteenth-century culture in which class and gender division had not yet solidified as they did in the years of intense industrialisation in the nineteenth century. Before the middle and working classes became identified once and for all as different species and before bourgeois men and women were consigned to their respective spheres in the years of imperial consolidation and expansion, English hegemonic culture had undergone numerous cycles of 'feminisation' and 'masculinisation', of shifting definitions of public and private activity, which may have produced other forms of identity.

That public life – citizenship, association, belonging – seems to have been so comfortably absorbed by the nineteenth-century nation-state is symptomatic of capitalism's power to make capitulation look like choice. The most powerful agents in the creation of the apparent consensus between nation and state or in raising national consciousness were the owners of intellectual property: the members of the eighteenth-century public sphere. As Nancy Armstrong and Lennard Tennenhouse have argued, the class emerging in the wake of the civil war were the

owners of knowledge before they were the owners of money.[25] Monop-
olising first cultural and then economic capital, the newly allied landed
and trading magnates, their scribbling representatives and their oppo-
nents discursively transformed the state by inscribing its mechanisms on
individual consciousness, making the citizen feel part of a collective
process, and of an imagined, national community.

To privilege the 'scribbling' classes as the makers of national identity
in the eighteenth and early nineteenth centuries might be seen at best as
a gesture of post-structuralist solipsism, or at worst a naive representation of print as somehow more powerful than property. However, the
notion of 'writing' as an agent of historical change encapsulates the
conceptual fragility and the material force of the myth of English
national identity and participatory politics as they were constructed in
the eighteenth century. Writing represents one of English culture's most
amorphous domains, at once private and public; the writer is its most
virtual subject, invisible yet inscribed and representable. The transformations wrought upon eighteenth-century society by 'print culture' have
been well documented, and literary critics have granted fiction and its
related forms a privileged place in the production of modern national
identity.[26] While realist novels and newspapers are understood to be the
forms that effect the internalisation of the state by the individual,
sentimental and domestic fiction – fictions about individuality, interiority and privacy – account for the sense of community that is forged
between otherwise isolated reading subjects.[27]

The process by which the collective is individualised and identity is
privatised through fiction is often referred to as a process of cultural
feminisation. The gendering of this metaphor of historical change can
be explained as a symptom of the fact that new political subjectivities in
the eighteenth century generated and depended on the exaltation of the
middle-class domestic woman – albeit in fiction. That is, the shift in
social relations enacted by eighteenth-century fiction is one in which
woman is literally, bodily central. This shift is particularly significant
for women writers and their public status, because the fictional domestic
woman is even more significantly a writing woman. Samuel Richardson's Clarissa and Pamela are signs both of the transition from aristocratic to middle-class desirability, and of a culture in which literacy is the
new mastery. The fictional figure of the domestic woman gave a new
respectability to the woman writer in the middle of the eighteenth
century, as she was increasingly distanced from the public notoriety and

political intrigues of women at court, represented earlier in the century, for instance, in Aphra Behn's and Delariver Manley's scandal narratives.

Just as the domestic woman stood for a subjectivity which was inclusive, familiar and natural – a sign of the nation seen through the anti-aristocratic gaze of the professional bourgeoisie – so women writers could be seen to perform respectable intellectual labour, distinguished from the bodily labours of the working class and the cultural consumption of the aristocracy. This image was always vulnerable, however. Despite their new cultural and economic authority and invisible visibility in print, women writers continued to teeter on the brink of scandal in social and moral terms. Fiction, because of its close affinity with the marketplace, was in constant need of moral recuperation and the production of political or publicly directed non-fiction was obviously no guarantee of respectability.

The risk of moral impropriety was exacerbated in the revolutionary decade of the 1790s, evidenced by the terms of derision which greeted women writers who associated themselves with the French *salonniers* and philosophes and radical associations and corresponding societies in England. The ready connection between Wollstonecraft's political activism and sexual licentiousness, for instance, revives the image of the courtesan, the debased femininity of court and aristocracy in scandal narratives. Conversely, women who adopted the learned discourses associated with professional middle-class men were caricatured as monstrously masculine; even those who, like Hannah More, joined the tirade against revolutionaries, in particular revolutionary feminists, undermined the logic of her own tirade against political women by taking up the pen, and were vilified for doing so. It was not just the woman writer's image of chastity and femininity that was at stake in the 1790s. In a decade when print culture underwent an unprecedented political radicalisation, the notion of writing as respectable, bourgeois intellectual labour came under assault. With social radicals putting their faith in writing and print as the key to the widespread dissemination of French revolutionary ideas, the fiction of the non-violent cultural revolution in writing turned into something more threatening to bourgeois culture itself. The prevailing metaphors of the Whig public sphere – exchange, conversation, contract – which supported the image of the writer as a cultural negotiator, a sharer of specialised knowledge, gave way to metaphors of rapid dissemination, electrical circulations and writers as conduits of truth. The reigning principle of radical corresponding societies of the 1790s, like the London Corresponding Society and those in Sheffield, Norwich and Manchester, was fast transfer of ideas from the parts to the whole; readers would achieve a communal identity by taking pleasure in and coming to direct and immediate knowledge of the political ideals of other correspondents.[28] This radical correspondent could be a member of a corresponding society, a political pamphleteer, a peddler of chapbooks, journalist, or – at a moment when any but the highest cultural forms smacked of dangerous demo- cratisation – a writer of fictions (whatever their actual political persua- sions). Such texts might be directed to a reading public made up not of connoisseurs but of anybody who could read or listen. Between 1795 and 1797, Hannah More sought to counteract the influence of such corre- spondence and of Painite pamphleteering, by saturating the same mar- ket with the ballads, bible stories, short fictions and serial narration of the *Cheap Repository Tracts*. In the advertisement to the 1818 edition of the moral tales, which were subsequently divided into 'Stories for the Middle Ranks' and 'Stories for the Common People', More explained her motivation for publishing the *Tracts*:

To improve the habits and raise the principles of the mass of the people at a time when their dangers and temptations, moral and political, were multiplied beyond the example of any other period in our history, was the motive which impelled the writer of these two volumes to devise and prosecute the institution of the *Cheap Repository*. It was undertaken with an humble wish to counteract, not only the vice and profligacy on the one hand, but error, discontent and false religion on the other. As an appetite for reading had from various causes been increasing among the inferior ranks, it was judged expedient at this critical moment to supply such wholesome aliment as might give new direction to the public taste, and abate the relish for those corrupt and impious publications which the consequences of the French Revolution have been fatally pouring in upon us.[29]

More's *Tracts*, then, offered a moral antidote to the 'corrupt and impious publications', which cultivated a pernicious reading aesthetic in the newly literate market. She sought to stem the flow of radical correspon- dence not by calls for censorship, but by altering public taste through the mechanisms of the free market: readers would choose the pleasures of reading her tracts over the radical pamphlets, and reap the moral rewards by volunteering to do so.

Against these images of reading communities – the radical version of the unconnected parts finding community in unmediated correspon- dence, and More's reactionary inversion, a controlling centre cultiva- ting counteractive tastes in those same parts – came specialised definitions of the writer whose perspective transcended simple politics, and whose creative products were untainted by the vulgar mechanics of theoretical plan or metaphysical system. The image of the Romantic writer, that is, was not just born in reaction to neo-classical models, but to the politically radical and conservative notions of representation and rapid dissemination of the 1790s. The Romantic writer, at least the Wordsworthian and Coleridgean versions, was 'representative' of the reading community in the sense of having specialised access to the collective psyche, standing in for the whole. His writing came to be defined as an exclusive, yet exemplary, kind of representation: Literature. As David Simpson suggests:

Literature, comes to be imaged as either immethodical and tending towards the sublime, in which case it can be contained by a cultivated aesthetic (for the sublime was always that), or the product of a method that never appears as such and cannot be understood or mastered by all and sundry.[30]

Significantly, Simpson finds a link between the language of state legislation and that of literary creation and criticism in this period: between Coleridge's description of the imagination as showing itself in the attempted 'balance or reconciliation of opposite or discordant qualities'[31] and Burke's portrait of 'the ideal patrician class' in *Reflections:* 'We see, that the parts of the system do not clash . . . We compensate, we reconcile, we balance. We are able to unite into a consistent whole the various anomalies and contending principles that are found in the minds and affairs of men.'[32]

These metaphors of mediation seem to be drawn from the discourse of the public sphere, but Burke is making a particular case for a representative class: a class which represents a political character, an English national style. The Coleridgean poetic similarly carves out a specialised place for the Romantic writer – above all, the Romantic poet – as the bearer of national culture. The Romantic poet is methodical in mind but lacks a discernible, imitable method in his poetry. The creative process is represented as a rigorous, masculine intellectual labour, producing a whole that is irreducible to its parts. As Simpson suggests:

These claims for a strong but inapparent element of method, discipline, and severe logic in literature, and especially in poetry, may be read as gestures toward a partial remasculinization of the aesthetic faculty, and as an effort to regrade it out of the merely bourgeois and into the abstract-intellectual sphere, into a realm of methodic classlessness.[33]

Fiction – in the broad sense I have been tracing here – is fundamental to modern national identity, carving out an interior space onto which to project a sense of belonging, but the Romantic invention of that more specialised category, 'literature' provides a new sense of the relationship between the nation, state and writing. Romanticism imagines literature as socially foundational, poetry as a 'prototypical communication'. It is under the aegis of Romanticism that the study of literature becomes a human science, the study of the foundations of society. The organic metaphors that predominate in this legislative and literary critical discourse display similar moves to obscure as they appeal to the origins of the creativity and nation. The Romantic poem and the Burkean nation-state, are each, as Marlon Ross suggests, 'an organic form that grows into itself by feeding on its origin'.[34] The Romantic carries on the sentimental project of tracing human sympathies, but his sensibilities are posited as the archetype, his representations as exclusive: the statesman acts as the representative of the nation whose sentiments he defines.

These constructions 'remasculinise' the nation-state and the literary domain, each tending towards the sublime, yet softened by sensibility. Until very recently, literary historians have bought into this construction in a literal sense, writing women out of the history of Romanticism and the history of nation-state formation. Their writing has long been seen as unrepresentative, consigned to a specifically bourgeois sphere. Literature and nations, this implies, are constructed without method, without system, by the organic processes of the right sort of politician or poet. The writing I consider in this study is perhaps more representative of 'Englishness' in the 1790s in its typicality and its diversity, its lack of a unified politics or poetics. Some of the texts, in particular those by Mary Wollstonecraft, and to some extent Charlotte Smith, drive to expose what we might think of as Romantic 'method', to demystify and make transparent the obscured origins of the nation-state to which they, as women, only marginally belong. Helen Maria Williams and Ann Radcliffe buy into the organic metaphors of literary circulation and national belonging, but feminise the sublime aesthetic on which the Romantic literary and legislative ideas were founded. In their writing, the images of commercial civility that circulated in the middle of the century still predominate, as they project the rapprochement of Whig state bureaucracy and affective national subjectivity. The predominant metaphors of their representations are of reciprocal commerce, rather than of specialised access to the collective psyche of the nation.

In her *Tracts*, Hannah More unequivocally imposes a method to shape the tastes of a patriotic, pious and economically productive readership, taking on a didactic rather than a representative role. Eschewing in her *Strictures* the 'enervating' idealism of 'so much English Sentiment, French Philosophy, Italian Love-Songs . . . fantastic German imagery and magic wonders', she recommends for the production of an efficient work force works more grounded in realist principle.[35] Her own contributions to this 'proper course of preparatory reading', the tales and fables in the *Tracts*, are imbued with principles of feminine domestic economy. The realist (albeit allegorical) impulse of More's fictions, with their attention to domestic detail and the materiality of their readers' lives, prepares the representational ground for that nineteenth-century domestic realism which, in more obvious ways than the Romantic idealist tradition, was to champion the cause of reform, and proved to be antagonistic to the prevailing mythologies of the imperial nation-state.

These, then, are some of the discourses of belonging that were in dialogue with what emerged as the hegemonic version of the Romantic nation-state: the organic union of parts and wholes, its origins submerged in the sublimity of process. These versions of nation use other metaphors of representation and other aesthetic economies to define the pleasures of participation. They issue from the imaginations of women, whose material participation or cultural place as subjects of the Romantic nation-state could not be taken for granted. Although they are ideologically diverse, the shared marginal status of these women and their writing in the histories of national-state formation and English literary character throws into relief the mechanisms of nationhood which the masculinist myth of the Romantic nation-state occludes.

The chapters that follow are part of a 'genealogy' of the present state of the nation, a means of articulating the historical, invented character of 'England.' To this end, I have traced the ways in which a small selection of English women writers – representative in their typicality – performed, promoted and resisted ways of belonging to the nation in the 1790s. In particular, I have emphasised the many and complex way in which gender inflects, and often circumscribes, both *their* versions of national belonging and the discourses of English nationhood which were circulating in the wake of the French Revolution and the ensuing revolutionary wars. In the 1790s and beyond, gendered assumptions about national subjectivity underpin accounts of national literary tradition, economic discourses on the wealth of nations, and political debates about democratic reform of the system of national representation. Such assumptions do not simply marginalise women in the histories of nations; they marginalise women in complex and multiform ways, involving the contradictory processes by which discourses of national belonging come to coincide with the interests of state and with the demands of international (now global) capitalism. Of course, part of the process of resisting such totalising forms of power is to identify the discursive gaps and contradictions, and that, in part, is what I have attempted to do here, by deconstructing the gendered language of nationhood. Of greater political urgency, however, is the institutionalisation of women's 'belonging' and of women's contribution to the definition of public and private value, so that the structures to which they belong do not simultaneously alienate them.

CHAPTER 2

Domesticating the sublime: Ann Radcliffe and Gothic dissent

In the context of recent debates about the English literary canon, the case of Ann Radcliffe provides a formula that is almost as clichéd as the imitations her fictions spawned. Her work was widely read and critically respected in the 1790s and the early nineteenth-century. However, like that of nearly all of her contemporary writers of prose fiction, Radcliffe's romances found no place in a Romantic canon based on poetry, and merited no more than a footnote in the rise of the novel and the great tradition. Our own Gothic revival – which has come about largely under the aegis of cultural studies, women's studies and psychoanalytic criticism – has thrown new light on Radcliffe's work. In our increasingly historically sensitive canons, 'The Great Enchantress' takes her place with other novelists, poets and prose writers in Romantic period studies.[1] Without rehearsing the history of Radcliffe's period of critical exile from the canons of English literature, I want to foreground aspects of her work that might account for it. Radcliffe's prose offers rational, didactic literary tourism through picturesque landscapes; in form, aesthetic and aspiration it had no place in a canon that, from the late nineteenth century, was represented by a poetry of nature mediated by the poet's specialised access to sublime experience. Perhaps understandably, the aspects of Radcliffe's fiction that I focus on here remained underrepresented when critical interest in the Gothic genre was revived in the 1970s and 1980s. Radcliffe's new feminist critics were keen to dismantle the image of middlebrow, perhaps counter-revolutionary Mrs Radcliffe and to unearth the 'anti-patriarchal', subversive psychodramas of her narratives.[2] To retrieve what I see as the manifest designs of Radcliffe's texts is not to reject the psychoanalytic readings that have unearthed their latent content. However, to understand Radcliffe in the context of literary nationalism requires a historical context, and that context illuminates the nuanced perspective of English middle-class dissent – and Radcliffe's own feminised version of it – in the 1790s.[3]

In the terms that I outlined in my introduction, Ann Radcliffe was a 'wandering woman' who understood women's participation in the nation to extend beyond maternal reproduction. It was perhaps the signs of extended female citizenship that provoked *The Anti-Jacobin Review and Magazine* to exile Radcliffe from their lists of English fiction writers in 1801, claiming that her sensibility was 'rather German than English'. She did travel as far as the Rhine, but a more significant explanation for *The Anti-Jacobin*'s displeasure is that her fictions are centred around female protagonists who move through landscape and who exceed the commonplace representational reduction of women to property, and indeed become proprietors. In class terms, Radcliffe was not a radical in her attitude to the relationship between citizenship and property. It is evident that Radcliffe inherited a contractual model of eighteenth-century citzenship in which belonging depends upon belongings, and a psychological model of innate class differences that rationalises the inequalities of property relations. However, if her class politics are little more than conventional for a woman of her social status – she was born into a middle-class trading family in Holborn and married the proprietor of the *English Chronicle* – her gender politics are more unusual. Her fictions fashion imagined communities in which women – at least middle-class women – belong on the same terms as property-owning men and in which female subjectivity shapes the character of the sexual contract. This contract evolves through the interpellation of her protagonists – both female and male – into a recognisably English culture, modelled on the mores of middle-class dissent. Through this process of acculturation, Radcliffe's ingénues become ideal citizens of public-minded private spheres. Enlightened, reflective and sustained by property, they establish familial structures based on mutual love and communal responsibility. If these aspects of her texts do not sharply distinguish Radcliffe's national imaginary from the emergent Romantic national idea – and, as I shall suggest, there are many correspondences between the two – then her long-time status as a Romantic 'other' has to be explained in other terms. It is those Romantic correspondences and differences in Radcliffe's work that I now want to address.

LITERATURE AND THE FOUNDATION OF NATIONS

When Emily St Aubert, in Radcliffe's *The Mysteries of Udolpho*, comes across a group of Tuscan peasants, delivering a classical invocation to a sea-nymph, she contemplates the scene with a mixture of pleasure and consternation: 'Emily had been early taught to venerate Florence as the seat of literature and of the fine arts; but, that its taste for classic story should descend to the peasants of the country, occasioned her both surprise and admiration.'[4] Like all of Radcliffe's heroines, Emily has been educated in the classics and she has, until this point, understood them as her own, private cultural capital. That is, she had regarded her familiarity with Shakespeare, Milton and Ariosto as a sign of her difference from the children of nature who work the land, not sketch it, write about it, or travel through it. Emily learns here that what she thought was privileged access is common knowledge. She quickly retrieves the moment as a testament to the power of the classics rather than the sensibility of the peasants, as the scene occasions her admiration for the story's power of transmission, not the performance.

The doubleness in Emily's response to this classical invocation – she now understands that the classic story is popular but fully accessible only to the refined imagination – is symptomatic of the social tensions in the discourse of eighteenth-century associationist psychology that underpins some aspects of Radcliffe's depiction of aesthetic appreciation.[5] The egalitarian potential of associationist psychology and the aesthetic discourses that relied on its stimulus-response model of the mind and body often gave rise to less than equal representations of a subject's susceptibility to artistic or other – moral and social – impressions. Thus Radcliffe's ('middling' class) protagonists have an abundance of original sensibility that needs only experience to refine it. They are supported by good, loyal servants who have limited aesthetic response or judgement and are persecuted by quasi-aristocratic libertines whose aesthetic faculty has exhausted their moral capacity, and who live by hedonistic systems of their own creation.

Such stock representations are given more cultural specificity – and a political charge – in Radcliffe's fiction, as she frequently alludes to contemporary educational philosophies to substantiate particular characterisations. *The Romance of the Forest*, for instance (which is said to have influenced Wordsworth's Gothic melodrama about the revolutionary terror, *The Borderers*) moves towards its resolution with the introduction of the Savoyard pastor Arnaud La Luc. His character is drawn directly from the portrait of the '*vicaire savoyard*' in Rousseau's *Emile*, although significantly Radcliffe changes his religion from Catholic to Protestant. In the education of his daughter Clara, La Luc's principles echo those put forward by Rousseau, as he allows her to learn by 'experience' rather than by 'precept' (p. 249). Radcliffe tellingly departs from *Emile*'s restricted view of women's education by having La Luc allow Clara to develop a taste for the picturesque arts, trusting her to develop self-command in her indulgence of these restrained pleasures through the exercise of reason and sensibility.

Rousseau's 'natural philosophy' informs many aspects of Radcliffe's fictions, but she differs from him in her representation of what we have come to recognise as a typically Romantic depiction of subject–object relations. Whereas for Rousseau and other 'pre-Romantic' naturalists, the encounter with nature is a formative, shaping experience in the construction of identity, Radcliffe's protagonists are Romantic primitivists, whose response to nature is figured as a reciprocal commerce between the self and a divinely created world beyond. Radcliffe turns the conventional romance battle for good and evil into a contest between benign and malign nature-worshippers: between a primitivism rooted in Christian precept and liberal ethics, like that of La Luc and St Aubert, and the moral libertinism of the Marquis de Montalt, Montoni or Schedoni, for whom the rule of law is no more than 'vulgar prejudice'. The libertine philosophy is exemplified in the following speech from the Marquis to La Motte in *The Romance of the Forest*:

There are certain prejudices attached to the human mind . . . which it requires all our wisdom to keep from interfering with our happiness; certain set notions, acquired in infancy, and cherished involuntarily by age, which grow up and assume a gloss so plausible, that few minds, in what is called a civilised country, can afterwards overcome them. Truth is often perverted by education. While the refined Europeans boast a standard of honour, and a sublimity of virtue, which often leads them from pleasure to misery, and from nature to error, the simple, uniformed American follows the impulse of his heart, and obeys the inspiration of wisdom.[6]

These sentiments are echoed in an exchange between Schedoni and the Marchesa in *The Italian*, as he persuades her that natural justice must prevail over the rule of law, and that Ellena should be put to death for threatening to dishonour the Vivaldi name. The distinction that Radcliffe makes between a more or less Rousseauan and a Sadeian rule of nature is crucial at this moment when, in England, critics of the French Revolution were confounding the two. Sentimentalism and liberal dissent were tarred with the same brush as Jacobinism, and all were signs of libertine culture. To the extent that her fictions gesture towards the events in contemporary France, Radcliffe invariably makes libertinism the sign of an *ancien régime*, rather than of a revolutionary class. To avoid the negative associations of sensibility, she socialises it, leading her sentimental protagonists towards progressive and benevolent community, rather than leaving them as inward and solitary Romantics. The ideal sentimental constitution for Radcliffe seems to be a rapprochement of what she has La Luc in *The Romance of the Forest* describe as the 'wisdom' of the English and the 'happiness' of the French. English wisdom, his friend Verneuil remarks, has a painful correlation with the frequency of English suicide, but French happiness, La Luc counters is 'airy thoughtlessness, which seems alike to contemn reflection and anticipation, produces all effect of it without reducing its subjects to the mortification of philosophy'. True wisdom, La Luc argues, 'is exertion of mind to subdue folly . . . a consequence of mind [not] of constitution' (p. 269). When posited as the fruit of intellectual labour rather than a quirk of national character, then, true wisdom and happiness become compatible and universally available: the model characteristics of the rational public sphere.

Literary culture plays a crucial role in educating Radcliffe's protagonists in the exercise of reason. In her fiction, reason is represented as a peculiarly English faculty, best inculcated through the power of the national language. Thus Adeline, Emily and Radcliffe's other protagonists are taught to appreciate the best of English literary culture, not so that they will imitate its good moral precept but, primarily, so that they come to self-knowledge and critical reflection. In *The Romance of the Forest*, for instance, Adeline frequently turns to 'the higher kinds of poetry' to 'withdraw her mind from the contemplation of its own misery':

and in these her taste soon taught her to distinguish the superiority of the English from that of the French. The genius of the language, more perhaps than the genius of the people, if indeed the distinction may be allowed, occasioned this.
She frequently took a volume of Shakspear [sic] or Milton, and having gained some wild preeminence, would seat herself beneath the pines, whose low murmurs soothed her heart, and conspired with the visions of the poet to lull her to forgetfulness of grief.[7]

The heady combination of English national genius and the protagonist's finely tuned sensibility provides a strong basis for individual and social cohesion. That literature might constitute, rather than reflect the social was, of course, an emergent Romantic idea, and as I have suggested, gave rise to the peculiarly elevated status of the author in English national culture. For Romantics, or at least, for Wordsworth in the Preface to the *Lyrical Ballads*, the literary writer, the 'man who, being possessed of more than usual organic sensibility' was able to feel and modify his feeling by thoughts, 'which are indeed the representatives of all our past feelings'. He continues:

as by contemplating the relation of these general representative to each other, we discover what is really important to men, so, by the repetition and continuance of this act, our feelings will be connected with important subjects, till at length, if we be originally possessed of much sensibility, such habits of mind will be produced, that, by obeying blindly and mechanically the impulses of those habits, we shall describe objects, and utter sentiments, of such a nature, and in such connection with each other, that the understanding of the Reader must necessarily be in some degree enlightened, and his affections strengthened and purified.[8]

Radcliffe's texts adumbrate Wordsworth's sense of the strengthening and purifying effects of good reading, particularly on her female protagonists. There is a difference, however, between Wordworth's manifesto for a literary and social revolution and Radcliffe's incorporation of a quasi-national canon in her fictions. The Romantic poet writes himself into his organicist literary canon, as he possesses a mind which is able to relate and to connect 'representative' feelings, which, when communicated, move the reader outward in social sympathy. Radcliffe narrates the second-hand effects of a literary (and, I shall suggest, visual) canon on an imaginary reader, but does not seem to claim those effects for her own work. In an English literary tradition that has been shaped by the ideals of Romantic organicism, it is perhaps the meta-narrative – or even didactic – quality of her work which makes Radcliffe's fictions look too 'mechanical' to be truly Romantic. The feelings of the reader are not organised by Radcliffe's sensibility. Instead, we witness how such a process might operate on an imaginary reading subject. What epistolary fiction had done for writers, fictionalising and putting into discourse the mechanisms of a newly privatised, yet professionalised activity, Radcliffe did for the reader. By foregrounding and idealising the anonymous side of the author-reader contract, she constructed a public, civic and representative identity for the reader of fiction, and, crucially, a morally acceptable persona for the female reader of romance. Radcliffe puts the reading and viewing subject into fiction, tracing her (and sometimes, his) interior reactions to varieties of aesthetic experience. In doing so, Radcliffe lays bare the concepts of culture, and the assumptions about the relationship between culture and consumption, on which the broader projects of Romanticism and 'literary nationalism' were founded.

ENGLISH ROMANCE

The reading matter of Radcliffe's protagonists tells another, perhaps more familiar, story about English literary history in the eighteenth century that bears reiteration here: the story of the revival of Gothic romance. It is a critical commonplace that mid-century novelists built their defences of novels on their distinction from the epistemology and ideology of romance.[9] The novel's apologists argued that the distance between the truths of their new fictional form and the fancies of romance reflected a historical and ideological split between an age of enlightenment and real and imagined eras of popular subordination, credulity and arbitrary rule. Novels stood to Protestant, Whiggish progressivism as romance stood to regressive, Catholic feudalism. The epistemic uncertainty of the late eighteenth century disturbed the confidence of the progressive novelists' claims to truth in representation. Diminishing confidence in the 'Enlightenment project' and rapid changes in the bases of political authority in Britain in the later part of the eighteenth century produced a new, if ambivalent fascination with pre-modern epistemology and its cultural and political signs, not least its national signs. Anxiety about English national identity, which was produced by British imperial growth, and new domestic political alliances (Whig and Tory, land and trade, Catholic and Protestant, Scottish and English) was reflected in the 'Little Englandism' which surfaced from the 1770s until the end of the century. This was expressed not just in the political associations and protests of radical patriots but in the literary domain. The production of genealogies of a vernacular English literary tradition, the lionisation of the English bards (Shakespeare, Spenser and Milton) and the unprecedented interest in regional folklore and customary culture demonstrated a consolidated effort on the part of the writing classes to construct an essential Englishness that, in its cultural traditions, mirrored the nation's customary constitution.[10]

This indigenous romance (or Gothic, as opposed to classical Greco-Roman) tradition did not of course reflect a homogeneous national culture or literary aesthetic; nor did the romances of the 'national bards' display uniform attitudes towards English political authority. In Elizabethan poetics, for instance, as Richard Helgerson argues, there were at least 'two versions of Gothic'. The first was 'associated with the immemorial customs and privileges of England and the English people . . . popular in the sense that it represents the communal will of the people' and championed, for instance, in Daniel's *Defence of Rime*. The second, represented by Spenser's *Faerie Queene*, was 'a Gothic of chivalry and romance . . . aristocratic and individualistic'.[11] Spenser's chivalric romance laid itself open to attack by classical humanists on both aesthetic and political grounds. They claimed it lacked uniformity of design, that it represented power as diffuse and dispersed, and depicted heroism residing in the private action of the knight-errant rather than the public virtue of the 'politic man'.

The next major national poem, *Paradise Lost*, was written in a period when romance had apparently gone underground. Milton explicitly rejected chivalry, abandoning his plan to write an Arthurian romance in favour of his classically designed biblical epic more fit for a modern imagination. His poem's status in the late eighteenth-century genealogy of English romance is secured, however, if not by its poetics then by its individualistic vision of power, which in some respects is more 'romantic' than Spenser's. Whilst Spenser's poem, despite its depiction of an anarchic knight-errant, ultimately upholds the absolute authority of the monarch, Milton transfers monarchic authority to the individual, via God. As Helgerson notes, in *Paradise Lost* the freedom of the individual moral agent arises in obedience to 'a thoroughly rational and God-centred state' (p. 61). It is an anti-militaristic, rationalist, contractual vision of power: a modern romance.

Over a century later, Radcliffe's romances are littered with references to the English and Italian romancers (Shakespeare, Milton, Ariosto and Tasso) although not significantly to Spenser. She seems to have found in these writers a romance ethos that could be allied to her other literary reference points: Homer, Horace and Petrarch. That is, she embraced the historicism, civic humanism and publicly oriented agency of classicism, but rejected its image of centralised power. Her fictions modify classicism's power with the subjectivism and individualism of romance, and eschew its aristocratic ethos in favour of a modern, middle-class sensibility. Radcliffe's fictions are romances about private, property-owning subjects performing public duty: a duty that is defined not in terms of military enterprise, but according to the values of Whig, commercial society and the rational public sphere.

Radcliffe's use of this inter-textual shorthand signals, more than anything does, how well established the romance revival was by the 1790s. For over two decades the aesthetic and political significance of the work of the English and Italian romancers had been exhaustively debated, and a cultural space had been cleared for new contributions to the canon in the form of the modern romance.[12] That blend of the marvellous with the probable, of pre-modern wonder, with modern rationality was defined most authoritatively and enthusiastically in the preface to Walpole's second edition of *The Castle of Otranto*. In a definition that echoes the old romance-novel distinction, Walpole suggests that ancient and modern romance are distinguishable as the fictions of two historical moments, divided by the revolutionary settlement of 1689. Rather than a clearly defined formal shift, it is the stamp of Miltonic bourgeois individualism that distinguishes the 'old' from 'new' romance. The republican poet is thus iconic for writers like Radcliffe, whose interests lay in its vision of individual moral agents debating their autonomy and negotiating a contract with a newly 'fraternal' patriarch.

Modern romance is intimately connected to Lockean social contract and public sphere sensibility. Thus, late eighteenth-century romance debates focused less on poetics than on what was at stake when the values of the middle class replaced those that had been occupied, in fiction, by aristocratic ideals, or when aspiration itself was geared towards such a lowly bourgeois plateau. This 'down-marketing' of the old romance was evident to the detractors and parodists of the new fiction. George Canning, for instance, listed disparagingly the old and new ingredients: for the 'merciless giant' find the 'austere guardian'; for the 'she-dragon', the 'maiden aunt'. The heroine 'retains her tenderness' but is 'divested of her royalty' whilst 'in the hero we must give up the knight-errant for the accomplished fine gentleman'.[13] With some subtlety, however, avarice could be characterised as virtuous. The individual pursuit of wealth could be represented as valuable to the public good and the notion of personal valour could be redefined in terms which were commensurate with the nation's commercial, rather than martial, success: industry, productivity, regulation, self-control. Fiction, including Radcliffe's, had a crucial role to play in this redefinition of heroic enterprise, for the puritan values of commercial productivity needed to be packaged with the pleasures of measured consumption. As I now want to suggest, in Radcliffe's romances, productivity and measured consumption are endemic to the aesthetic experience of reading and to the dissemination of modern national culture.

PRODUCTIVE PLEASURES

Radcliffe's romances celebrate the values of an industrious (albeit intellectually industrious) bourgeoisie, allied, in archetypal romance fashion, to the 'best' of aristocratic value: that is, to those aristocratic values of leisure and civility which are most palatable to a middle-class ethos. In her *Journey Made in the Summer of 1794*, when Radcliffe had the opportunity to makes notes on the manners of her real European neighbours, she found the rapprochement of bourgeois exertion and aristocratic repose thin on the ground. In the record of her travels through Holland, Germany and then through the English Lake District, her strongest praise, when she is not describing the landscape, is reserved for commercial centres. In Rotterdam, for instance, she singles out the new exchange building, as a sign of that 'permanent defender of freedom and knowledge against military glory and politics': commerce.[14] Business, she notes, erodes at least the outward signs of political differences. In Dutch cities 'where those of both parties must transact business together', the party-coloured cockades and ribbons which are worn by all classes in the rest of the country are not evident. She does not take an opportunity to draw attention to the more terrifying signs of partisanship in the cockades of the new French republic, but she draws attention to the inadequacy of state legislation to temper such signs of loyalty and their possible incendiary effect. She recalls a ludicrous bureaucratic intervention of 1785, when Dutch magistrates ordered that 'nothing orange-coloured should be worn, or shewn, not even fruits or flowers, and that carrots should not be exposed to sale with the ends outwards' (p. 40). The parallel with the increasingly legislative and interventionist French state of 1794 is not drawn; but the point that trade and the values of a commercial class produces a greater degree of national, if not international unity than the inorganic imposition of bureaucratic legislation would surely not be lost on Radcliffe's readers.

Although for Radcliffe, the industry of the Dutch pales in comparison with that of the English (p. 47), the social benefits of its system of production are thrown into relief when she crosses the border into Germany, where the feudal arrangements of landholder and peasant labourers persist. 'The latter' she notes 'are, perhaps, supplied with stock, and the grounds produce as much as elsewhere, though you may read, in the looks and manners of the people, that very little of its production is for them' (pp. 85–6). These signs of alienation continue in the towns and cities. Rheinberg, for instance, a town with a proud military history, is:

. . . half filled by inhabitants, whose indolence, while it is probably more to be pitied than blamed, accounts for the sullenness and wretchedness of their appearance. Not one symptom of labour, or comfort, was to be perceived in the whole town . . . Some small shops of huckster's wares were the only signs of trade.[15]

This Gothicised community lacks the virtuous avarice of Dutch commercial adventurers; denied the incentive of reaping the reward of their own industry, and of competing with their fellow traders, they have not replaced military with commercial enterprise. The social inertia is reflected in the paucity of carriages, poor circulation, inadequate accommodation and inhospitable innkeepers that intensifies Radcliffe's longing for the sociability of travelling in commercial England where, 'towards the end of a day's journey . . . you are not far from the cheerful reception, [and] the ready conveniences of a substantial inn'. Instead of the 'civility of an English landlord', in Germany the traveller can expect to be greeted by a character resembling one of her fictional assassins, 'a huge figure, wrapt in a great coat, with a red worsted cap, and a pipe in his mouth, stalking before the door' (p. 158).

England, of course, yields plenty of examples of the civilising effect of commerce. Her brief passage through Stockport and Manchester is distinguished favourably by the 'cheerful populousness' of the towns which are connected by 'an almost continued street of villages', and a busy but uncluttered road, teeming with passengers and carriages (p. 377). Such commerce might be expected to produce a uniform national character but when Radcliffe arrives in the Lake District, she is eager to point out that even in 'this age of communication and intelligence' inhabitants of different regions maintain strong local identities. It is this post-Enlightenment attention to local difference, she argues, that governments need to observe in order to ensure the appropriate policy for the happiness of their subjects. This point is reinforced when, travelling through Holland, she reflects on the ignorance of local needs exhibited by many governments:

How much the means of political happiness depend, for their effect, upon the civil characters of those for whom they are designed, has been very little seen, or insisted upon. It has been unnoticed, because such enquiries have not the brilliancy, or the facility, of general speculations, nor can command equal attention . . . A juster effort of understanding would aim at rendering the application of principles more exact, rather than more extensive, and would produce enquiries into the circumstances of national character and condition, that should regulate that application. A more modest estimate of human means of doing good would shew the gradations, through which all human advances must be made. A more severe integrity of views would stipulate, that the means should be as honest as the end, and would strive to ascertain, from the moral and intellectual character of a people, the degree of political happiness, of which they are capable.[16]

Her portrait of England suggests that attention to the 'civil character' not just of the national people but of their regional variety has produced that organic union of parts and the whole, which was emerging as the ideal of Romantic nationalists. In anticipation of Wordsworth's Preface to the *Lyrical Ballads*, Radcliffe celebrates the 'superior simplicity' of the people of the Lake District, who 'do not bend with meanness, or hypocrisy, but shew an independent well meaning' (p. 397). In this instance, it seems that lack of commerce with a world beyond the local region has proved to be a protection from the competitive impulse that degrades the city dwellers:

They are without the baseness . . . of becoming abject before the persons of one class, that by the authority of an apparent connection with them, they may be insolent to those of another; and are free from the essential humiliation of shewing, by a general and undistinguishing admiration of all persons richer than themselves, that the original distinctions between virtue and vice have been erased from their minds by the habit of comparing the high and the low.[17]

Wordsworth, in the Preface, was to find in these kinds of self-enclosed communities a model for poetic language, 'because, from their rank in society and the sameness and narrow circle of their intercourse, being less under the influence of social vanity, they convey their feelings and notions in simple and unelaborated expressions' (p. 282). Although Radcliffe seems to have been attracted to the simplicity of the indigenous rural community, she does not offer a wholly pastoral vision. She clings to the idea of 'commerce' in its range of associations and sees it as a levelling and unifying activity. Perhaps Radcliffe's social ideal turns on the delicate distinction she makes between the proud independence of the rude 'statesman' (the name attributed by the lakelanders to a man who 'had land of his own'), whom she discovers sheltering under 'the lee of an heaped up pile of slates', and the insularity of the young man in Nibthwaite who 'knew not how far it was to Ulverston, or as he called it Ulson, though it was only five miles' (p. 460; p. 484). It is actually property that separates the autonomous freeholder and the unworldly labourer, but Radcliffe passes over this fact. She chooses to foreground commerce, the *exchange* of property and the social face of private ownership, as the guarantor of progressive, rational community.

Her attitude towards the relationship between the 'moral and intellectual character of the people' and the environment in which they live seems to come close to Coleridge's response to Wordsworth in *Biographia Literaria*, when he offers his description of the shepherd-farmers in the vales of Cumberland and Westmoreland. In a statement which is reminiscent of Hannah More's prescriptions for the moral health of the working classes, Coleridge ranks two principal causes which account for the 'thoughts, feelings, language and manners' of the rural dwellers, not necessarily connected with their 'occupations and abode':

As the two principal I rank that independence which raises a man above servitude or daily toil for the profit of others, yet not above the necessity of industry and a frugal simplicity of domestic life, and the accompanying unambitious, but solid and religious education which has rendered few books familiar but the bible and the liturgy and hymn book.[18]

Country life or country labours, he argues will not 'improve' without education, 'or original sensibility, or both' (p. 191). Comparing the poor in Liverpool, Manchester and Bristol, with the poor in agricultural villages, he finds well-managed urban Poor Laws as conducive as 'the ordinary dispensation of poor rates in agricultural villages' to reasonable conditions and respectable behaviour. The most telling comparison is that between the Swiss mountain community and the peasantry in the mountains of North Wales. The former's 'stronger local attachments and enterprising spirit' are evidence that the 'desirable influences of low and rustic life in and for itself' are less prejudicial in character formation than 'a particular mode of pastoral life', which, in the case of the Swiss exists 'under forms of property that permit and beget manners truly republican'. Where such conditions do not prevail, as among the peasantry in North Wales, 'the ancient mountains, with all their terrors and all their glories, are pictures to the blind and music to the deaf' (p. 191).

Radcliffe implies such a case throughout her *Journey* and in her fiction, where 'original sensibility' prevails over education in determining the moral capacity and social worth of characters, where both education and original sensibility have more influence than accident of environment, and where property relations dominate all manner of behaviour. In the fiction, Radcliffe presents *choice* of environment, where choice is possible (for the middle classes and nobility), as an obvious outward sign of moral disposition, and she establishes a formulaic shorthand of interior decor, external improvements and prospect as an index of the proprietors' sensibility and moral worth. Moral excellence is found in the rurally retired: those who, like La Luc and St Aubert, have had commerce with the world but have chosen the repose of nature.[19] An excess of commerce, which leads to a surplus of income for the individual, on the other hand, is signalled by an orientalist taste; too rich, sensuous and an index of a dangerous libido. In *The Romance of the Forest*, for instance, the danger that Adeline faces after being abducted by the

Marquis de Montalt become only too apparent when she surveys the chamber in which he incarcerates her:

The airy elegance with which it was fitted up, and the luxurious accommodations with which it abounded, seemed designed to fascinate the imagination, and to seduce the heart. The hangings were of straw-coloured silk, adorned with a variety of landscapes and historical paintings, the subjects of which partook of the voluptuous character of the owner; the chimney-piece, of Parisian marble, was ornamented with several reposing figures from the antique. The bed was of silk the colour of the hangings, richly fringed with purple and silver, and the head made in the form of a canopy. The steps, which were placed near the bed to assist in ascending it, were supported by Cupids, apparently of solid silver. China vases, filled with perfume, stood in several of the recesses, upon stands of the same structure as the toilet, which was magnificent, and ornamented with a variety of trinkets.[20]

Radcliffe famously used landscape and architecture to signal mood and the moral inclination of her characters. Perhaps because her use of place was so well established by her final published work, *The Italian*, it relies to a much lesser extent on elaborate architecture to summon up the sublime. The vaults, passages and chambers of the ruined abbey in *The Romance of the Forest*, and the galleries and chambers of Udolpho, which take on more terrific dimensions in the dreams of the persecuted imaginations of Adeline and Emily, are replaced by the attenuated terrors of the house by the Adriatic Sea, and the almost wholly internalised environment of the Inquisition. This may be partly to do with a refinement of technique, but it is also connected with the greater emphasis that Radcliffe places on the complexity of subjective experience, in particular the workings of conscience as an internal arbiter of moral truth. Moral fitness is signalled less by externals in this text than by the way characters behave under pressure.

CATHOLIC TASTES

The turn of events in the revolution by the time Radcliffe wrote *The Italian* perhaps explains why this text sets up more complex and, to some extent, bolder debates about moral truth and the progress of evil than her earlier fiction. Schedoni is a more shaded villain, whose descent into crime is described as the hardening of guilt. The young protagonists lack the guidance and protection that is afforded Adeline and Emily. Vivaldi's father is ineffective and his mother is vindictive. Sentimental surrogate parents appear only in the attenuated versions of Bianchi and Olivia. They must rely on their own resources in a paranoid environment where every potential benefactor is an inquisitor in disguise.

The restraint and near-silence of the heroine Ellena is thrown into relief in an environment of compulsive confession. This is figured in the Marchesa's relationship with Schedoni; in the chain of confessed crime which leads to the disclosure of Schedoni's guilt; in Vivaldi's 'confessional' disposition (his constant declarations of love are represented with a parodic touch) and the typical comic loquaciousness of the servant Paulo, which nearly gets him locked away in the Inquisition. Whilst these characterisations are partly a canny realignment of the gendered roles of her previous romances (the narrative is focalised through the feminised hero, who suffers at the hands of his avaricious mother, whilst the heroine, Ellena, comes into the narrative as self-possessed as she leaves it) there is a fairly obvious religious dimension to this aspect of the text: the triumph of diffuse and individualistic Protestant conscience over ritual and institutional Catholic confession.

Radcliffe's settings are, of course, European, where Counter-Reformation culture had taken hold with oppressive force (a point she makes repeatedly in her *Journey*). However, in a century when, until the late 1750s, Jacobitism had threatened Britain with the return to a Roman Catholic monarchy, when war with Catholic France seemed more or less constant, and when Catholics were being granted new privileges by increasingly tolerant legislation, the appeal to English Protestant readers of fictions about the triumph of rational faith and natural religion over superstition and dogma must have been evident to Radcliffe. Walter Scott, of course, capitalised on the 'auld romance' and old danger of Jacobitism more directly, by providing fantasies of two cultures united by the modernising forces of Georgian Britain.

The market for Radcliffe's and Scott's fantasy resolutions spoke of the real sense of unease. Anti-Catholic feeling in England remained potent beyond the end of the century. Its impact was evident in the 1780s (while England was again at war with France), when the Protestant Association petitioned parliament against what it saw as increasing Catholic toleration, after the legislation of 1778 allowed Catholics to become property owners. E. P. Thomson records how the failure of parliament to debate the issue led to the Gordon Riots, in which first property belonging to wealthy Catholics, and then the property of apparent Catholic sympathisers was attacked by crowds of 'journeymen, apprentices and servants'.[21] Of course, this kind of popular 'mob' aggression was also directed against dissenters; for instance, in the Priestley Riots of 1791, the targets were the wealthy traders and the liberal intellectual reformers of Birmingham. From Thompson's perspective, the Gordon Riots were just another sign among so many others – from the Wilkite mobs to the Birmingham rioters – of spontaneous, or possibly externally orchestrated, popular resistance to the impact of free market and industrial economy on an increasingly self-conscious 'working class'. This argument does not detract from the fact that 'Catholic' was the sign of both foreign and domestic Counter-Reformation, of aristocratic alliances between Tory old money and European landowners, of popular subjection and superstition: the feudal nemesis of rational, Protestant, constitutional liberty.

Throughout her fiction, and in her *Journey*, Radcliffe explicitly condemns the repressive nature of Catholicism. Protagonists find themselves incarcerated in convents and abbeys alongside castles and caves, all sites where free will and rational choice is subordinated to ritual persecution and 'ideal' terrors. Adeline's sketch in *The Romance of the Forest* of the Lady Abbess of the convent in which she spent her childhood is typical of her portraits of Catholic clergy:

The Lady Abbess was a woman of rigid decorum and severe devotion; exact in the observance of every detail of form, and never forgave an offence against ceremony. It was her method, when she wanted to make converts to her order, to denounce and terrify rather than to persuade and allure. Her's were the arts of cunning practised upon fear, not those of sophistication upon reason. She employed numberless stratagems to gain me to her purpose, and they all wore the complection of her character. But in the life to which she would have devoted me, I saw too many forms of real terror, to be overcome by the influence of her ideal host, and was resolute in rejecting the veil.[22]

Of course, the pleasures of Radcliffe's Gothic fiction depend upon the record of the repressive character of Catholicism, as they put into discourse all that is banished from the rational epistemology of Protestantism: superstitions, taboos and rituals. Catholic dogma and folkloric superstition may both be presented as the way of the unenlightened, but the doubled perspective of Radcliffe's Gothic blurs the boundaries between acceptable and unacceptable fancy. In place of the 'ideal host' of Catholic transubstantiation, which exists in a transcendent, unknowable realm, Radcliffe posits the 'ideal' state that exists in the Romantic subject's capacity for imagination, fancy and vision. Gothic fiction, as much as Romantic poetry, foregrounds the 'ideal' quality of experience. Radcliffe suffuses her texts with spirit, so that matter and image, at least for the protagonists, become indistinguishable. They dream of ideal terrors, while real ones stalk them in their sleep; they conjure up mental pictures of the dead or the absent which to the reader are as vivid as the 'real'; they see portraits and faces haunted by resemblances of others. This is not just empty sensation. These incessant resemblances are, as Terry Castle argues, part of a breakdown between 'mind and world' in Radcliffe's Gothic.[23] The obsessive replications and conjuring up of images in Radcliffe's texts are what Freud comes to characterise as the doubling that occurs in the 'infantile psychic life' of the uncanny, where the subject fails to distinguish between the self and not-self, and which Todorov describes as the condition of the 'fantastic' where the 'transition from mind to matter has become possible', and ordinary distinctions between the real and the unreal have broken down.[24] I would follow Castle in arguing that psychoanalytic and formalist readings of these border states do not go far enough to explain their significance in Radcliffe's fiction.[25] This sense of insubstantiality is compounded in a world in which the material has an ideal value as exchangeable property. Thus the shadows, disembodied voices, and, to use Castle's phrase, the 'spectralisation of the other', are signs both of rationalism's limits and of the increasing 'ghostliness of things' on the marketplace. In *The Mysteries of Udolpho*, Radcliffe brings together these signs of modern experience – the ideal value of the material, the impulse to make spirit materialise – in the terror that lurks at the heart of Udolpho castle. The ghastly figure that Emily sees behind the veil turns out to be a waxen image, a *momento mori*, on which the former proprietor of Udolpho gazed as a penance and a chastening reminder of his mortality. Its preservation after his death has a more material purpose, however:

> . . . he had not only superstitiously observed this penance himself, which, he had believed, was to obtain a pardon for all his sins, but had made it a condition in his will, that his descendants should preserve the image, on pain of forfeiting to the church a certain part of his domain, that they also might profit by the humiliating moral it conveyed. The figure, therefore, had been suffered to retain its station in the wall of the chamber, but his descendants excused themselves from observing the penance, to which he had been enjoined.[26]

The preservation of the waxen form, and the evacuation of the original content (its significance as a *momento mori*), has an even more particular cultural context, echoing the effects of the Reformation and the transference of Catholic property, ritual and culture to Protestantism. Here, in an inversion of that process, the preservation of a sign of Catholic ritual literally prevents the estate from falling into the hands of the church.

PROTESTANT AESTHETICS AND THE MODERN SELF

The preservation and dispersal of the forms of Catholic culture have been theorised as part of the experience of modernity and of subjectivity in modern England. Michel Foucault, for instance, addressing the formation of the modern subject, draws attention to the status of the confessional, which, whilst dispensed with ritually in Protestant culture, appears in disseminated form, in relationships beyond that of the penitent and the confessor.[27] This includes the self's relation with itself. The modern individual is characterised by its analysis, recording, modification and displacement of its own behaviour: in effect, its self-production through an on-going internal confession. For Foucault, this internalisation of institutional ritual is central to the construction of modern bureaucratic power. When given religious authority, such power becomes even more compelling. The rituals of Catholic culture, emptied of original content, dispersed and individualised, become the forms of Protestant identity. In this view, it is the dissenting varieties of Protestant worship, outside the ritual of the established Anglican church, which form the strongest alliance with the power mechanisms of the bureaucratic state. Dissenting subjects find everywhere signs of their liberty from institution, but, in conscience-ridden self-regulation submit to an order beyond their own design.

Perhaps the archetypal post-Reformation subject is thus the Romantic artist, paying homage to nature, and coming to self-knowledge and self-regulation through that worship. This self is expressed, or rather, reproduced, in the locodescriptive poem, where the poet's experience is given form and order in the terms of the predominant aesthetic categories of eighteenth-century landscape description – the sublime, the beautiful and the picturesque. The mechanisms of the Romantic (or proto-Romantic) subject's production through nature are most clearly laid out in the 'meta-narratives' which circulate alongside the poetry: in the poetic theory; in tour guides and travel journals (like Radcliffe's and the guides to the Lakes by Clarke, Gilpin, Gray, Hutchinson, West and later Wordsworth)[28]; and in narrative fictions like Radcliffe's that use the picturesque tour as a means of narrative development.

Radcliffe's landscape descriptions are often self-conscious attempts to put into narrative form the paintings of Claude Lorrain and Salvator Rosa, but by the time Radcliffe was writing, the picturesque had an established tradition in England, popularised by her near contemporaries, Gilpin, Price and Knight. The picturesque is an aesthetic that, through its privileging of cultivated, accessible wilderness, its association with the middle-class recreational tour and, as I shall argue, with English Protestant culture, is a peculiarly controlled and productive source of pleasure.

The picturesque vies with the sublime in Radcliffe's fictions, to provide the doubled experience of Gothic as it was characterised by Richard Hurd.[29] Readers take pleasure in subjection (to suspense, to terror, to superstition, to the sublime), in the rational knowledge that their liberty is secured. Liberty is figured in the relief of the imaginary landscapes, in the privileged cultural artefacts and even in the narrative movement of Radcliffe's fictions, which all come to us as picturesque experience refracted through the consciousness of her liberal protagonists. Radcliffe's fictions thus doubly avert the reader from the subjection of the sublime and the wanton pleasures of Gothic, ensuring the ascendance of a more productive, if fragile and, I shall argue, feminising aesthetic of the picturesque.

The picturesque has been described as *the* aesthetic of post-Reformation culture. Alan Liu, for instance, has analysed the picturesque in relation to various features of English historical representation and politics.[30] As the aesthetic of Reformation, it was, he argues, the aesthetic of English nationalism, for 'the meaning of Reformation in England was also . . . nationalism. It was *state*' (p. 88). Whilst Liu, following Foucault, too readily reads all national culture as state culture, his analysis of the picturesque landscape in terms of Protestantism and Whig ideology is suggestive and astute, and a brief summary of his argument provides an illuminating context for Radcliffe's use of the picturesque as a sign of English culture.

As the basis for his argument about the religious significance of the picturesque, Liu compares eighteenth-century landscape painting, topographical poetry and picturesque tour guides with sixteenth- and seventeenth-century Catholic iconography. The latter's motifs of journey and narrative forms which foregrounded human subjects, were, he argues, the means 'through which the [Catholic] Church told the story of human history in such a way as to authorise itself as the culminating temporal mold [sic] of that history' (pp. 85–6). Liu considers picturesque art (with its evolution towards subjectless images of landscape, before which the spectator reposed, and in which narrative, both movement within the scene and interpretation of the scenic journey, is arrested) to be the repressed form of Catholic iconography, a '*Protestant* method of rehearsing culture':

If the picturesque made all experience bow to form, such form was a new reform – specifically, a syncretistic or 'Anglican' reform tolerating many of the old forms but unmindful of their past significance. Picturesque arrest was evacuated liturgy. Fixed in a ritual posture of religiosity named repose, back turned to the world, and eyes adoring a mirror with hinged case not unlike a reliquary, the picturesque tourist stood in worship. But what he worshipped was one of the two Protestant arts substituting for the image of the Virgin or of the saints: landscape . . . Where once there rested the image of the Mother of God, now there reposed Mother Nature.[31]

With similar ingenuity, Liu argues that this Protestant art was a sign of changing property and economic relations and an imaginative form of social control. The picturesque, he argues, was a landscape version of the panopticon through which the Whig state supervised, regulated and encouraged the productivity of its subjects. In this formulation, the picturesque tourist is an imaginative overseer, surveying the landscape with such an eye for detail that, as Liu suggests, picturesque tour guides frequently stood in for official surveys in rural parishes. The picturesque, then, not only mimics bureaucracy, but also supplements and naturalises it.[32] Protestant and bureaucratic, the picturesque also has explicit political features. In the 1790s, two of the principal theorists of the picturesque, Uvedale Price and Richard Payne Knight, were Foxite liberals, whose political sympathies and aesthetic doctrines were read by some as evidence of their Jacobinism.[33]

THE RETURN OF THE REPRESSED

Protestant, bureaucratic and Foxite, the picturesque in the 1790s seems to be the aesthetic of the English liberal Whig imagination, and the rational sensibility of Enlightenment culture. However if, in Liu's terms, picturesque representation is 'evacuated liturgy', the empty form of a repressed Catholic culture, there is always the possibility that the repressed may return, in a more compelling form. Radcliffe's narratives are predicated on the tension of the possibility of the eruption of the sublime, and the collapse of picturesque repose. The disruptive potential of a repressed Catholic content, which is endemic to picturesque representation, becomes apparent if a historical, narrative dimension is introduced into the arrested scene. Despite Liu's emphasis on the anti-narrative quality of picturesque representation, it is not simply an aesthetic that is produced by particular spatial arrangements within the frame (pictorial or verbal), for it also has a temporal dimension. Picturesque objects rely for their effects not just on 'nature' (or the imitation of it) but on the passage of time (or the imitation of it). The roughness so cherished by the picturesque practitioner is produced both by the cultivation of wilderness and by the impact of history. If the spectator chooses to read or interpret that history, they reintroduce narrative into the frame, and the scene resists the arrest of the reposing gaze. For example, the landscape ruin, perhaps an abbey, or a castle, which is a significant feature of picturesque representation, and which is, in many ways, continuous with the 'heritage' mentality with which the picturesque became associated with the establishment of the national park, may prove to be more evocative of a national past with values very different to those of the culture which has appropriated it. To the rational Protestant eye, such ruins may seem more sublime than picturesque, signs of a Catholic culture that leave the spectator as object rather than subject. As Ann Janowitz suggests in *England's Ruins*, the anxiety which these other histories produce in the state is registered in the ruin of the monasteries in the sixteenth century and in seventeenth-century parliamentary orders to demolish castles 'in order to prevent further occupations in as yet unimagined civil wars'.[34]

Through the doubled perspective of Radcliffe's narrative, wherein the reader is both subjected to and distanced from each aesthetic experience, Radcliffe's Gothic mobilises the political and historical ambiguity of the ruin. She avoids the national and cultural discomfort of recalling an earlier English past and a Counter-Reformation present by 'painting' them in Europe. When these ruins – the abbey in which the La Mottes and Adeline take refuge in *The Romance of the Forest*, the war-ravaged castle of Udolpho, the fortress of Paruzzi where Vivaldi hears the portents of the monk in *The Italian* – appear in the distance, under the arranging eye of the surveyor, they may indeed be picturesque; but when the distance between subject and object is less well-defined, or at night, when outlines are obscured and their walls seem infinite, the ruins take on the character of the sublime. Similarly, whilst protagonists are free to wander inside, and to enjoy the curious intricacy of galleries and chambers, the picturesque prevails; when they are incarcerated, walls close in and sublimity returns.

La Motte's reflections on entering the ruined abbey in *The Romance of the Forest* are typical of the mixed response to history that such places also arouse:

He entered what appeared to have been the chapel of the abbey, where the hymn of devotion had once been raised, and the tear of penitence had once been shed; sounds, which could now be recalled by imagination – tears of penitence, which had been long since fixed in fate. La Motte paused a moment, for he felt a sensation of sublimity rising into terror – a suspension of mingled astonishment and awe! He surveyed the vastness of the place, and as he contemplated its ruins, fancy bore him back to past ages. 'And the walls,' said he, 'where once superstition lurked, and austerity anticipated an earthly purgatory, now tremble over the mortal remains of the beings who reared them!'[35]

The memories, or fancies, of a past culture that are provoked by picturesque objects are marked by an elegiac and progressive duality. The sense of loss and melancholy that is provoked by the light of deteriorating objects, of the dead and their irretrievable histories, suffuses Radcliffe's texts. Melancholy, the pathological idealisation of the dead or lost, must give way to mourning, however, in order for the subject to progress. In *The Romance of the Forest*, for instance, Radcliffe uses an ancient manuscript as a literal return of the repressed: the return of Adeline's murdered father, in the form of a narrative that reveals his identity. Its deteriorating condition ('the paleness of the ink . . . baffled her efforts to discriminate the letters' (p. 128)) produces gaps in the narrative which both arouse her curiosity and almost thwarts her ability to interpret the text. Its picturesque status almost arrests the manuscript's narrative and other kinds of historical evidence have to come to light, facilitated by the machinery of romance, before Adeline can resolve the mysteries of her past.

Picturesque artefacts like the manuscript or the ruin are elegiac talismans, through which protagonists summon up feelings of nostalgia or memories of the dead or the absent – feelings and memories that haunt the subject. Progress from the un*heimlich* to the *heimlich* depends at least metaphorically on property, on the subject's possession of him or herself and of the picturesque artefact as an object, separate from the self. Only once identity and the property on which it depends are secured does the protagonist's pursuit of irretrievable or unpalatable histories give way. In an English national context, the individual *bildungsroman* takes on a broader significance, wherein the progress of Radcliffe's protagaonists comes to stand for the repression of a feudal Catholic past and the interpellation of Protestant subjects into liberal, English culture.

PROGRESSIVE PILGRIMS

Radcliffe's fictions, of course, teem with more conventional aspects of picturesque landscape description, as her protagonists progress around the mountains, valleys and coastlines of Europe. These journeys are variously motivated: the more or less recreational search for health and change of scene; journeys which the protagonists take against their will, in the thrall of kidnappers; or flights to liberty, often in fear of pursuit. In *The Romance of the Forest* and *The Mysteries of Udolpho*, a party travels with the convalescent La Luc along the Mediterranean coast and Emily and her father take an excursion after the death of Mme St Aubert. These journeys resemble Liu's formulation of the picturesque tour, 'motivated by a desire for some special significance (whether conceived as meaning or feeling) missing at home: a sense of eventfulness whose site is in- herently "out there", other, or elsewhere' (pp. 7–8). The travel writer or tour guide buries this motivation beneath the burden of descriptions. In *The Romance of the Forest*, La Luc adopts the technique of the tour guide when he turns the journey into a pedagogic opportunity, providing for his companions a commentary not unlike that of Radcliffe's own travel journal:

The time passed with mingled pleasure and improvement as La Luc described to his attentive pupils the manners and commerce of the different inhabitants of the coast, and the natural history of the country; or as he traced in imagination the remote wanderings of rivers to their source, and delineated the characteris- tic beauties of their scenery.[36]

It is Radcliffe's fictional project, however, to foreground the subjective experience that motivates the journey and shapes landscape description. Thus Adeline, travelling with La Luc, finds significance in the feelings that are aroused by the scenes that she frames through her imaginary and real sketches and poems. These 'freeze frames' are filled with narrative significance, a sense of personal history as they trigger mem- ory and force her to contemplate the future:

The present moment brought to her recollection her voyage up the Rhone, when seeking refuge from the terrors of the Marquis de Montalt, she so anxiously endeavoured to anticipate her future destiny. She then, as now, had watched the fall of evening and the fading prospect, and she remembered what a desolate feeling had accompanied the impression that those objects had made. She had then no friends – no asylum – no certainty of escaping the pursuit of her enemy. Now she had affectionate friends – a secure retreat – and was delivered from the terrors she then suffered – but still was unhappy.[37]

In her unhappiness, which is provoked by the absence of her lover, Theodore, Adeline finds melancholy comfort in the picturesque pros- pect of the moonlight on the ocean: 'She continued to muse till the moon arose from the bosom of the ocean, and shed her trembling lustre

upon the waves, diffusing peace, and making silence more solemn . . .
Her tears had somewhat relieved the anguish of her mind, and she again
reposed in placid melancholy' (p. 295).

Momentary repose is the best the picturesque travellers can hope for
in Radcliffe's fictions, until they reach the moment of plenitude, are
reunited with lost love objects, gain new identities and are free to enjoy
the independent retirement of the picturesque estate. Before repose
becomes permanent, however, protagonists face arduous journeys; they
are bundled into carriages or flung on horseback at night by abductors
and their agents; they are often forced to travel without the benefit of a
view, save occasional, unconnected glimpses of unfamiliar landscapes.
Views, of course, bring their own kind of freedom. When Emily St
Aubert, takes her first journey to Udolpho accompanied by her aunt
and uncle Montoni, she has full access to the sublime and picturesque
scenes along the way, but is not at liberty to direct her own route. She
maintains her sense of independence, however, by looking on the
landscape with the eye of a prospective proprietor, imagining the least
inhabitable spots in more verdant, productive and pastoral guise:

> The snow was not yet melted on the summit of Mount Cenis, over which the
> travellers passed; but Emily, as she looked upon its clear lake and extended
> plain, surrounded by broken cliffs, saw, in imagination, the verdant beauty it
> would exhibit when the snows should be gone, and the shepherds, leading up
> the mid-summer flocks from Piedmont, to pasture on its flowery summit,
> should add Arcadian figures to Arcadian landscape.[38]

Significantly, the same landscape provokes Montoni and Cavigni to
dispute the route of Hannibal's passage over the Alps. Whilst the men
thrill to the thought of such adventure, Emily dwells only on the loss and
destruction that such a journey must have entailed, imagining 'soldiers
and elephants tumbling headlong down the lower precipices'. Madame
Montoni, meanwhile, notices nothing of the present scene, contemplating instead the imagined 'splendour of palaces and the grandeur of
castles, such as she believed she was going to be mistress of at Venice
and in the Apennine, and she became, in idea, little less than a princess'
(p. 166). Between the ruthless, but ambivalently romantic adventurer,
Montoni, and his avaricious wife, Emily's pastoral projections are a
model of the benign investments of the picturesque traveller. Like
Radcliffe in her *Journey*, Emily takes pleasure in the signs of cultivation and the decorous labours of the peasant community.

The imaginative investments made in the course of the picturesque
journeys have an improving effect on the travellers. As I have suggested,

the journeys in these texts, however meandering, are always purposive: they are more pilgrimage than recreation. As in many eighteenth- and nineteenth-century novels, pilgrimage is a recurrent trope in Radcliffe's fiction. For instance, when Emily finally escapes from Udolpho, and travels back to France, she journeys as a 'forlorn pilgrim' from tyranny to face the memory of loss:

> With a full heart, Emily hailed the waves, that were to bear her back to her native country, the remembrance of which, however, brought with it a pang; for there she had no home to receive, no parents to welcome her, but was going, like a forlorn pilgrim, to weep over the sad spot, where he, who was her father, lay interred.[39]

The pilgrimage may be forlorn, but for Emily, its end-point is liberty and coherent identity, as she dispels melancholic longing in the transition to mourning for the dead, reunion with the living and a coherent repertoire of memories and narratives of her past to give meaning to her future.

In *The Italian*, where picturesque description is less evident than in Radcliffe's earlier romances, the 'recreational' tour is only suggested in the framing narrative of the English travellers to whom the story is related. The environment that Radcliffe depicts is not conducive to the genteel traveller. Whilst the abducted Ellena takes an enforced carriage-ride to the monastery of San Stefano, and catches glimpses of a landscape that is more arid than is usual in Radcliffe's texts, the principal journey is undertaken by Vivaldi, the main protagonist through whom most of the narrative is focalised. As he wanders from village to village in search of Ellena, Vivaldi comes across a group of pilgrims, and adopts their costume in the hope of gaining access to Ellena's holy prison. Perhaps significantly, then, a fake pilgrim, adopting the look of a Catholic, secures Ellena's release from her convent to lead her to a more enlightened place. Their journey to freedom is hampered by the confusion over guides, from whom the Protestant pilgrims must discriminate the good from the bad. In this text, the picturesque tour becomes a paranoid journey through environments that border on the sublime. Ellena's and Vivaldi's paranoia is borne out when, on the verge of marriage and the liberty that their union will secure, Vivaldi is charged with stealing a nun from the convent and is summoned to the Inquisition in Rome, whilst Ellena is abducted again and taken to the house by the Adriatic. In each place, a battle is waged between liberal conscience and different forces of unreason. Whilst Vivaldi faces the irrational forces of the Counter-Reformation institution, Ellena awaits her doom in the hands of anarchic moral relativist Schedoni and his brutal accomplice, the assassin Spalatro.

CORRECTING THE SUBLIME

The threat that Schedoni poses to Ellena is not only violent but potentially sexual and, because of the supposed familial connection, incestuous. In the following confrontation between the two, for instance, the initial dynamic is as erotic as it is terrifying. Walking along the beach near the house where she has been taken to die, she comes across the monk, who, asking who she is and where she comes from, is told of her fears:

'Poor insect!' added Schedoni, 'who would crush thee?'

Ellena made no reply; she remained with her eyes fixed in amazement upon his face. There was something in his manner of pronouncing this, yet more extraordinary than in words themselves. Alarmed by his manner, and awed by the encreasing [sic] gloom, and swelling surge, that broke in thunder on the beach, she at length turned away, and again walked towards the hamlet which was yet very remote.[40]

On each such occasion in Radcliffe's fiction, the awakening of the tyrant's conscience averts catastrophe. This process can be read in aesthetic terms, as the correction of sublime power by the passive agency of a reposing, picturesque object.

Ellena's sexually charged encounter with the sublime turns into another kind of scene when, overcome by fear and excitement, she faints and becomes a picturesque object (the sleeping or fainted form of the heroine being reminiscent of the half-veiled, dishevelled Eve, described in Gilpin's *Three Essays* as the archetype of picturesque femininity). Radcliffe gives agency to this enthralled feminine object, as she passively effects her own release from the arrest of the sublime. Schedoni yields to her vulnerability, her helpless beauty – '[a]s he gazed upon her helpless and faded form, he became agitated' (p. 223):

While he was yet unable to baffle the new emotion by evil passions, he despised that which conquered him. 'And shall the weakness of a girl,' said he, 'subdue the resolution of a man! Shall the view of her transient sufferings unnerve my firm heart, and compel me to renounce the lofty plans I have so ardently, so laboriously imagined, at the very instant when they are changing into realities!'[41]

Just as Schedoni is about to throw Ellena into the sea, he succumbs to the pathos of her delicate, faded, feminine form. Here, and throughout her fictions, Radcliffe depicts a picturesque scene, which initially agitates and arouses the spectator, but ultimately chastens desire. This alters the erotic dynamic of the picturesque described by both Gilpin and Price. For Price, the picturesque is 'the coquetry of nature', effecting an aesthetic release for the spectator from the chains of the sublime. For, in its 'variety, its intricacy, its partial concealments, it excites that active curiosity which gives play to the mind, loosening those iron bonds with which astonishment chains up its faculties'.[42] A similar dynamic is suggested in Gilpin's description of the picturesque traveller who thrills to the chase of previously undiscovered objects, experiencing a release from the sublime as his eye roves across the landscape:

> The first source of amusement to the picturesque traveller, is the pursuit of his object – the expectation of new scenes continually opening and arising to his view. We suppose the country to have been unexplored. Under this circumstance the mind is kept constantly in agreeable suspence [sic]. The love of novelty is the foundation of this pleasure. Every distant horizon promises something new; and with this pleasing expectation we follow nature through all her walks. We pursue her from hill to dale; and hunt after those various beauties with which she everywhere bounds.
>
> The pleasures of the chace [sic] are universal . . . Care is left behind; and every human faculty is dilated with joy – And shall we suppose it a greater pleasure to the sportsman to pursue a trivial animal, than it is to the man of taste to pursue the beauties of nature? to follow her through all her recesses? to obtain a sudden glance, as she flits past him in some airy shape? to trace her through the mazes of the cover? to wind after her along the vale? or along the reaches of the river. After the pursuit we are gratified with the attainment of the object.[43]

The release of picturesque travel, and of surveying the scene, is described here in terms of sexualised pursuit, arousal and consummation. The traveller/spectator is a libertine; the scene is teasing, coy and objectified. Radcliffe's texts transform this dynamic. Her picturesque scenes may arouse curiosity, but they remain chaste and move the spectator to repose. The libertine traveller is thwarted in his desire to take pleasure from the coquetry of nature and move on, whilst the genteel seek to populate and cultivate all they survey in the picturesque scene.

The narrative movement of Radcliffe's texts is informed by principles of picturesque description, as the reader is transported through the text by means of scenic contrast, rather than episodic transition. Such contrast is often temporal as well as spatial, as protagonists compare visions of the future with memories or their present predicament. Valancourt's projection of his separation from Emily in *The Mysteries of*

Udolpho is typical:

O Emily! This countenance, on which I now gaze – will, in a moment, be gone from my eyes, and not all the efforts of fancy will be able to recall it with exactness. O! What an infinite difference between this moment and the next! Now, I am in your presence, can behold you! Then, all will be a dreary blank – and I shall be a wanderer, exiled from my only home![44]

Scenic contrast in this instance transforms the happy present into an unhappy future, or worse, no future at all. At other moments, however, imaginative projection releases protagonists from the unbearable circumstances of the present. These temporal shifts and scenic contrasts anticipate Walter Scott's 'definitive' narrative principle of history and modernity, as the protagonist–agent links and interprets his or her past, present and future to effect change. In Radcliffe's fictions, the metaphorical prospect and retrospect of the visual picturesque is given a narrative dynamic, as in each scene the present revises the past, projects a future shaped by benign providence and offers to the protagonists the possibility of progress. The controlling consciousness, which motivates this emplotment, is so passive that movement through the narrative seems agentless. Such unobtrusive narrative propulsion corresponds with what Ian Duncan, in *Modern Romance and the Transformations of the Novel*, refers to as the performance of a dialectic of 'privacy and persecution' in Radcliffe's fiction, wherein female desire and sensibility passively enact the transformation of a masculine will-to-power (p. 35). Both the narrative technique and its progressive historical register, he suggests, differ from examples of male Gothic in which there is a 'fatal dialectic of repression and riot', in which individual agency is 'blocked or transgressive' (p. 37).

PICTURESQUE RETIREMENT

This progressive dynamic of Radcliffe's narrative, the sense that historical change brings improvement, depends upon the cultural capital which each of her fantasy proprietors bring with them to the picturesque journey and to the restored estate with which each of them is rewarded. Each comes to belong through self-possession, which amounts to a separation from the world beyond them, but they remain socialised by force of their 'original sensibility'. They retire from 'commerce', but are not at odds with its values; indeed, their retirement depends on the preservation of commercial order. Her enlightened protagonists ostensibly become part of a 'representative' middle class. The independence that is afforded them by property allows them to establish both benevolent contact with and imaginative distance from the local community. That the protagonists are female, of course, throws into question their 'representative' quality in the Romantic sense, and perhaps explains why Radcliffe's fictions would long be regarded as unrepresentative of the English literary character of the 1790s. There might, however, be another, political reason for Radcliffe's marginalisation, connected with her apparent unwillingness to revise the liberalism of her early romances in the aftermath of the revolutionary terror.

Whilst the sublimity of Catholic feudalism is unequivocally overturned by the agents of the Protestant picturesque, there remain, in each of Radcliffe's romances, the signs of other kinds of consciousness which trouble the democratic imagination in the 1790s. As I have suggested, in each of Radcliffe's fictions, the reader, positioned as Hurd's sceptic, takes temporary pleasure in superstition and submission, but retains critical distance from popular epistemology. However, Radcliffe's last published fiction of the decade, *The Italian*, closes with an image of popular consciousness that is less easy to contain, discursively and politically. In the final scene, the loquacious Paolo, giving thanks for his release from the Inquisition and for the marriage of his benevolent masters, leads his friends in a celebratory chorus:

'O! giorno felice! O! giorno felice!' flew from his lips with the force of an electric shock. They communicated his enthusiasm to the whole company, the words passed like lightning from one individual to another, till Vivaldi and Ellena withdrew amidst a choral shout, and all the woods and strands of Naples re-echoed with – 'O! giorno felice! O! giorno felice!'[45]

Here rapid dissemination and spontaneous energy, albeit aroused in celebration not revolutionary discontent, pushes the liberal protagonists to the margins of their own nuptial celebration. The festivities themselves take place against the customary Anglicised estate, in which '[t]he style of the gardens, where lawns and groves, and woods varied the undulating surface, was that of England, and of the present day, rather than of Italy' (p. 412). The estate, however, is overshadowed by the more sublime natural feature of Vesuvius, described here by Paolo as 'spouting up fire, just as it used to do before we got ourselves into the Inquisition!' (p. 413) *The Italian* leaves us with the ambivalent image of the energy of popular action associated with the eruptive potential of the volcano, threatening to subsume the liberal proprietors, their picturesque estate and their implicit principle of imperceptible agency. In the aftermath of the French Revolution, Radcliffe offers an uncertain vision of historical progress, signalling either doubt in the liberalism which she had once confidently espoused or fear of the popular consciousness for which liberals had claimed to stand.

Perhaps this uncertainty, which saw Wordsworth and Coleridge retreat into their respective visions of poetic and legislative representation and which was endemic in the Romantic national idea of the organic union of parts in the whole, forced Radcliffe to give up her attempts at imaginative reconciliation in the modern romance, at least in the public domain. She wrote for remuneration no more after *The Italian*, leaving the historical romance *Gaston de Blondeville* and the narrative poem *St Alban's Abbey* unpublished. This retreat from publishing has no recorded motivation, but if the ideological cause I have offered here is too insubstantial, then another might suffice. Radcliffe had by this time come into property. Free from economic necessity and the competition of the fiction writer's marketplace, Radcliffe kept the fruits of her intellectual labours in the private domain and abandoned her commerce with a reading public whose demographic profile and political sentiments might be at odds with her imagined community. That she did so meant that her last published fiction was a more shaded, morally complex exploration of modern subjectivity than her early work and, given the reactionary culture of the late 1790s, a bold reaffirmation of the dissenting principles with which she began the decade.

CHAPTER 3

Forgotten sentiments: Helen Maria Williams's 'Letters from France'

> She wept. – Life's purple tide began to flow
> In languid streams through every thrilling vein;
> Dim were my swimming eyes – my pulse beat slow,
> And my full heart was swelled to dear delicious pain.[1]

In March 1787, *The European Magazine* published a Shakespearean sonnet by a pseudonymous poet, 'Axiologus', which was entitled 'On Seeing Miss Helen Maria Williams Weep at a Tale of Distress'. The poet was William Wordsworth; it was his first published poem, although it was not reproduced under his name during his lifetime. Some thirty-five years later, this formative moment of sonneteering seems to have dropped out of Wordsworth's memory, when, in a letter to Walter Savage Landor, he recalls his first foray into authorship and his early attempts at the sonnet. He records 1793 as the year 'when I first became an author', inspired not by the sentimental effusions of a 'minor poetess', but by a more sublime, masculine model:

Many years ago my sister happened to read to me the sonnets of Milton, which I could at that time repeat; but somehow or other I was singularly struck with the style of harmony, and the gravity, and republican austerity of those compositions. In the course of the same afternoon I produced 3 sonnets, and soon after many others; and since that time, and from want of resolution to take up anything of length, I have filled up many a moment in writing Sonnets, which, if I had never fallen into the practice, might easily have been better employed.[2]

It is possible to read this suppression of an earlier creative moment in terms of the multiply anxious trajectory of masculine Romantic poetics: anxiety about the association of poetry, particularly the sonnet, with women; a fear of the commercialisation of culture of which such an association is a sign; about the less ancillary dread of national feminisation in the face of a threat of French invasion; about Wordsworth's internal struggle for a 'manly' mode of poetic address which conceals his own crisis of masculinity.[3] Lost amongst such rationalisations – formal, national, political, psychological – is the subject of Wordsworth's sonnet; in looking for answers to Wordsworth's dilemma, that is, we repeat his suppression of a memory of Helen Maria Williams.

This chapter addresses the subject rather than the form of Wordsworth's sonnet, to consider in part what Helen Maria Williams might have stood for in the mind of the male Romantic poet and a masculine national poetics. It also implicitly addresses the reversal of literary status, or at least literary 'celebrity', which has been enjoyed by Wordsworth and Williams in the course of the last two centuries. By the time that Wordsworth reconstructed his own literary history, Williams was more popularly known for her 'foreign correspondence', her *Letters from France*, which were published in eight duodecimo volumes, and reproduced in extracts in newspapers and magazines.[4] These letters were one of the few 'eye-witness' accounts of the Revolution produced for an English audience. Wordsworth is known to have had two volumes of the letters and a volume of Williams's poetry in his possession at the time of his death, and in his correspondence he was open in his admiration of her poetic ability, even though he does not seem to have been keen to advertise his formative emulation of the female sonneteer.[5]

Williams escaped the kind of criticism from Wordsworth which he meted out to Anna Laetitia Barbauld, who, he claimed, 'was spoiled as a poetess by being a dissenter, and concerned with a dissenting academy'.[6] He had tried to meet his early muse during a visit to Paris in 1791, having obtained letters of introduction from Charlotte Smith, but Miss Williams was not at home when he called.[7] By 1814, Wordsworth still does not seem to have come to Williams's attention, if a record in Henry Crabb Robinson's diary, describing a visit to her Parisian apartments, is anything to go by. 'We conversed a little on literary subjects,' he wrote, and continued to describe how 'Mrs C. [Clarkson] and I repeated some sonnets, etc., by Wordsworth, of whom Miss W. had never heard before.'[8] In 1820, Crabb Robinson, who was helping Williams find a publisher for her latest and last work, seems finally to have arranged an introduction between the poetess and the bard.

From that point on, the canonical fortunes of the two would reverse so sharply that it scarcely seems possible that there was a time that Williams was more widely read than Wordsworth. As Andrew Ashfield suggests, in his introduction to Williams's poetry in a recent anthology of *Romantic Women Poets, 1770–1838*, 'with the possible exception of Mary

Robinson, she was the most vigorously excluded in subsequent literary histories'.[9]

In the 1790s, Williams's attitude to the French Revolution was similar to Wordsworth's; both celebrated the Gironde years then retreated from the Jacobin terror. Whilst Wordsworth, so lachrymose at sixteen, eventually withdrew into an opaque manly Englishness, or a Miltonic republican austerity, Williams maintained her the early Gironde-inspired sensibility, a sentimental transparency and faith in cosmopolitanism. Williams's transparency became invisibility, however, when, despite her contemporaneous popularity, she disappeared from the English literary canon. Williams's sense of political and social belonging, which I shall delineate in this chapter, left her in exile from a literary establishment looking for a manly English tradition.

By the time young Axiologus sent his sonnet off from Hawkshead to the editor of *The European Magazine* in 1787, Helen Maria Williams was an established figure in English literary and cultural circles, having had two volumes of her poetry published by Cadell in the previous year. Before she moved to France in 1790, she had held court at a salon in Portman Square, and had published polite, sentimental verse, some of which was explicitly political in its condemnation of slavery, colonialism and warfare. While many of her contemporary hostesses had shared her passion for liberal causes in the 1780s, not many extended their sympathies to the burgeoning cause of the French Revolution, nor opted to live at its epicentre.

Having left behind the genteel circles of her London salon for a Parisian equivalent, Williams became the darling of the liberal periodicals, including *The Analytical Review*, *The European Magazine* and *The Monthly Review*. In the latter she was 'a successful candidate, both in verse and prose, for the public favour'; an 'amiable letter-writer', whose second volume of letters, like the first, 'abounds with just and liberal sentiments, is written with elegance and spirit, and relates a great variety of pleasing anecdotes'.[10] Predictably, she was less warmly received by *The Gentleman's Magazine*, and later in the decade was admonished by *The Anti-Jacobin Review and Magazine*. She appears in *The Anti-Jacobin's* anonymously published, annotated version of Richard Polewhele's 'The Unsex'd Females' (as 'HELEN, fir'd by freedom, [who] bade adieu/ To all the broken visions of Peru'), and her literary career is glossed in the following footnote:

Helen Maria Williams is, doubtless, a true poet; but is it not extraordinary, that such a genius, a female and so young, should have become a politician; that the fair Helen, whose notes of love have charmed the moonlight vallies, should stand forward, an intemperate advocate, for Gallic licentiousness; that such a woman should import with her a blast, more pestilential than that of Avernus, though she has so often delighted us with melodies, soft as 'the sighs of the zephyr, delicious as the airs of Paradise!'[11]

Her transition from London's blue stocking society to a Parisian salon, and from the sonneteer and novelist to correspondent from a war zone (although she continued to produce poetry) laid Williams open to the commonplace reactionary critique of the political woman, and the ready association between female radicalism and sexual licentiousness. In 1793, the conservative commentator on feminine propriety, Laetitia Matilda Hawkins addressed her two volumes of *Letters on the Female Mind, its Powers and Pursuits* to Williams, condemning the presumption and immorality of this female politician.[12] Many reviewers focused on her relationship with the dissenting entrepreneur John Stone, as a means of undermining the authority of her public voice.[13] Even sympathetic critics and biographers of more recent years have privileged the image of Williams the coquette, buying into her self-portrait as a woman who was led into politics by her heart not her head.[14]

This image was forged partly in the 1780s, when she moved in the socially diverse milieu of the London literati: the middle-class woman's alternative to a formal university or academy education. Under the mentorship of Andrew Kippis, a leading figure in English dissenting circles, she was helped to publish her first work, the anti-war poem *Edwin and Eltruda: A Legendary Tale* (1782) and to move from England's provincial margins, in Berwick, to the capital and centre of literary activity. In London's salon culture, Williams mixed with the polite and the avant-garde of the literati and both radical and conservative figureheads of the political world; a liberal coterie of England's most 'enlightened'.[15] Most of Williams's output of the 1780s reflects the social, political and literary interests of the more liberal element of the salon set. She published sentimental poetry, in a range of forms – principally odes and sonnets – on public issues, focusing on their impact on the individual and the domestic sphere.[16] Her contemporaries credit her along with William Lisle Bowles and Charlotte Smith with the revival of the sonnet, and she published in both the Shakespearean and the Italian forms. Perhaps her best known piece, *Peru; in Six Cantos* (1784) epitomises the mix of public address and private sentiment, gender propriety and presumption that marks Williams's poetry. It takes on the 'masculine' subject matter of warfare and empire, but condenses the epic scope into the frame of the more acceptably feminine epyllion, and surveys the impact of war through the lens of individual tragedy.

The salon in Portman square, like that of other English women of the late eighteenth century, was, somewhat like her poetry, a sign of the liberal mix of English 'public sphere' culture. The gendering of its guests reflected that 'mix', as men and women shared the conversations, correspondence and the literary production of the London salons. Williams seems to have followed a fairly conventional route into these circles, supported by a male mentor and living with her mother and sisters. As I have suggested, however, contemporaneous and subsequent portraits of Williams depict her less as a 'learned lady', like the so-called second generation blue stockings, Frances Burney or Hannah More, than a cultured coquette, with more in common with the affected Della Cruscans: Hester Piozzi, Robert Merry, Edward Jerningham and John Moore. Williams did demonstrate to some degree the Della Cruscan taste for Tuscan culture and poetics, and in the late 1780s she, like Merry and the Italians Alfieri and Pindemonte, was drawn to France and the dawn of a new age of liberty and republican patriotism that was heralded by the fall of the Bastille. When she moved for good, first to Orléans and then to Paris, in 1791, one of her acquaintances saw more material benefits in her emigration: 'Our little democratic friend is not doing a foolish thing by leaving England, I do believe. Such is the advantage of exchange between London and Orléans, that they say the very difference may make it worth her while.'[17]

Williams's transition from the London salon to Paris marks a turning point in her literary career and her canonical fortunes, as well as her personal history. Although her *Letters from France* brought her into contemporary popular consciousness, they seem to have precipitated her subsequent disappearance from English literary history.

To some extent, Williams's move to France was initially encouraged by her acquaintance with the French du Fossé family, whose history she was later to trace in her *Letters*. Her stay was prolonged by her internationalist idealism, or at least by her desire to unite the salons of London and Paris through her correspondence. This ambition was to leave her in national and literary exile. When international relations between England and France broke down, Williams found she was no longer a citizen of the world, a correspondent for the universal public sphere; she was cast out, at least temporarily, by the French authorities as an

English infiltrator and by the English establishment as a Jacobin collaborator.[18]

Even before the outbreak of terror and warfare, Williams was attempting to bridge a gulf in national cultures which was in part based on the perception of the role of women in the English and French 'public spheres'. The rules of association in the salon cultures of Paris and London up until the 1780s were arranged along different gender axes.[19] In English coffee-house culture, the rules of polite conversation maintained Whig sociability. Although this was a feminised code, women only sporadically participated in the actual conversations of this civil domain. As a model of Englishness, Whig feminine sociability was always threatened by a competing manly, patriotic version which came to the fore at war years, and which certainly became hegemonic during and beyond the 1790s.[20] The masculine and feminine conceptions of the public sphere were underpinned by different versions of political economy – one focusing on consumption and on the creation of luxury, the other on pared-down productivity and hard-nosed competition. Models of literary value followed these economic trajectories just as much as they followed discourses of moral propriety. In the 1790s and the war years that followed, a masculine poetics of production was in the ascendant; if the writer was to correspond in the process of creation, it was with the breeze not the consumer. Epistolarity had had its day.

In the extra-literary domain, the transformation of civil 'conversation' into hard copy – journals, periodicals and newspapers – was male-dominated throughout the century, and although women were undoubtedly more than consumers of print culture, they were not, predominantly, in control of production. The trajectory of gender relations in the Parisian salon, the physical centre for the French Enlightenment republic of letters, is slightly different. As David Hume had noted with some consternation in 1742, in France there was a closer connection between conversation and written discourse (what he called the *conversible* and *learned* worlds) than in England, and women were sovereigns of both.[21] The influence of the *salonnier*, that is, went not just as far as feminising and harmonising the conversations of the philosophes (as in the English coffee house), but governed the actual production of polite letters too. It was not until the 1780s that London's hostesses seemed to hold such sway. The literary output of the English blue stockings attests to the successful translation of conversation into text and an extended sphere of influence for literary women by the 1780s. The apotheosis of the authority of women of the conversible and learned worlds of London was signalled by the onset of the kind of critical ridicule that the Parisian *salonniers* had suffered for some decades. Whilst the *salonniers* were criticised for their ambiguously seductive influence on literary men, London hostesses were berated for their wholesale appropriation of masculine intellect; the *salonnier* was a co-quette, the blue stocking a castrator.

In England and France, the crudest alternatives to these feminised 'associations' were the masonic societies that explicitly excluded women. However, more subtle shifts in gender relations occurred within the more 'enlightened' circles of salon society and the literati themselves. By the 1780s, the French sphere of influence was easily read by the champions of liberty as undemocratic, and the character of the republic of letters and the salon as too 'courtly'. Such anxiety, endemic to salon culture, was manifest in the 1780s when alternative sites of intellectual sociability such as the *musées* and the *lycées* were established. As Dena Goodman notes, the *musées* 'proclaimed a new democratic spirit, where a letter of introduction was not required for admission, where the aristocratic rules of polite conversation did not obtain, and where women no longer held the keys of access or the powers of governance' (p. 233). These spaces anticipated the Jacobin clubs of the 1790s, which marked what Habermas sees as the transformation of the literary to the political public sphere in France.[22] The *musées* largely excluded women from their activities, inviting them in, as Goodman suggests, as objects, observers and adornments of the process and space of masculine culture, but no longer as arbiters, governors or participants.

Helen Maria Williams left London and entered the Parisian scene at a crucial turning point in the literary public spheres of England and France. In Paris, Williams witnessed the eradication of the republic of letters, and the transformation of the literary to the political public sphere. She recorded this process in an eight-volume 'correspondence' with her English readers – including the readers of the miscellanies in which extracts of the letters were reproduced and serialised – at a moment when correspondence itself was being explicitly politicised in England. With letters cast into the realm of politics, and the literati coming to define themselves in opposition to mere politicians, Williams's *Letters* would be consigned to the non-literary realm; her poetry, it seems, was cast out of the English Romantic canon at the same time.

It is tempting to argue that Williams was marginalised for impropriety or for being a female politician; but as I have suggested, plenty of her contemporaries, including the young Wordsworth, welcomed her letters in the 1790s. Her canonical fate seems to have been fixed more by the anxieties of the following decades in which her letters read as the anachronistic sign of a feminised public sphere, which was in the process of being remasculinised by the literary community and the political establishment. At a time when English culture was being entrusted to the few, Williams's *Letters* are reminders of a culture of conversation – those *ideally* democratic conversations which, when put into print, would extend beyond the walls of the salon or drawing room. They speak of a culture governed by feminine codes of conduct and subjectivity, to a culture striving to construct a 'manly' character; they address matters of public and social concern in terms of domestic relations and the immediacy of experience at a time when the social and political worlds were being mythologised as transcendent, and part of a broader trajectory of historical continuity. In a final transgression, Williams stands as a persistently cosmopolitan character in an era of literary and economic nationalism.

Ironically, although Williams's *Letters* would leave her in exile, she seemed to write in the hope of joining an international community. As an epistolary correspondent, she sought membership of the French republic of letters and tried to extend its boundaries across the English Channel. Earlier in the century, French salons had benefited from the models of sociability and conversation which had disseminated from English coffee houses, and it seems that Williams felt it was time for the French to reciprocate and to send back to the English the superannuated, Gallic version of Enlightenment and society. She was warned before her journey that 'French liberty had destroyed French urbanity', but she set out to prove otherwise, believing that 'the French will carefully preserve, from the wreck of monarchical government, the old charter they have so long held of superiority in politeness'.[23] By capturing the images and the sentiments of the new order of things in letters (the established form of French Enlightenment discourse) and sending them on to her English readers, she would help to transform English political sensibility, breathe new life into the worn-out matron of English liberty and unite the men and women of letters – and their readers – in both countries.

Williams opens her correspondence with this spirit of courtly democracy and open urbanity; of easy circulation and permeable boundaries between nations, stations and subjects. The first volume, which was written while Williams was still a visitor, not yet resident in Paris, is characterised by movement, as Williams follows the familiar route of the eighteenth-century polite tourist around the abbeys, museums and commercial centres in and around Paris. Her optimism about the chivalric and cosmopolitan character of the French seems to be vindicated when she and her sister gain entry to the National Assembly without tickets: their foreignness and femininity being enough to satisfy the rules of French urbanity (1, p. 42). In these early letters, she is a sentimental traveller, feeling her way from the Palais Royal to the Maison de Ville to Versailles. She consciously evokes Sterne when she encounters a friar who resembles his monk, and a post-boy who recalls the idea of La Fleur (1, p. 89), although inadvertently she seems to be reminiscent of Yorick, whose enthusiasms blind him to the dangers of travelling through France without a passport in the middle of war. In these early days, she finds everything '*a là nation*' (the 'cant term' for all that is agreeable) as opposed to '*aristocratie*' (all that is not) (1, p. 74). All signs of the struggle for political liberty, which in Williams's eyes reached its violent zenith at the fall of the Bastille, are allied to the pursuit of social pleasure, commercial success and the preservation of French national culture. Although she notes a sign of dissent at the National Assembly, when a decree to institute rewards for literary merit meets the objection of a member who 'said the State stood in need of husbandmen, not poets' (1, p. 208), she travels with the confidence that the leaders of the French Revolution 'are men well acquainted with the human heart' who 'have not trusted merely to the force of reason, but have studied to interest in their cause the most powerful passions of human nature ' (1, pp. 61–2).

This mixture of pleasure and progress in French politics is overtly symbolised for Williams at the early state celebrations of the Revolution, where she participates not as an interested tourist but as a member of 'the public'. When she arrives in Paris on 13 July 1790, in time to witness the Fête de la Féderation, she declares her enthusiastic affiliation to a Utopian community. Following the Declaration de paix au monde in May of that year, this was a moment of optimism for revolutionary internationalism. Williams could think of herself unproblematically as a French patriot, without turning her back on her English sensibility or her self-declared status as 'citizen of the world'. To be a French patriot was, after all, to be unfettered by notions of ethnic origin. Her early enthusiasm for the Revolution, like that of other English 'liberals', is based on the assumption that she is about to witness the transformation of the French political system into something which is reminiscent of England's 'balanced' constitution: a limitation on the authority of king and aristocracy, but not their abolition. Williams embraced the signs of a new order, the symbols of a new French nation and was particularly drawn to the female figure of liberty, the sign of secularity, reason and nature. Perhaps naively, she reads liberty less as a replacement for representations of the king and church, than as a sign of the difference between the French and English attitudes towards femininity and the public sphere: 'Upon the whole, Liberty appears in France adorned with the freshness of youth, and is loved with the ardour of passion. In England she is seen in her matron state, and, like other ladies at that period, is beheld with sober veneration' (1, p. 71).

Williams demonstrates her enthusiasm for this public icon by appearing as the figure of liberty in a play called 'La Fédération, ou La Famille Patriotique', in which she and her sister and the family Du Fossé perform an entertainment for the latter's tenants. Liberty, replete with cap and scarf was performed frequently in pageants and festivals, by young women embodying the image of nature, closing the gap between surface and substance, representation and thing, in a demonstration of Rousseau's ideal of 'transparency'.

Whilst Williams is excited and arrested by the sublime spectacles of the Fête de la Fédération, it is the signs of yielding beauty which reassure her that French liberty is also feminine and consoling, like the procession of 'five hundred young ladies ... dressed in white, and decorated with cockades of the national ribbon, leading by silken cords a number of prisoners newly released from captivity' (1, p. 62). Whilst Burkean commentators railed against the monstrous inversions of gendered identity in the Revolution, Williams saw only signs of an enhanced compatibility between masculine and feminine subjectivity, in both the public and private domains. This was emblematic, she suggests, in the aesthetic combination of sublime spectacle and beautiful iconography in the symbols of the new French republic.

THE PLEASURES OF COMMERCE

This gendered complementarity is evident too in the relations between men and women in the private sphere (that is, in Habermas's terms, both the commercial and the domestic spheres) and the public domains (literary and legislative) – and in the commerce between them. For instance, she notes that the coffee houses on the boulevards admit women as freely as men 'for the English idea of finding ease, comfort, or festivity, in societies where women are excluded, never enters the imagination of a Frenchman' (2, p. 80). Similarly, familial sentiment extends into the social domain. Whilst a London tradesman sits down at the end of the day with his family, 'a bourgeois at Paris usually concludes the day at one of the spectacles' (2, p. 79). This is not, for Williams, a sign of the Frenchmen's neglect of his family, but of the extension of 'home' into the broader community. The French bourgeoisie, it seems, have an economy wherein work and leisure, public and domestic life are less radically divided, and consequently less defined by gender, than they are in England. Williams is struck by the fact that a French girl preparing to marry a merchant, will be instructed in arithmetic, to allow her to act as a clerk for her future husband (2, p. 63). This arrangement allows the husband and wife to spend their working hours together, ensures the woman's security after her husband's death, and allows the wife to keep abreast of her spouse's affairs. The wife of an English merchant is not so involved, and the consequences for England's economy are dire, she suggests. Kept away from the workplace, and ignorant of her husband's real economic situation, she 'indulges herself in a mode of living which hastens on his ruin, and receives like a thunder-stroke the intelligence that her riches were a dream, and that her husband is a bankrupt' (2, pp. 63–4). The men and women of the English bourgeoisie, that is, exist in an economy of division, deceit and delusion, living beyond their means and doomed to insolvency; their French counterparts work together in mutual trust, shared responsibility and flourishing fortunes.

For Williams, then, the French economy is regulated by the participation of its women, and by the intercourse between the domestic and the commercial realm (the 'doubled private sphere').[24] Similarly, the economy thrives on the feminised pleasures of the marketplace, which entice the consumer to spend. Williams's description of the Place du Martroy in Orléans in an early letter epitomises the tenor of the first volumes of correspondence with respect to French commerce, emphasising the pleasures of consumption rather than the rigours of production as a source of economic strength:

Pleasure and business are united on the Place du Martroy! for not only does it present fine sights, and resound with patriotic songs, but there, by way of interlude, the corn-market is held: gowns, petticoats, sweetmeats, grapes, and Bastilles of sugar are also sold in little booths erected for that purpose, and which sometimes disfigure the square. But the French are an amiable, accommodating people, and permit many things of this kind which would not be suffered in England.[25]

This image of marketplace permissiveness, of a civic space turned over to private enterprise, is typical of Williams's 'commercial humanist' perspective on France in the early years of the 1790s, and is perhaps influenced by her acquaintance with figures like the British entrepreneurs John Hurford Stone and Thomas Christie, and J.-B. Say, a French businessman and follower of Adam Smith. She represents France as a country miraculously released from the bondage of feudalism and enjoying its freedom in commercial activity. She celebrates the advent of paper money and the creation of national debt as signs of liberty. Repelling the critique of these economic moves by contemporary commentators as diverse as Arthur Young, Thomas Paine, William Cobbett and Mary Wollstonecraft, she conceptualises the new 'insubstantial' currency as a stand-in for the real commodity which, despite its temporary absence, will miraculously regenerate, accumulate and redistribute itself under the new social and economic system:

If the French money has 'made unto itself wings, and fled away,' so also has the corvée, the gabelle, the arbitrary impositions, the seigniorial rights, the enormous taxes which the poor paid to the rich, and which produced famine, where nature had scattered plenty: while they have left behind them the blessings of liberty, equal taxation, mild laws, trial by jury, the spirit of commerce. Paper money, when the crisis of the revolution is past, will, by a process only known to free states, be transformed into pure gold.[26]

This confidence in credit is symptomatic of Williams's broader imaginative investment in the future of the republic, and of the commonplace Whig connection between economic freedom and other kinds of unrestricted commerce. From this perspective, the pursuit of commerce does not preclude the generation of a public sphere of the kind envisaged by Habermas: a sphere of literate men, whose interests are not market-led. The political and literary public sphere, for Williams, transcends the material demands of the marketplace, but is informed by similar principles of exchange, unrestricted production and self-regulated consumption. Further, its liberty is bolstered by the existence of a successful private, commercial sphere. Williams's idealised version of the public sphere – the French republic of letters – is less distinct from the doubled private sphere (the realm of affective and commercial relations) than Habermas's ideal projection, which depends on a radical separation from or the denial of the private, and thus has a different gendered identity. Williams sees the French spheres as undifferentiated along gender lines, or, at least, that women participate significantly in the labours of the public intellectual sphere and the private spheres of commercial and domestic life.

Even in the early letters of 1790 and 1791, however, Williams is aware that the political changes in France have brought with them some unwelcome side effects, particularly in the gender relations of the public sphere. She notes that the 'gallantry, the ... constant attention to women' which prevailed before the Revolution is diminishing:

The men, engrossed by political concerns which involve the fate of their country, and on which their own lives and fortunes depend, have no longer leisure or inclination to devote as much time as they did formerly to the women; and I think the French ladies stand a fair chance of being soon as much neglected as the English. Not only the age of chivalry, but the age of petits maitres is past.[27]

This is the first of a number of allusions to Edmund Burke's indictment of the barbarity of the Revolution, his prophecy that the order of beauty, of consoling courtly femininity would disappear under the aegis of state rationalism. Williams is eager to make a distinction, however, between Burkean chivalry and the romance of Enlightenment; between a dusty Gothicism that enslaves women and the court's subjects and the sparkle of urbanity that liberates them. In her second volume she writes of the dawn of a new age of chivalry, wherein all classes of people are elevated, united in the cause of 'general will' which has overcome feudalism:

Living in France at present, appears to me like living in a region of romance. Events the most astonishing are here the occurrences of the day, and every newspaper is filled with articles of intelligence that will form a new era in the history of mankind. The sentiments of the people also are elevated far above the pitch of common life. All the motives which most powerfully stimulate the mind in its ordinary state, seem repressed in consideration of the public good, and every selfish interest is sacrificed with fond alacrity at the altar of the country. For my part, while I contemplate these things, I sometimes think that the age of chivalry, instead of being past for ever, is just returned; not indeed in its erroneous notions of loyalty, honour, and gallantry, which are as little 'a l'ordre du jour,' as its dwarfs, giants, and imprisoned damsels; but in its noble contempt of sordid cares, its spirit of unsullied generosity, and its heroic zeal for the happiness of others.[28]

Insistent on the image of Paris as an undivided paradise, one happy salon, Williams describes her attendance at the lycée, which was first formed in 1785: 'a charming institution, where learning seems stripped of its thorns and decorated with flowers, and where the gay and social

Parisians cultivate science and the belle-lettres, amidst the pleasures and attractions of society' (2, pp. 129–30). The *lycée* was, like the *musée*, founded by members of the republic of letters, partly to counteract the influence of the salon and the influence of the *salonnier*. This does not seem to concern Williams. The *lycée*, from Williams's account, was attended by men and women and replicated the milieu and function of the salon in its continuum of leisure and intellectual labour. Significantly, instruction at the *lycée* was given by men, an arrangement that Williams found conducive to her taking pleasure in instruction, if not increasing her knowledge: 'Of their knowledge in the different sciences they teach, I, in my ignorance, am little qualified to judge. But I can feel the charms of eloquence, and therefore find that chemistry, when taught by Mons. Fourcroy, is the most engaging, the most enchanting science in the world' (2, p. 131).

She represents the English pursuit of knowledge, on the other hand, as an antisocial ascetic affair, with male scholars engaged in 'sober meditation, and serious solitude' (2, p. 129). So intent is Williams on celebrating the charms of Parisian society in the midst of political transformation, that she seems oblivious to the downgrading of female influence in the formation of French public opinion, noting without concern the formation of clubs where the gentlemen discuss the journals of the day and politics without the company of women (2, p. 133).

There are soon signs of division, however, which disturb Williams's ease. As I have suggested, in the first letters after her arrival in France in 1790 Williams appears to wander freely, under the guidance and hospitality of her many literary friends and acquaintances, confident that she was '*à là nation*'. Some months into her second visit, whilst she watched a procession of the citizens of Paris from the Palais de Bourbon, in the apartments of the man of letters and ex-librarian to the exiled prince, de Condée, she became aware that 'the people' may in fact view her as '*aristocratie*'. Apprehending the danger, she rhetorically distances herself from the kind of crowd whose spontaneity she had once embraced, and resorts to a guarded, but Burkean condemnation of the unreasonable nature of the mob:

The people do not reason very logically; and therefore, instead of concluding, as they ought to have done, that since the aristocrates of the Palais de Bourbon were fled, those who remained behind were probably good patriots, their conclusions took quite another turn. They could associate no ideas of patriotism with the Palais de Bourbon, and accused us of aristocracy as they approached.[29]

Although on this occasion the citizens' sympathies are aroused when they discover she is English, the moment anticipates both the proscription of French men and women of letters under Robespierre's régime (his purge on the 'aristocracy of talents'), and an end to Williams's peripatetic freedom, when she is imprisoned along with the other English residents of Paris.

In Williams's Edenic narrative of the Revolution, then, the 'fall' is precipitated by the ascension of the Paris Commune, the 'gloomy and saturnine' Robespierre and 'One next in him in power, and next in crime', Danton (3, p. 7). The organicism and undifferentiated harmony of the early Revolution is supplanted by dislocation and division: 'the enchanting spell is broken, and the fair scenes of beauty and of order, are transformed into the desolation of the wilderness, and clouded by the darkness of the tempest' (3, p. 6). The spread of the Satanic 'faction' inverts the codes of salon culture which, through Williams's somewhat glazed eyes, had extended its codes of attentive politeness and urbanity throughout all orders of Paris. Now, in the sections of Paris 'which for the most part are under the influence of this faction', the citizen '... in order to gain applause, must harangue in the grossest language of the lowest vulgar; and a person of education is hooted for that reason only; any superiority of mind being considered as an aristocratical deviation from the great principles of equality' (3, p. 23).

In the succeeding volumes, Williams records the impact of the Mountain on Parisian culture. She chronicles the radical separation of the mediating, consoling literary public sphere from the legislative; of the commercial from the domestic; of the public from the private. The arts, sciences, taste, genius and literature are, she claims, being sent into 'everlasting exile' (3, p. 24). Public spaces – boulevards and squares – become theatres of execution, and hotels and salons are turned into prisons. Commerce ceases for warfare, the citizen is swapped for the soldier, and the king for a despot. Like Lear, Williams saw a 'moral and natural world ... at melancholy variance ... while one unfolded the prospect of beauty, harmony, and order, the other presented a hideous perspective of carnage and desolation' (4, p. 52).

Examples of easy circulation and free exchange of ideas are now replaced by stories of intrigue, conspiracy and subterfuge. She records the corruption of public information after attacks on printing houses and the attempts of the Jacobins to suppress representations that caricature or represent their behaviour in an unflattering light. For Williams, this perversion of 'public opinion' is exacerbated by the wilful misrepresentation of events in England. No man, she claims 'could form any adequate idea of that great event from English newspapers' (with the notable exception of the *Morning Chronicle*, which 'owes its superiority to the impartiality and talents of its editors ... to their stricter adherence to the authority of the French journals' (4, p. 211): and, no doubt, to the fact that they received their information from Williams). The worst offender, she claims, is Edmund Burke, who could be held responsible for both the circulation of poor information about the Revolution, and for the 'evils' that he predicted:

... in all probability, his predictions, and those of the writers who followed him on the same side in France, were in great measure the causes of the evils they foretold. Mr. Burke predicted the death of Louis the sixteenth, at a time when not a human being in France had such an idea in his mind.[30]

However, always the optimist, and not shy of self-contradiction, Williams notes that Burke's respondents – she cites Christie, Mackintosh, Rous, Macaulay Graham, Wollstonecraft and Brooke Boothby – 'made a powerful impression on the thinking part of the English nation', effacing the 'momentary effect of Mr. Burke's eloquence' (4, p. 220). The stigma of misrepresentation would fade, and be eclipsed by the light of indelible principle:

In the early ages of the world, the revolutions of states, and the incursions of barbarians, often overwhelmed knowledge, and occasioned the loss of principles: but since the invention of printing has diffused science over Europe, and accumulated the means of extending and perceiving truth, principles can no more be lost.[31]

Williams's Blakean faith in the transparency and enlightening force of print culture ('good will remain written in brass – the evil will evaporate like water' (4, p. 150)) is premised on the existence of a 'literary' public sphere, which supplements knowledge with pleasure and truth with consolation. However, in the aftermath of Robespierre's purge on men and women of letters the French public sphere recedes to a realm of pure politics. Williams's initial agenda to continue the exchange of ideas between France and England and to participate in an international republic of letters shifts to the more defensive ambition of justifying the Gironde revolution to her English readers. In the remaining volumes she goes to some lengths to characterise the Gironde as an amalgam of the best of the old régime (chivalry, taste, civility) with the new (democracy, equality), and to distance their ambitions from those of the Jacobins.

From 1793, with press and publishing freedom under threat, and intestine wars raging, Williams looks afresh at the 'commerce' between French regions that she had celebrated for its openness just a few months earlier, in the hope of finding a cause for the breakdown of revolutionary enlightenment. Poor internal communication, she now notes, accounts for the volatile political alliances of the French people. Trying to explain the royalist insurrection in the region between the Loire and the Charente, for instance, she characterises the area as an unilluminated blackspot, whose people lack informed principle and are therefore prone to the persuasions of anyone seeking shelter from Paris, and hence of exiled royalists. In this analysis she again characterises commerce as continuous with intellectual progress and enlightenment:

However innocent and pastoral the life of the shepherd and husbandmen has been represented, and however productive of those vices that corrupt and enervate mankind the commercial intercourse between nations may have been found; this communication brings with it an interchange of knowledge and manners which improves and embellishes society, while the permanent habitudes of the former serve to retain him in a state which adds nothing to the common stock of knowledge, and contributes nothing to the progressive improvement of the world.[32]

Whilst such regions had once inspired in Williams 'new images of plenty' (2, p. 9) they now seem stagnant, circulating nothing.

Although Williams does not see commerce as an inhibitor of enlightenment, she begins to see that the commercial realm itself is not a guarantor of culture or civilisation. As she records Robespierre's attack on the literary public sphere, she articulates a sense of a more radical distinction between the men and women of letters whose influence over the early Revolution was so benign, and the traders and labouring classes who have been thrust into positions of public authority:

The greater part of mankind in all ages, even when accustomed to the most elevated rank, have abused power: how then could it be hoped that unlimited power would not be abused, which was confided to men who were for the most part ignorant and unenlightened; men who, till that period, confined to their shops and their manual occupations, were suddenly transported into splendid hotels, with authority to unlock cabinets blazing with jewels, to seize upon heaps of uncounted gold, and with a stroke of their pens disperse as many warrants for imprisonment, as caprice, envy, or mistaken zeal might prompt.[33]

In this inverted order, where the bourgeois and the labourer have become legislators, the property of the few has become the property of 'the nation'; this is *not* the revolutionary end Williams had in mind. For her, the seizure of private property signals the end of commerce and of private pleasure; it halts the formation of a true middle class, a literate and liberal public sphere which mediates between the interests of the nation and the state; and ultimately it thwarts the possibility of both commercial and cultural international relations.

True to Williams's belief in the irrepressible nature of liberal civility, however, she notes how the palaces, hotels and apartments that housed prisoners before their executions came to serve as impromptu salons. According to Williams, the more democratic ideals of the republic of letters persist, if not thrive, on this reduced scale. '[U]nited by the strong tie of common calamity', she says, strangers became friends and the poor shared the repast of the rich (5, p. 20). Even in these circumstances, space was found, by means of a public room and private apartments, to separate the members of the former third estate ('priests, physicians, merchants, shop-keepers, actors and actresses, French valets and English waiting-women') from 'those who were most likely to find satisfaction in each others' society': the men and women of letters, (5, pp. 26–7). The prison community, that is, shares in the 'small stock of goods' but is divided in their pleasures and their tastes. The continuum between the literary and the commercial classes seems to have fractured.

THE TYRANNY OF TRANSPARENCY

From Robespierre's accession, the ideal of social transparency – both a sentimental and early revolutionary ideal – becomes synonymous with the scrutinising gaze of the faction. Those who were once eager to proclaim their virtue retreat to an opaque inwardness. The literary community, once the proponents of revolutionary truth, is now the faction's prime suspect, and is subject to continual surveillance. Openness and obliqueness lead to the same end, however: 'One person was sent to prison, because aristocracy was written in his countenance, another because it was said to be hidden at his heart' (5, p. 207).

In the last four volumes, Williams's vocabulary is littered with references to espionage, conspiracy and fear of disclosure. She illustrates the absurdity of the network of espionage with an anecdote about a piece of correspondence between a steward and the count and countess he served ('who had distinguished themselves from the beginning of the revolution by the ardour of their patriotism and the largeness of their civic donations' (5, pp. 24–5)). The message referred to a broken marble hearth, the French word for which is *foyer*, which also means the central point of a system:

The steward sent a letter, in which, among other things, he mentioned that the 'foyer must be repaired at Paris.' The letter was intercepted and read by the revolutionary committee. They swore, they raged at the dark designs of aristocracy. 'Here,' said they, 'is a daring plot indeed! a foyer of counter-revolution, and to be repaired at Paris! We must instantly seize the authors and the accomplices.'[34]

The count and countess were conducted to the Luxembourg, where Williams made their acquaintance. The episode illustrates not only the paranoid excesses of the revolutionary committee, the extent to which the 'interiors' of French citizens were subject to scrutiny but, from Williams's perspective, the degree to which those interiors (homes, minds and hearts) remained elusive. She emphasises the irrepressibility of affective community by describing how the count and countess have the consolation of 'finding themselves in the society of many of their friends and acquaintances, for all the polite part of the fauxbourg St. Germain might be said to be assembled at the Luxembourg in mass' (5, p. 26). They find a home from home. The many references to such makeshift 'domesticity' – or, at least, polite society – indicate the premium that Williams places on the autonomy and resilience of civil society and the inviolable interiority of the civilised individual.

Whilst in prison Williams's sociability is put under pressure. She records how access to those outside the Luxembourg was forbidden except through letters, and she recognised that these were now subject to the scrutiny of the sentinels. In any event, correspondence ceased to bring consolation, and newspapers – 'stamped with conspiracy, vengeance, desolation, and death' (5, p. 34) – inclined Williams and her fellow prisoners into further depths of privacy and dreams of transcending the social world: 'We sometimes quitted the crowd in the public room, and shutting ourselves up in our own apartment, endeavoured, amidst the evils of the world, like Sterne's monk, to look beyond it' (5, p. 34). Such desires find some fulfilment when Williams and the other English women prisoners are ordered from the Luxembourg to a convent. Here again, Williams finds solace in the 'tie of common calamity' which binds the women together. However, as if to illustrate the extent to which her cosmopolitanism was also cracking, she notes the 'bond of union' which was produced by 'the tie of common country' which 'appeared so strong, that it seemed, as Dr Johnson said of family relations, that we were born each others friends' (5, p. 186). In this community which is united by nation and gender, Williams discerns, and indeed envies, another level of distinction: 'that of belonging to the privileged class who gained their bread by the labour of their hands, and who alone were exempted from the penalties of the law' (5, p. 188).

This exemption was typical of Robespierre's France as Williams represents it; any activity which accrued value for the individual which was disproportionate to its public value – a surplus private value – was proscribed. Labour or pleasure that could not be publicly evaluated was only of private worth. In the commercial domain, Robespierre found an easy solution, when he initiated what Williams refers to as a purge of the 'aristocracy of commerce'. As no one should enrich himself 'while he enriched his country by the supply of its wants', Robespierre and the revolutionary committee '... conceived the project of reducing every article of merchandise and subsistence to what they called the maximum, and obliged every merchant and shopkeeper to sell his goods to the public at the prescribed rate, whatever might have been the first cost' (5, pp. 151–2). The imposition of the maximum, an economic measure which Williams claims was 'calculated to please the lower class of people' (5, p. 152) was, for her, a direct attack on the values of commercial humanism, on individual enterprise and freedom of expression. Given the commonplace connection between economic and cultural commerce, Williams's account of the attack on the 'aristocracy of commerce' is followed naturally by the purge of the 'aristocracy of talents': the execution of men and women of letters and the imposition of standardised national culture, which was to be defined by the central state.

By the time that Robespierre turned on the literati, most of Williams's fellow English enthusiasts who had visited France in the first flush of revolutionary excitement had retreated to England. If they retained cosmopolitan faith, it was from a safe distance. Williams chose to stay, and when she fled briefly it was to neutral Switzerland, not to England, where she was being received with increasing hostility by a nation preparing for war. Williams's persistence seems to have been motivated by her desire to vindicate the ambitions of her French friends who would not survive Robespierre's purge. The list of Williams's acquaintances who succumbed to the guillotine, or to suicide to escape it, reads like a check list of the French republic of letters: the Rolands, Brissot, Vergniaud, Gensonné, Rabaut Saint-Étienne, Sillery, Fonfrede, Ducos, La Source, Dupré and Pétion. After their deaths, she joined a new community, not united by common pleasure but by sympathy and mutual pity; they were a nation in mourning, communing with their dead:

There scarcely exists a family, that has not been bereaved by tyranny of some dear relation, some chosen friend, who seems from the grave to call upon them with a warning voice to watch over the liberties of their country. The love of public affairs in the people of France is now blended with all the sympathies and affections of their natures: it is heard in the signs of general mourning; it speaks in the tears of the widow and the orphan; and is not only imprinted by every argument that can render it sacred and durable to the understanding, but clings to every feeling of the heart.[35]

Robespierre attempted to unite the mourners by other means, by the creation of a new culture, a new economy of pleasure. Williams describes scenes of public festivity, like those which, she says, were once marked by spontaneous enthusiasm, but which are now choreographed and regimented. She records her contempt for Robespierre's Festival of the Supreme Being, which was orchestrated by 'the celebrated painter, David ... he, whose mind the cultivation of the finer arts had no power to soften; ... who, instead of cherishing that sacred flame of enlightened liberty which is connected with the sublimer powers of the imagination, was the laquey of the tyrant Robespierre, and the friend of the man of blood, Marat' (6, p. 74). David's art violates the mediating, consoling power of the public sphere and makes a mockery of private affections by demanding their performance in state ceremony. At his command, Williams notes, 'mothers are to embrace their daughters ... fathers to clasp their sons ... the old are to bless the young ... the young to kneel upon the old' (6, p. 86). Such spectacles are mere simulacra of the festivals that celebrated the early Revolution, in which the undirected sentiment of one was the sentiment of all:

Ah, what was then become of those civic festivals, which hailed the first glories of the sublime federation of an assembled nation, which had nobly shaken off its ignominious fetters, and exulted in its newborn freedom! What was become of those moments when no emotions were pre-ordained, no feelings measured out, no acclamations decreed; but when every bosom beat high with admiration, when every heart throbbed with enthusiastic transport, when every eye melted into tears, and the vault of heaven resounded the bursts of unpremeditated applause![36]

Williams's descriptions of Robespierre's cultural regeneration again echo Burke's prophecies of a state gone mad with rationality, and where sensibility, affection and pleasure are subject to legislation. Williams, however, resists the temptation to compare the Jacobin order of things with Burke's version of an English public sphere, which contests or agrees upon historically immanent value, and provides space for interpretation, mediation, fluctuating signs, and differential values. If France is now dictated to by an individual who is driven by the 'resentment of disappointed wit', a failed aspirant to the republic of letters, that is because of the superiority of that republic, not because of its failure.

Robespierre's regulations on cultural expression and commercial enterprise inevitably alter Williams's sense of citizenship, however. As we have already seen, her sense of national belonging recedes to a purely English identity when she is imprisoned in a convent. She is unable to imagine the international community that she had hoped to unite through her correspondence. Whilst the French literati are led to the guillotine, sympathy for the revolutionary idea, for its version of nationhood and for its cultural implications is fading fast in England, and Williams is left adrift. Although the cosmopolitan ideal persists amongst Romantics well into the next century, Romantic nationalism firmly takes root, underpinned by a myth of unregulated but representative culture, of unique but 'characteristic' English writers. Williams, mourning the loss of friends and an ideal of an international culture, reluctantly concedes that Burke's terrible prophecies seem vindicated. Looking upon the scenes of the Festival of the Supreme Being she reflects on a new sense of alienation:

From this profusion of gay objects, which in happier moments would have excited delightful sensations, the drooping soul now turned distasteful. The scent of carnage mingled with these lavish sweets; the glowing festoons appeared tinged with blood; and in the back ground of this festive scenery the guillotine arose before the disturbed imagination. I thought of that passage in Mr. Burke's book, 'In the groves of their academy, at the end of every vista I see the gallows!' Ah Liberty! best friend of mankind, why have sanguinary monsters profaned thy name, and fulfilled this gloomy prediction![37]

These Gothic projections haunt the later volumes. When she describes her movements outside the prison in these months, the sentimental traveller is displaced by the h(a)unted exile; images of plenty dematerialise to shadows and phantoms. When she is first released from prison, she returns to her apartments in Paris with a sensation of the uncanny, of a home half-recognisable. The Parisian parks where she once walked for pleasure are now 'haunted by vulgar despots . . . spies of the police' (6, p. 2).

The easy circulations of the early letters, then, stop short with Robespierre's accession to power, the proscriptions and her imprisonment. Having journeyed throughout France with no more than letters of introduction to ease her passage, Williams is forced to quit Paris, equipped with a pass, 'the mark of Cain' (6, p. 5), which entitles her to live in a nearby rural region, on condition she presents herself daily to the municipality. Under this régime she envies first the new-found esteem of the labourer, then, like Rousseau, she covets the peasant's 'lonely hut! for now I had almost lost the idea of social happiness' (6, p. 4).

If ultimately she fails to emulate the peasant's ease in solitude, she has a chance to mimic his economy when her belongings are confiscated by the state and the resources she had received from England are stopped by an Act of Parliament restricting correspondence between the two nations (5, p. 181). Her only belongings are her papers, most of which she had destroyed for fear of interception. The remainder 'consisting only of a few poetical scraps' was subject to police inspection: 'Odes, elegies, and sonnets were instantly bundled up and sent to the municipality, notwithstanding my assurances that the muses, to whom they were addressed, far from being accomplices in any conspiracy against liberty, had in all ages been its warmest auxiliaries' (5, pp. 181–2). Finding that her published letters had come to the attention of the committee of public safety, she spent the winter of 1793 'with the knife of the guillotine suspended over me by a frail thread' (5, p. 173). She took a 'singular', but unexplained opportunity to flee her adopted *patrie* for Switzerland, describing her journey in terms that would befit any of Radcliffe's heroines:

I proceeded on my journey, haunted by the images of gens d'armes, who I fancied were pursuing me, and with a sort of superstitious persuasion that it was impossible I should escape. I felt as if some magical spell would chain my feet at the frontier of France, which seemed to me a boundary that was impassable.[38]

When the boundary does open up to her, she finds herself in what seems to be 'the only speck on Europe's wide surface, where men meet for any other purposes than those of mutual destruction' (5, p. 176). Basel affords safety but she records an overwhelming sensation of exile from family and friends. Even her letters receive no reply. From the status of *salonnier* in a republic of letters bound neither by the walls of the salon, nor the borders of country, she is reduced to the status of a motherless Gothic heroine, in flight from phantoms and despots, exiled from home and comfort, in mourning for France, once 'our mother' now 'our grave' (6, p. 65). These are the consequences of revolutionary nationalism in France and a reactionary nationalism in England, both of which close down the possibility of international community, and of cosmopolitan patriotism.

NATIONAL ROMANCE

The narrative that Williams constructs in her letters is evidently under-written by romance: Edenic, chivalric, sentimental, Gothic. The Revolution is a Mannichean struggle, first between the *ancien régime* and the national assembly, then between the Jacobin faction led by Robespierre and the Gironde. The Revolution is family romance, with a fantastic twist: the country desires new parents, the new parents turn into wicked magicians. Williams's own narrative of desire is, somewhat oddly, written always from a moment of imagined plenitude, not loss, as though she looks back on dangers now passed from a regained paradise. For instance, she prefaces the seventh volume, which records the events leading to Robespierre's death, with a glimpse of the state of Paris at the time of writing, noting the return of French culture, of the mingling of public and private pleasures, undifferentiated by gender:

... literature and the arts, covered with sack-cloth and ashes during the reign of our jacobin vandals, again revive, the national library offers every other day its treasures of literature to the public, and its long galleries and ample tables are filled with persons of both sexes, who, amidst the silence which is there observed, enjoy the charm of meditation, or the pleasure of study.[39]

Romance narrative appears in more localised forms in the *Letters*, too, as Williams punctuates each volume with simple romantic vignettes and anecdotes about and from acquaintances, which illustrate particular moments in the Revolution's history. In the first volume, for instance, there are seven letters devoted to the story of the Du Fossé family. This is narrated as a romance between a young man and his love-match, which was thwarted by the patriarchal values of the *ancien régime* and revived by the Revolution, a decree of the National Assembly, and the death of the father. Williams draws attention to the romantic apparatus that shapes their story: 'Such is the history of Mons. du F-. Has it not the air of romance? and are you not glad that the *dénouement* is happy? – Does not the old Baron die exactly in the right place; at the very page one would choose?'[40]

In Volume Two she brings us the story of Auguste and Madelaine, a young aristocrat and a daughter of a modest, middle-class family, whose love is obstructed by pre-revolution convention, and thwarted further by Madelaine's decision to become a nun (2, pp. 156–82). By the miraculous force of the new order, their romance is liberated by a revolutionary decree forbidding the profession of new nuns just as Madelaine is about to take the veil. Again, Williams prepares the reader for the heightened emotional register of the story, claiming in fact, that its air of romance is remarkably understated:

... in some parts of the narrative you will meet with a little romance; but perhaps you will wonder that you meet with no more; since the scene is not in the cold philosophic climate of England, but in the warm regions of the south of France, where the imagination is elevated, where the passions acquire extraordinary energy, and where the fire of poetry flashed from the harps of the Troubadours amidst the sullen gloom of the Gothic ages.[41]

Other sentimental vignettes involve more public figures, as Williams turns 'news' into narrative. The letter which records the king's execution, for instance, combines sentiment and sensation, as it recounts the last visit from his children, the terrible drama of the beheading and the implicit sacrilege of his burial (4, pp. 27–40).

Williams's *Letters* came to the attention of a popular readership in England through the publication of one of the political apologues, the 'Memoirs of Mons. and Madame Du F-' in the December 1790 issue of *The European Magazine*. After its publication, in serialised form, it reappeared seven times in other miscellanies throughout 1791. Stories from her later works, *A Tour in Switzerland* (1798) and *Sketches of the State of Manners and Opinions in the French Republic* (1801) were similarly widely reprinted in contemporary miscellanies. According to Robert Mayo, Williams's status as the principal interpreter in England for political changes in France was based on the publication of these short stories, divested of their epistolary apparatus.[42] The 'correspondence' is reserved for a more specialised, or wealthy, readership, who were able to buy the volumes of *Letters* as they were published, under the mentorship of *The European*'s editor. It is possible, however, to see each complete volume of *Letters* as a kind of miscellany edited by Williams. Whilst Mayo suggests such a parallel between the *Letters* and the miscellanies that popularised them, when he refers to William's work as 'an animated medley of anecdote, gossip and hearsay, personal impressions, reports published in the papers, and summaries of political events' (p. 260), he fails to notice the political risk that Williams took in compiling and circulating such 'medleys'. He ignores the transcriptions of memoirs, letters and tribunal defences of the proscribed members of the 'republic of letters' that Williams 'smuggles' out in each of the later volumes.[43] Just as the political analogues translated the Revolution into the terms of magazine fiction, appealing to a 'popular', or middle-brow readership, so the transcriptions are a mediated continuation of the exchange of ideas between English and French men and women of letters, which was being closed down by governments on both sides of the Channel. As we have seen, the reproduction of extracts of her own letters in English newspapers drew Williams to the attention not only of the English reading public but also of the French committee of public safety, and she only escaped execution by fleeing to Switzerland. Her desire to circulate the manuscripts and publications of Robespierre's victims put her in similar danger. She frequently refers to the confiscation of written materials, apologising, for instance, for being unable to publish more of Madame Roland's papers than her defence to the tribunal in an appendix to the fifth volume:

With keen regret I must add, that some papers in her justification, which she sent me from her prison, perhaps with a view that at some happier period, when the voice of innocence might be heard, I should make them public, I was compelled to destroy, the night on which I was myself arrested; since, had they been found in my possession, they would inevitably have involved me in her fate.[44]

Madame Roland, like Sillery, La Source, and Brissot, succumbed to the guillotine. Williams, instead of joining and extending their community, as she had hoped on her arrival in France, finds herself lucky to be able to memorialise it and keep alive its ideals through her own publications. She supplements the transcripts of their trials, letters and memoirs with character sketches, pen portraits of the leading literary figures, most of whom perished during Robespierre's reign.[45] The fifth volume of letters reads as a catalogue of executions, and a tribute to the 'fortitude' with which the victims, particularly the women, met their fate. She adds to the list of literary victims those who martyred themselves for the sake of their country by more direct action: Amée Cecile Renaud, who attempted to assassinate Robespierre, and Charlotte Corday, who assassinated Marat (5, p. 128). Corday (a woman 'who appears to have lived in a state of literary retirement with her father, and by the study of ancient and modern histories to have imbibed a strong attachment to liberty' (5, pp. 122–9)), provides her own memorial, presenting to the judges at her trial three letters, one an 'affectionate and solemn adieu to her father', the other two written to Barbaroux, which record her 'adventures' from leaving home to the trial.

These women are particularly important for Williams as an antidote to the popular, pejorative image of all women associated with the Revolution. Williams herself provides sensational glimpses of the furies of the guillotine (5, pp. 133–4), the women who gathered at executions to pour insults on the victims; of Robespierre's band of female bodyguards, and the 'certain class of women of Paris, who gave themselves the title of revolutionary women' and were complicit with the Mountain's régime. In Williams's text, however, such women are simply more signs of the monstrous perversions of Robespierre's régime, unconnected with the consoling yet seductive icons of liberty, nature and reason; the women of the true revolutionary republic of letters.

The character sketches and execution reportage that Williams styles after the iconography of martyrdom, and supplements by the self-vindications of the martyrs' letters, memoirs and transcriptions of trial defences, urge her readers to distinguish between the perpetrators and victims of Revolutionary terror; and between the true revolution and its anarchic simulacrum. Noting with indignation the way in which the English confound the philosophes with 'the faction' ('They might with as much propriety talk of the faction of Sidney, of Russel, and of Hampden' (6, p. 76)), she looks forward to the time when:

> ... history will judge between Brissot and Robespierre, between the Gironde and the Mountain. History will not confound those sanguinary and ambitious men who passed along the revolutionary horizon like baneful meteors, spreading destruction in their course, with those whose talents formed a radiant constellation in the zone of freedom, and diffused benignant beams over the hemisphere till extinguished by storms and darkness.[46]

She offers her defences, with their appeal to a burgeoning Romantic individualism, not just to the tribunal of English public opinion, which seems to have lost its sense of value, but to the less contingent arbiter of 'history'.

EPISTOLARY EXCHANGE

What here, then, of the 'private' address of the letters? It is possible to suggest that the register of Williams's chronicle should be understood as 'public' only in terms of the extracts that are published in miscellanies and newspapers, divested of epistolary apparatus: the apologues and obituaries that popularise and 'translate' the revolutionary ideals in England. The format of epistolary address, that is, seems to demand that we understand these volumes as in some way 'private' texts, necessarily inviting us to read and interpret the author, as much as, if not more than, the letters themselves. Letters might imply personal address, but we discern little of Williams's 'private' self in these texts, or, at least, of the disclosures one would expect to find in a diary, familiar letters or, at a later moment, in autobiography. Such biographical detail about

Williams has been gleaned from the correspondences of her contemporaries and from her later work, translated into French, her *Souvenirs de la Révolution française.*[47] The 'personal' dimension of the *Letters*, if by that we understand the foregrounding of the authorial subject, has its roots in other recognisable narrative traditions, as Williams mediates her experience to extend it beyond the 'personal' into the 'private' (affective and commercial) and the 'public' domains. As I have suggested, in the early letters she is the genteel, sentimental 'tourist', guiding the reader through the cultural highlights from Paris to Rouen. The private register of these letters is to be found in Williams's fairly conventional aesthetic categorisation of the sights of her tour, as she couches her feelings in the language of sensation. In later volumes she writes as a Gothic heroine, at turns incarcerated and in flight, only writing when in temporary repose. All eight volumes, that is, are a form of 'public' address, as Williams gives order, or a kind of order, to the range of experiences which she hopes will encourage her English readers to share her sentiments about revolutionary France. To this extent, the epistolary format signals her desire to continue a tradition that was established earlier in the century by French philosophes and *salonniers*, who opened up the conversations of the salons to a broader public sphere, through writing and print.[48] The register of epistolary exchange that Williams adopts is recognisably more 'spontaneous', 'organic' and democratic than that of seventeenth-century letters, but, like other correspondences of the eighteenth century, this spontaneity, organicism and democracy is largely discursive: the sign of an expanded public sphere rather than the unmediated expression of an individual's private subjectivity.

The 'miscellaneous' nature of Williams's *Letters* – and the readiness with which extracts were reprinted in periodicals and newspapers – demonstrates the discursive nature of the texts, and the close link between the epistolary commerce of the republic of letters and other print media in the eighteenth century. The increasing 'catchment area' of the correspondence of philosophes and salon in the eighteenth century led to the establishment of newsletters and journals, which, like their English counterparts, established and extended the domain of public opinion by the circulation of reader's letters. Editors mediated this extended public, who acted, as Dena Goodman says of the philosophes, as 'intermediaries among its members and between the public and the state', but simultaneously 'submitted themselves to the tribunal of public opinion constituted by their own readership'.[49]

The bound volumes of Williams's correspondence mediate between a

French and English republic of letters, as she offers her portraits of Brissot, Roland *et al.* to the judgement of public opinion, and commits them to print for the tribunal of history. The extracts that were published in miscellanies and newspapers widen this tribunal to a broader readership, who, if less interested in the demise of urbanity, would be drawn to the narratives of 'everyday life' (turned into romance) and the immediacy of news from France. If this public were sympathetic, all of the ideals of cosmopolitan patriotism would not be lost.

As I have already suggested, Williams's is not the only epistolary voice in the volumes; there are letters by her colleagues John Hurford Stone and Thomas Christie and the various kinds of transcripted text written by her acquaintances. There are, however, no direct 'replies' from her readers, and although she does preface some letters with references to responses, this 'correspondence' exists largely in Williams's paraphrase. Sometimes, she represents this other voice as corrective, asking her to tone down her enthusiasm: 'Yesterday I received your letter, in which you accuse me of describing with too much enthusiasm the public rejoicings of France' (1, p. 145). She turns the admonition into a polemical opportunity, however, by simply repeating the eulogy instead of tempering her excitement to the taste of this embarrassed reader. One named correspondent (among a number of others) appears in the second volume: her friend Dr John Moore, whose own journal of his residence in France in 1792 stands, with Williams's *Letters*, as the fullest 'eye-witness' account by English citizens of the Revolution.[50] Williams composed a response is to Moore's 'Poetical Epistle, written in Wales, to Helen Maria Williams', written in kind, as a 'rhyming letter' inspired by a pastoral scene near Orléans, and describing men, women and children gathering the vintage: a scene which had inspired in Williams a 'new image of plenty' (2, p. 9). The rhyming letter is, significantly, a reproduction of one that she had already sent to Moore; that is, she extrapolates part of a personal correspondence, and like the sentimental vignettes and other transcriptions, introduces it into the volume at an appropriate moment, making it public.

To some degree, it is impossible to locate any purely 'affective' dimension of the letters, as the sentiment can always be read as another kind of 'private' discourse, the entrepreneurial kind, as the commercially minded Williams woos the readers of epistolary fiction. Williams frequently uses the licence of the sentimental epistolarian, inscribing her emotional state into the narrative, appealing to a readership already trained in epistolary fiction and the language of sensibility.[51] In fact, the letter form had been so thoroughly absorbed by the epistolary novel by the end of the century – in France and in England – that the 'self-inscription', the personal sentiments of any correspondent were bound to invoke pre-existing models and narrative strategies from the fictional domain as well as the albeit fluid codes of salon conversation which were inscribed in the correspondence of the *salonniers* and philosophes.

Williams thus orchestrates her 'first-hand' experience for a heterogeneous audience. This orchestration has been more pejoratively described as poor history, impressions 'frequently formed on very imperfect, one-sided, and garbled information, travestied by the enthusiasm of a clever, badly educated woman and uttered with the cocksureness of ignorance';[52] or, by Adams, as 'flighty' political romance: 'so embarrassed is she by the multitude of things to be put down that she sometimes cannot follow an exposition through' (p. 99). These nineteenth- and early twentieth-century readings repeat contemporaneous accounts of 'sentimental Helen,' who struggled with the burden of masculine political commentary. Williams, of course, invested shamelessly in this characterisation, foregrounding her own lachrymose sentiment and editing the chronology of her narrative, often at the expense of simplicity, so that the best of the Revolution is always in the foreground. For instance, on numerous occasions Williams proleptically refers to the narrative future, flagging up some triumph for liberty, but in quick succession pulls herself back to the present of the writing situation, and then to her ostensible subject, an event in the narrative past:

My pen, wearied of tracing successive pictures of human crimes and human calamity, pursues its task with reluctance; while my heart springs forward to that fair epocha which now beams upon the friends of liberty – that epocha when the French republic has cast aside her dismal shroud . . .

But whither am I wandering? Before we reach those fair and cheerful regions, we must pass through the nethermost abyss.[53]

This 'struggle' to keep that narrative in order is an obvious technique of serial narration: a teasing glimpse of an end, before the chronological order of events resumes. As well as building narrative tension, this technique is valuable in terms of the *Letters'* status as political journalism; Williams must let her readers know that the horrors she presently describes have passed, that liberty is still in the ascendant. In doing so she attempts to maintain their sympathy as well as their attention before she provides them with the chronicle of tyranny:

I must not conclude without informing you, that the dark picture which you have been contemplating is relieved by a bright and soothing perspective. The past seems like one of those frightful dreams which presents to the disturbed spirit phantoms of undescribable horror, and 'deeds without name;' awakened from which, we hail with rapture the cheering beams of the morning, and anticipate the meridian lustre of the day.[54]

The chronology of the letters is often ambiguous (most of the letters in the first volumes are undated, making it difficult to discern the relationship between the time of writing and the narrated events). Part way through Volume Five, the dating system changes altogether, in line with Robespierre's new calendar which replaced the seven-day week with a ten-day decade, and gave names to the days and months to reflect nature and reason. The calendar was, in Walter Benjamin's terms, a 'tiger's leap into the past', a reincarnation of the Roman republic, measuring time by marking new days of public significance, and turning them into 'monuments of historical consciousness'.[55] Williams submits to the new calendar on her letterhead, but effectively dismisses its public significance. She records it with some resignation as an opportunity to erase the memory of her recent personal history:

...for my own part I felt myself so little obliged to the months of my former acquaintance, which as they passed over my head had generally brought successive evils in their train, or served as the anniversaries of some melancholy epocha, that I was not much displeased to part with them for months with appellations that bring to mind images of nature, which in every aspect has some power of giving pleasure, from Nivose the month of snows, to Floreal the months of flowers. I therefore soon learnt to count the days of my captivity by the new calendar.[56]

The renaming of the months, and the reordering of 'public time' is part of the broader attempt by Robespierre to establish a new French history and to erase the memory of the past, not least through the destruction of the old national culture. Williams resists the obligation to forget. The resistance is born partly of her position as exile, as citizen of the world, and of the contradictions endemic in the idea of the revolutionary general will. From Williams's perspective, the will to imagine a collective identity around a nation cannot be divorced from that nation's history and its internal differences; differences which, she seems to believe, can be smoothed by commerce, and accommodated by a Whig public sphere, or a republic of letters, or other kinds of imagined, media(ted)/ing community. If this sounds like Burkean Romantic nationalism, the difference lies in Williams's situation. By not retreating to England, she signifies her faith in the 'extra-national' public sphere; not the Romantic national kind, the part which stands for the whole and which speaks with the logic of imperialism, but a (albeit ideal) democracy of correspondents from a heterogeneous, international public.

The irony of Williams's attempt to keep the memory of the republic of letters in circulation, and to maintain international relations between France and England, is the speed with which she was forgotten and symbolically exiled. (In material terms, she had exiled herself from England in 1791). William Beloe, writing of Williams in 1817, charts her demise from successful London hostess to relative obscurity:

> She received before she went to France the respect and attention of many of the most considerable persons in this country, both for talent and rank. What is she now? If she lives – and whether she lives or not, few know, and nobody cares – she is a wanderer – an exile, unnoticed and unknown.[57]

Mary Favret reads this fall from grace as a symptom of a society that fails to erase 'walls between a woman's place and the public forum' (p. 295); but it is also a sign of the changing character of that 'public forum', which was becoming hegemonically masculine and doggedly nationalistic even as Williams wrote her early letters.

The terms, if not the sentiment, of Beloe's somewhat premature reflections on the forgotten Williams (she was still significant enough in 1820 to be sought out by Wordsworth) recalls young Axiologus's sentimental sonnet, written thirty years earlier. In the poem, the 'wanderer' is the spirit that leaves the poet's heart on watching Williams weep:

> Life left my loaded heart, and closing eye;
> A sigh recalled the wanderer to my breast;
> Dear was the pause of life, and dear the sigh
> That called the wanderer home, and home to rest   (ll.5–8)

In 'the pause' before the wanderer returns, the poet joins his subject, Helen Maria Williams, in her tears. Composed again, he, like his wandering spirit, comes 'home to rest'.

Unlike Wordsworth, who briefly followed the wandering Williams to France, she made her home elsewhere and never returned to England. Her implicit belief in the 'sociable commerce' of an international public sphere became outdated in her own lifetime, and her public status changed considerably. As Wordsworth tailored his poetry, or at least his poetics, to a wartime austerity, a manly national public, and reaped the canonical reward, Williams drifted into literary exile.

The value of returning to her *Letters* in the present context, to remember Helen Maria Williams in our constructions of Romanticism through the revisionary lens of feminist literary history, is not simply to come to terms with a woman's 'private' intervention into politics or a feminine, sentimental construction of history; it is also to understand the changing nature of 'the public sphere' in which the women and men of the Romantic period shaped, and had their histories shaped by, our national literatures.

CHAPTER 4

Exiles and émigrés: the wanderings of Charlotte Smith

SILENT EXILE: "DESMOND" AND THE LIMITS OF
COSMOPOLITANISM

On 19 July 1790, a young Englishman wrote a letter from Paris to his mentor in England, to report with 'the most heartfelt satisfaction, that nothing is more unlike the real state of this country, than the accounts, which have, been given of it in England'. Like his countrywoman Helen Maria Williams, the young man had been overwhelmed by the 'animating spectacle' of the 14th July storming of the Bastille, and could only conjecture that the 'scenes of anarchy and confusion' which were being circulated in England 'have no existence but in the malignant fabrications of those who have been paid for their mis-representations'. The English public, he now understood, was being duped by its government's *agents provocateurs*.

The letter from a young gentleman in Paris is fictional, taken from Charlotte Smith's novel of 1792, *Desmond*.[1] It is part of a correspondence between the eponymous hero, Lionel Desmond and his guardian, Erasmus Bethel, which makes up one strand of the epistolary novel that marked a turning point in Smith's fictional writing. It was her first overtly political novel and the only work of British fiction to comment directly on the events of the French Revolution as they unfolded.[2] Set between June 1790 and February 1792, the novel incorporates references to the significant events of the early Revolution (the Fête de la Fédération, the march on Versailles, the flight and re-entry of the king) and ends at a time when hopes for a constitutional monarchy were still in tact.

Smith would have been familiar with Williams's account of the Fête de la Fédération, one of the few eyewitness reports of the scene, and with the 'malignant fabrications' of English counter-revolutionary agents, which were also reported by Williams. Many other aspects of *Desmond* exploit the sentimental and melodramatic potential of Williams's *Letters*, or perhaps simply elaborate on Williams's own use of fictional topoi to dramatise the Revolution. In Smith's novel, sentimental Helen, who writes with the 'language of the heart', is recast as Lionel Desmond, a passionate advocate of reason, who travels to France to distract himself from his love for a married woman. He finds appropriate diversion in the revolutionary celebrations and, like Williams, he mingles with liberal, pro-revolutionary aristocrats. In another echo of the *Letters*, one of Desmond's aristocratic acquaintances, Montfleuri, narrates the history of his family. The story is reminiscent of one of the prominent vignettes of Williams's first volume, the history of the pro-revolutionary, aristocratic family, du Fossé, whose plight and redemption by the Revolution Williams narrates as a 'national romance'.

By 1792, Smith had evidently not only become familiar with Williams's *Letters*, but had absorbed the range of British public opinion on the events of the early revolutionary years. *Desmond* effectively reproduces in fictional summary the pamphlet debate between Burke, Wollstonecraft, Paine and others; in fact, some of the material to which she alludes must have been published after she began to write the novel and then incorporated, as it became available. Perspectives on the Revolution and on other related matters thus seem to accumulate throughout the novel. This effect is achieved by and suited to its epistolary format, in which characters develop in the course of the exchange of ideas and sentiments. The narrative unfolds in letters between the eponymous hero, his mentor, Bethel, and other ancillary characters, principally Desmond's married amour, Geraldine Verney, and her younger sister, Fanny. Despite the linearity of the narrative – the letters are arranged chronologically with no two written on the same date or upon the same event – Smith manages to convey multiple perspective, by incorporating reported conversations, rumour and gossip into her characters' correspondence. Letters report discussions about the Revolution, conducted in French salons and in those classic spaces of the English public sphere: coffee houses and booksellers. French responses range from the enlightened Montfleuri's invocations of Voltaire and Rousseau in what amounts to a brief prehistory of the Revolution and an eloquent attack on the abuses of the *ancien régime*, to his uncle, de Hauteville's aristocratic defence of social inequality, to the exploitation of political instability in France by émigrés like de Boisbelle and de Romagnecourt, who go to England both to escape the Revolution and to take advantage of the profligate lifestyles of their English counterparts.

The English debate is often presented satirically, as Smith sketches a range of social types (who were to reappear in her later fictions) to represent various shades of ill-informed political sentiment: the passive ignorance of Geraldine's mother and of Waverley, her vacillating younger brother (who spends his time in France at houses of fashion, oblivious to the tumult around him); the middle-class attachment to rank, represented by Mrs Fairfax, her daughters and the 'professionals' who gravitate around her, Wallingford, Sidebottom and Cranbourne, the despised lawyer[3]; the boorish conservatism of the 'hereditary patriot' Lord Newminster (p. 146), who is a walking, or usually supine, argument for republicanism, to whom the Fairfax circle genuflect and in whose honour they lament the abolition of titles by the National Assembly, and with it 'the very name of nobility' (p. 148). English opportunism is represented by Robert Stamford, who has used his knowledge of the fluctuations of the British economy to his own advantage. This is 1790s England as sketched by a reformer's hand: entirely corrupt, its social ranks distinguishable only by their degree of self-interest, deference and dependence, and its institutional fabric on the brink of collapse. Allusions to the Birmingham riots and to the appearance of French counter-revolutionary agents outside Bath, who are ready to put down reform agitation, embellishes the sense that the condition of England in 1792 is perilously like that of pre-revolutionary France.

Smith ironically comments on the level of misinformation and conjecture which passes for news and debate in both countries by lacing characters' conversations and the letters that report them with gossip, scandal and rumour pertaining to characters' private affairs; in particular Desmond's purported affair with Geraldine Verney. A letter from Bethel, for instance, reports how Desmond's uncle Danby 'came bustling up to me in the coffee-house . . . to tell me, that all he had foreseen as the consequence of your imprudent journey to France, was come to pass, that you were assassinated by a party who your politics had offended; and would probably lose your life in consequence of your foolish rage for a foolish revolution' (p. 135). It is up to Bethel to inform Danby that his nephew was wounded in the course of a 'mere private quarrel'. There is much play of this kind with characters' relative interest in the Revolution and more quotidian matters, and Desmond, for all his revolutionary sentiments, is constantly rebuked (by Danby), teased (by Bethel) or admonished by himself for his preoccupation with Geraldine Verney.

Desmond's multiple perspectives, the overlapping of official discourses and unofficial dialogue on the Revolution, of public and private opinions on international and intimate matters, and of news and gossip, are conveyed largely through the epistolary format, which can contain economically a variety of social registers, as well as simply alter narrative perspective as each new letter begins. The epistolary format of the novel also signals its affiliation to a particular strand of sentimental fiction, and Smith's protagonists compare themselves explicitly with those of Frances Sheridan's *Sydney Bidulph*, Rousseau's *Julie ou la Nouvelle Héloïse* and Goethe's *The Sorrows of Young Werther*. Although, as Janet Todd suggests in her introduction to *Desmond*, Smith's narrative is 'a happier retelling of all three novels' (p. xxx), it shares the metonymic charge of 'correspondence' that circulates in those texts, and their revolutionary suggestions of sexual, social and economic exchange between writers and readers. *Desmond* is, then, a continuation of an established tradition of 'radical' epistolary fictions, and, as I have suggested, it is in part a fictionalisation of Williams's pro-revolutionary *Letters from France*. A further epistolary influence, however, which has been overlooked by most critics of *Desmond* is the most public letter exchange of 1790: that between a young political idealist, Jean-Francois du Pont, and Edmund Burke, which culminated in the publication of the *Reflections on the French Revolution in France, in a Letter Intended to Have Been Sent to a Young Gentleman in Paris*. The parallels between du Pont and Bethel and Desmond and Burke are not seamless. Bethel himself voices anti-Burkean sentiments, and sends Desmond a copy of Paine's *Rights of Man*, commending its blunt delivery and its 'sound sense' (p. 167). However, the dynamic between the revolutionary *ingénue* and the prudent elder statesman is reminiscent of the rhetorical address of Du Pont's private letters and *Reflections*. Here Burke/Bethel is characterised as a reformed rake, who is then disappointed in love, and bears the wounds inflicted by his first wife who left him for the arms of a French man. Despite remonstrating with Desmond against his impetuousness in private affairs, Bethel remains prone to the charms of beautiful women. He comes to sympathise with Desmond's attraction for Geraldine, responding to her 'loveliness in distress': terms that Smith paraphrases from Burke's *A Philosophical Enquiry into the . . . Sublime and Beautiful*. Eventually, Bethel gives way completely to his weakness for beauty, when he falls in love with Geraldine's sister Fanny, only to lose out a second time to the more chivalric allure of a Frenchman when Fanny marries Montfleuri. It seems that Smith is picking up on Wollstonecraft's caricature of Burke as a sentimental hack, who camped it up in *Reflections* with his bathetic eulogy on Marie Antoinette. If this is the case, Smith's satire is gentler. Bethel's political prudence is informed by a history of personal disappointment, and his advice to Desmond is that of a man who is aware that his moment as lover and politician is being eclipsed by a new generation of idealists. This is an analogy that could readily be extended to Edmund Burke in 1790.

Despite the connection between Bethel's private and public prudence, and between Desmond's amatory and political passions, the love-plot in *Desmond* does not simply reiterate the revolutionary argument (unlike, for instance, the romantic allegories in Williams's *Letters*, which amount to fantasies about the Revolution as a transformation of sentiment, a feminisation of culture, which is wrought by and productive of the political reorganisation). Even in the early years of the 1790s, Charlotte Smith seems to have been less certain than Williams about the potential of a class-based revolution to yield new gender relations, or the desirability of gender relations as they were imagined by those associated with revolutionary politics. In both the pro- and counter-revolutionary imaginary, women were valued primarily as bearers and moral guardians of the nation. Lionel Desmond reproduces this value system when he falls in love with Geraldine, not only despite her status as a mother but *because* of the exemplary nature of her maternal sentiments. Desmond is thus subject to the gender critique that cuts across the revolutionary/counter-revolutionary argument in the novel, and that draws attention to the persistent connection between national well-being and an objectified maternal body in the new and old nation, in French and English patriotism alike.

Desmond is thus shot through with Wollstonecraft's critique of chivalry in her *Vindication of the Rights of Men*, and adumbrates her analysis of women's objectified status in her later *Rights of Woman*. The gendered critique of Desmond's otherwise laudable sentiments is issued largely through implication rather than direct commentary, although there is a moment early in the first volume when Smith provides a footnote that contradicts one of her hero's more romantic political visions. Visiting Montfleuri's estate, Desmond comments on the rational happiness of the peasantry (another allusion that is reminiscent of Williams's *Letters*). A comparison with the contentment of the English peasantry elicits a footnote from Smith, which cites the unhappiness of the English rural poor. If Bethel finds Desmond's revolutionary sympathies quixotic, this intervention indicts that quixotism from a more revolutionary perspective.

Desmond's complicity with a conservative social vision is mainly thrown into relief in the course of Geraldine's correspondence with her younger sister. Here, she gives voice to less temperate sentiments about the lot of women than may be expected from a figure who is invariably represented by the men in the text as an icon of maternal endurance.[4] Whilst Fanny rails, it is Geraldine who comes closest to articulating Wollstonecraft's views on the inadequacy of women's education and the bondage of their financial dependence. When she responds to a letter from Fanny, in which the younger sister describes the restrictions that have been placed on her reading, Geraldine can only lament that even though *she* had free access to all manner of reading matter, her head was not turned by even the most extravagant romance, and that she thought only of being a 'quiet wife, and a good nurse, and of fulfilling, as well as I can, the part which has been chosen for me' (p. 195). Her dissent continues with a caustic description of her mother, as a woman whose idea of happiness 'consists in being visited by the opulent, in having . . . the reputation of having very good parties . . . and of being considered as a perfect judge of etiquette, and a woman of the highest respectability' (p. 235): again, this is reminiscent of Wollstonecraft's attacks on women of fashion in her *Vindication* and her short fiction, *Mary*.

Most commentators suggest that Smith, unlike Wollstonecraft, ultimately concedes to the logic of romance (by which, as she frequently tells her readers, she is contractually bound) when Geraldine is rewarded for her patience by her husband's death and his blessing on a union with the enlightened Desmond. The romance is surely undercut, however, by the silence that haunts the text (and much of the early commentary on it): the unrepresented voice of Geraldine's double, Josephine de Boisbelle.[5] The sister of Desmond's friend Montfleuri and abandoned wife of a French émigré, Josephine is figured as equal in charms, virtue and unhappiness to Geraldine, but she is rewarded neither by self-representation (there are no letters from Josephine), nor by the dubious prize of a romance conclusion. The narrative twist that seals Josephine's fate – her sexual relationship with Desmond – is only ever implied in euphemistic references to his 'unworthiness' for Geraldine. The final revelation that Josephine has given birth to Desmond's child – the 'consequence of her indiscreet attachment' (p. 404) – merely provides another opportunity for Geraldine to demonstrate her magnanimity by extending her family from three to four, whilst Josephine is consigned to exile in Italy and the prospect of remarriage to a distant cousin, who, we learn, has commercial interests in the East Indies.

It has been argued that this uneven distribution of rewards is symptomatic of Smith's attempts to explore as far as possible the adultery plot, whilst remaining within the bounds of romance propriety (Geraldine's 'other' gives way to sexual passion so that Geraldine can be rewarded for her virtue) and that Smith capitulates to a discourse of national difference by marking out Geraldine as Josephine's natural superior and therefore the natural recipient of Desmond's favours.[6] However, such readings overlook the gender-consciousness of the novel, and depend on too radical a separation between its 'romance' plot and its intervention in the Revolution debate. Geraldine and Josephine, like other women in the text, are frequently figured as objects for exchange between men. Verney's attempt to sell off his wife is only the crudest version of an acceptable practice. The women are discussed throughout as interchangeable love-objects: Fanny is recommended by Bethel to Desmond as a more suitable match than Geraldine, and then by Desmond to Bethel as a candidate for his second wife; Josephine evidently stands in for Geraldine whilst Desmond is in France, and, later, when she is lying-in in England, she is mistaken for her English double, precipitating a surge of local gossip; ultimately, Geraldine is given to Desmond by the penitent Verney and Josephine is given to a man who is explicitly connected with colonial appropriation.

Whilst Geraldine and Josephine are interchangeable at one level, it is the cosmopolitan Desmond who articulates the difference between them. When describing Josephine, Desmond implies that the qualities that make a French woman charming do not apply to English women:

She has a pretty voice and plays well on the harp. Yet all she does has so much of national character in it, that it would become only a French woman, and I think I should not admire one of my own countrywomen, who possessed exactly the person, talents and manners of my friend's sister.[7]

Josephine's performance of her gender is constitutionally national: her feminine accomplishments may not be inherently female but they are inherently French. It is apparently Josephine's national body that marks the limits of her interchangeability with Geraldine:

I have once or twice, as Madame de Boisbelle has been walking with me, tried to fancy her Geraldine, and particularly when she has been in her plaintive moods. I have caught sounds that have, for a moment, aided my desire to be deceived. – But, as the lady herself could not guess what made me so silent and inattentive . . . some trait, in the character of her country, has suddenly dissolved the charm, and awakened me to a full sense of the folly I was guilty of.[8]

Desmond understands his folly to be less his indiscreet attention to a married woman, than his 'desire to be deceived' that he could love a Frenchwoman *as* an Englishwoman. For the otherwise cosmopolitan and Francophile Desmond, the limit of Josephine's and Geraldine's transferability is, in part, marked by their nationality. Alison Conway has argued that the national difference of Josephine's body is necessary to the nationalist logic of the plot, as it functions to make Geraldine's and Desmond's bodies appear more alike. Further, she argues that Josephine and Desmond's child (the child being a revolutionary symbol of the future of the nation) provides a bond between French theory and English history without the presence of the errant French body. This is a persuasive reading, but it repeats Desmond's own reasoning, and overlooks the polyphonic effects of the novel that undercut his perspective. It also overlooks another difference between Josephine and Geraldine. When Desmond first meets Geraldine, she is a mother; when he first meets Josephine, she is merely a wife. In his desire to elide the difference between them, Desmond cannot make Josephine English, but he can make her a mother. In doing so, he guarantees her exclusion both from the old order and the 'new international'. Desmond cannot sanction Josephine's romantic 'return' to the new order, however; not because she is French, but because she is now a mother.

That Smith chose not to make Josephine absent through death but through exile is symptomatic of the way in which, throughout the novel, she draws attention to the way that fantasies of familial and national reorganisation are fatally woven together: fatally, that is, for women. She demonstrates that the new sentimental family on which the new nation will be modelled does little to transform the status of women, either as national or familial subjects. With Josephine in exile in Italy, Desmond can indeed fantasise about the success of an intimate revolution, of revolutionary cosmopolitanism, as he describes to his mentor his image of a newly defined family: 'My Geraldine, You, my dear Bethel and your sweet Louisa – my friend Montfleuri, and his Fanny' (p. 408). As the use of possessive pronouns in this sentence suggests, this revolution in sentiment is still dependent on the subordinate status of women. The limits of the Revolution are made explicit by the silence of the extra mother who is absented from this familial scene. In the new international order, Geraldine can be sanctified as a mother, but Josephine is surplus to requirements. Rather than capitulating to nationalist sentiment, Smith demonstrates the pervasively patriarchal logic of revolutionary thought, its attachment to the familial model of the nation, and to the subordination of women.

The trope of exile that dominates the ending of *Desmond* is recurrent in Smith's fiction and her poetry. This can be attributed both to a 'Romantic' preoccupation with a generalised condition of alienation and to the more particular impact of revolution and war on the discourse of national belonging. As I suggested in relation to Williams's *Letters*, the national self-consciousness of the 1790s necessarily produced the spectre of the non-national, defined either as ethnically 'foreign' or more pervasively, and less tangibly, as alien to the national self-image. Thus, in France, the aristocracy was soon declared as non-national by the revolutionary hegemony, when the National Assembly decreed the abolition of titles in June 1790. The response of many aristocrats was to literalise their condition, and to leave France for more hospitable shores. Ironically, for many, this friendly place constituted England, a sign perhaps of the long-standing connections between British and European aristocracy that transcended broader national antagonisms. As I have suggested, *Desmond*, which opens in June 1790, incorporates a response to the wave of emigration that began in that month. Here, such ties constitute an international libertinism, exemplified by the exploits of Verney, de Boisbelle, a number of profligate English peers and French aristocrats who make up their party and who see in the Revolution an opportunity to capitalise on economic and political instability. Desmond and Montfleuri, whose mutual acquaintance with the thoughts of Locke, Rousseau and Voltaire speaks of the enlightened cosmopolitanism that fuelled the Revolution, throw their opportunism into relief. As I have suggested, however, Smith's text problematises the opposition between international libertinism and cosmopolitanism, from a gendered perspective. It is a problem founded not only on the status of women in the old and new orders, but also on the logic of Romantic nationalism that shapes cosmopolitan thought. Whilst libertines exhibit an indifference to the sentiment of place, of cultivation and generation, the sensibility of the cosmopolitan is, paradoxically, informed by his attachment to place. Desmond signals this when he writes to Bethel on his arrival from Paris: 'Were my heart less deeply interested for my friends in England, I should be quite absorbed in French politics' (p. 66). Desmond's inability to detach himself from his native place even in such distracting circumstances is echoed in Montfleuri's conversion of his family's Gothic pile into a productive estate, and of a disused monastery into a 'house of industry': both organic commitments to the new French nation. These signs of investment in his native place are, of course, highlighted by Verney's ready transfer of Linwell to Stamford and by Stamford's forced cultivations and grotesque improvements of the estate. Just as Verney's wantonness extends to his relation with his wife, selling her off to de Romagnecourt, so Desmond's attachment to England extends to his feelings for Geraldine. Though the spirit is willing, the cosmopolitan, at least the English cosmopolitan, cannot be in two places at once. The French Montfleuri is able to marry Fanny and join the new family group in England; but Desmond can only attach himself to one woman, one estate, one nation. As Josephine reports to her brother, explaining the terms of her intimate acquaintance with Desmond: 'he had promised nothing; . . . he used no art to betray her, but, on the contrary, had told her that his whole soul was dedicated to another' (p. 405).

GOING HOME: "THE BANISHED MAN" AND EUROPEAN
ÉMIGRÉS

Smith wrote *Desmond* while she was living at Brighton, a gathering place for London literati and French émigrés. She focused her attention on the latter for the 'public poem' she wrote in 1793, *The Emigrants*.[9] The poem is in two books, each delivered by a meditative female speaker, who reflects on her own forlorn condition, on the situation of the 'Men/ banish'd for ever and for conscience sake/ From their distracted Country' (ll. 96–98), and on the tyrannical turn of the Revolution. The first book is set on the cliffs to the east of Brighton, on an early morning in November 1792 (by which time France had been declared a Republic and Robespierre was in control of the French Convention). The speaker is roused from her own melancholy reflections by 'Sad Heralds of distress!' (l. 96): the 'dejected looks' of an approaching group of émigrés. The passage that follows, incorporating descriptions of the fallen condition of the typical victims of the Revolution, members of the clergy and aristocracy, serves both as advocacy of tolerance for the French exiles while they are in England, and builds to a chastising warning to Britain's political representatives – 'Pensioners/Of Base corruption', 'worthless hirelings of a Court!', 'pamper'd Parasites' (ll. 316–17; l. 329; l. 330) – of the fruits of inequality:

> Study a lesson that concerns ye much;
> And, trembling, learn, that if oppress'd too long,
> The raging multitude, to madness stung,
> Will turn on their oppressors; and, no more

> By sounding titles and parading forms
> Bound like tame victims will redress themselves![10]

Although reviews of the poem censured it less for its political force than for its self-referentiality,[11] the critical allusions to the French clergy and the French aristocracy, here and in *Desmond*, were noted by Thomas Lowes, who saw them as symptomatic of the increasingly 'democratic twist' in Smith's behaviour and attitudes in the early 1790s. Having 'liked her well enough for some time', he had been disgusted when she condoned the massacre of the Swiss Guards at the Tuilleries, from which time he no longer sought her company. In an arch comment on her malleable political opinions, however, he noted that '[n]ot long after this Augusta [Smith's daughter] married an emigrant French noble-man, and I understand that her style both in her conversation and novels altered considerably'.[12]

Certainly, by the time Smith wrote her next novel on the Revolution in 1794 – *The Banished Man*[13] – she, like most of her 'radical' contempora-ries, looked with horror on the turn of events in France, and chose to focus her narrative on the plight of a virulently anti-republican French aristocrat. She was at pains to note in the novel's preface that although her protagonist is, like her son-in-law, 'under the exigencies of banish-ment and proscription', he 'resembles in nothing but in merit, the emigrant gentleman who now makes part of my family'. Despite Lowe's insinuation of a sea change in Smith's politics, and despite its reception in *The European Magazine* as a prophylactic against 'admitting the spe-cious reasonings of republicanism' into England,[14] *The Banished Man* is not such a radical departure from *Desmond*. Rather, it reiterates the ideals of the early Revolution, directing the critique towards the tyranny of the new régime in France, and provides a continuing argument for the republican cause elsewhere in Europe.

The Banished Man, as its title suggests, is an exploration of the condition of exile, engendered not only by the wave of French aristocratic emigra-tion in 1790, but by the advance of the French republican army into Europe in 1792, which displaced large numbers of the population of the Austro-Prussian empire. As in *Desmond*, Smith fictionalises recent politi-cal history, adopting and frustrating Gothic conventions which, in the wake of Radcliffe's romances and to some extent Williams' *Letters*, are already overdetermined by the semiotics of the Revolution and broader cultural crisis. Setting her novel between October 1792 and July 1793, Smith eschews the thin, ahistorical disguise of Radcliffean Gothic. The Gothic setting that is revealed in chapter one, Castle Rosenheim, is not a rococo metonym of an internally divided, transitional England. Rather, situated beyond the French border somewhere into an Austro-Prussian empire, Rosenheim is part of the territorial netherland that is Western Europe during the revolutionary wars. Abandoned by the retreat of the imperial troops and exposed to a siege by the French republican army, the occupants of the castle are discovered as they experience the disorienting effects of war. The novel opens on a sleepless night, with the householders – the stoic Baroness de Rosenheim, her more sentimental daughter, Mme d'Alberg, and their servants – transfixed by the simultaneous sound of a storm and cannon-fire. Their fears are exacerbated by the absence of the Baron and his son-in-law, the Count D'Alberg, who are stationed with the imperial army at Vienna. When the household finally retires to bed, Mme D'Alberg is disturbed by the sound of human groans, mingled with the noise of the wind and rain. Finally able to distinguish one noise from the other, she recognises the voice of a Frenchman. When she sends for assistance from a servant, the household is thrown into a state of emergency, and the shout goes up that Sans Culottes are at the castle walls.

Here, then, is a familiar Gothic context: female virtue in distress; a fatherless household, besieged by real or phantom interlopers; superstitious domestics who exacerbate, and in some cases, manipulate, the heroine's anxieties. Smith seems set to round off the formula with the arrival of a chivalric hero when, instead of Sans Culottes at the wall, Mme D'Alberg discovers an ageing French royalist and his son, Armand D'Alonville. The discovery of a wounded father, supported by his son (a scene economically resonant with Burkean imagery of state violation and national loyalty) sets in train the romantic expectation of the union of the daughter of the house with the sentimental stranger. This is frustrated when Smith restores Mme D'Alberg to her husband after the first few chapters. For readers familiar with Smith's novels, this merely sets the scene for a repetition of the adultery plot in *Desmond* and the earlier *Ethelinde*. Smith frustrates this possibility, too, however, by turning her attention away from Mme D'Alberg at the end of Volume One, until she is reintroduced in marital harmony, at the end of the fourth volume. As the reviewer in *The European Magazine* suggests, this is not a novel for those seeking a love interest.[15] Smith is self-conscious about the disorientation she produces in her reader by abandoning this potential love-plot. In an imagined dialogue between the author and a friend in the preface to the second volume, the latter remarks on the novelty of reaching the end of the first volume with no sign of a romantic heroine. In this novel, the reader, like the hero, will have to go further afield to find consolation. D'Alonville, the displaced French aristocrat, has a peripatetic destiny to fulfil before he can be relocated, or find a new home. His insubstantial and misinterpreted arrival at Rosenheim, when he is no more than a disembodied voice, mistaken first for the sound of the wind and then for a Sans Culotte, suggests how far the Revolution has divested him of his history, and the extent to which his national language has become a divided sign. This is reinforced when D'Alonville recounts his recent history: a story of displacement, first from a private home and then from a nation. In D'Alonville's account of his arrival at Rosenheim, all of France, royalist and patriot, is on the move, one half in flight from the other. This internal conflict and its diasporic effects are dramatised in the plight of D'Alonville's family itself. The father, a royalist, is betrayed by his eldest son who has joined the republican forces, but is consoled by the loyalty of a younger son, with whom he is forced into exile: a ready analogy with the plight of the French monarch and his divided subjects.

This story is immediately reiterated with the death of D'Alonville's father, the battle-scarred and broken-hearted Fayolles, and by the decision of the Rosenheim household (reconfigured to include D'Alonville as a surrogate son) to leave the castle to the ravages of the Sans Culottes and to find refuge in Koblenz.[16] D'Alonville's fate is not merely doubled at a personal level, but is recapitulated in the stories of the many other exiles he encounters as he wanders back and forth across the French border.

D'Alonville's wanderings take him to Austria, Germany and England, attempting to retrieve his family property and gathering around him a surrogate family of other émigrés and travellers: the Marquis de Touranges, a French aristocrat searching for his wife and mother; his companion, the Abbé de St. Remi; and Ellesmere and Melton, two English travellers, with whom D'Alonville journeys through the German states, before joining them in their return to England. Whilst in Dresden, the party is joined by another exile: the Polish patriot Carlowitz, who provides the novel's most powerful counterpoint to D'Alonville's embittered attacks on republicanism. Poland, having been inspired by the French and American revolutions to establish a democratic government, had moved towards a constitutional monarchy in 1791, but was subsequently invaded and partitioned by Russia, Prussia and Austria. Carlowitz is the subject of a lost nation, a proud patriot with no country. His arguments with D'Alonville not only provide a historical gloss on the broader conflict in Europe, but are also an outlet for republican discourse that can no longer be articulated sympathetically through a French subject.

Rather than capitulate to counter-revolutionary sentiment, then, as Lowes argued, the novel reasserts the cosmopolitan fantasy that underpinned early revolutionary philosophy. Again, Smith demonstrates that transnationalism is supported by a familial structure, albeit a liberal one, for D'Alonville's invented community also includes a wife. The double deferral of D'Alonville's love-plot is brought to an end with the introduction, in Volume Two, of Angelina: an English woman who fulfils all expectations of a Gothic heroine. The gender critique of *Desmond* does not disappear, however, but shifts its focus. The female exile is not now an abandoned lover, but the single mother of Angelina: the beleaguered English novelist, Charlotte Denzil, to whom D'Alonville is introduced by Ellesmere.

Through Denzil, Smith brings back into focus the criticisms of the British public that she had voiced in *Desmond*. *The Banished Man* provides another gloss on the public/private dichotomy by demonstrating the vulnerability of women in respect to property law and their dependence on public representatives. In an obvious dramatisation of Smith's own predicament, Denzil narrates how she is prevented by a legal wrangle from living in property that is legally hers. Dependent on benefactors and the money she earns from writing novels, Denzil is constantly in flight from debtors and beleaguered by feelings of obligation. When she is offered a home by a 'philanthropic' aristocrat, she describes in a letter to a friend how the worst debts are those that are to be repaid by ill-defined means and she makes a veiled gesture to the promise of a home in return for sexual favours. She dreams, she says, of being able to divest herself of the binds of patronage, which are doubled by the demands of the publisher and bookseller, and 'to pack up my children and my books, in which consist all my riches, and, like a female Prospero, set forth for some desert island – or any island but this dear England of ours' (2, p. 217). Her fantasy of bringing to an end the nomadism and dispossession of modern authorship, the obligations of patronage and the demands of the marketplace, is curtailed by the fact that her only possession is 'learning', a 'commodity [which] would not be marketable in any other country' (2, pp. 219–20).

Denzil is just one version of Smith's fictional self-portrait. Her tendency to represent herself in her texts was vilified by some contemporary reviewers but is equally celebrated by recent readers of Smith's work.[17] Her fiction and, of course, her poetry catalogues her life of debt and her frustration with the legal bureaucracy which tied up the trust fund bequeathed to her children by her father-in-law. Her self-referential technique varies from direct authorial intervention, usually prefatorial, to transparently autobiographical characterisation, such as Geraldine Verney or Denzil, to analogy with characters in financial or other distress. Whilst Smith's success in capitalising on her indebtedness, or 'selling her sorrows' is neatly illustrative of the ways in which women writers manipulated the literary marketplace, the acumen and humour of the authorial performance should not blind us to the extent of the critique of British 'public' life which is built into these episodes, and which goes beyond the demonstration of the author's private need. Indeed, Smith's fictions do not allow for the easy separation of private and public interest, as they play out the way in which one produces and redefines the other. In *Desmond*, private interest largely signals public corruption, from Verney's libertine profligacy to Desmond's misplaced chivalry. *The Banished Man* conducts an extensive debate on what constitutes the difference between public and private interest. From the opening scenes, for instance, the German almoner and steward to the Rosenheim household, Heurthosen, is figured as an opportunist who puts personal interests before the needs of the family he serves. When the family debate the risk of allowing the emigrants to take refuge in the castle, he argues with primitivist logic: 'I would have everybody . . . consult their own security first; – it is the first law of nature' (1, p. 56). He evidently acts on this principle when he leaves the family to their fate when the carriage taking them to Koblenz goes off the road and falls into a swollen river. His demonstrable lack of integrity in the opening scenes anticipates his later return as Citizen Rouillé, who, less through conviction than self-preservation, has thrown in his lot with the cause of French republicanism. We rejoin Rouillés amongst a circle of republican *salonniers* to whom D'Alonville is introduced by his brother in the hope that the charms of its society will procure his conversion to the republican cause. Instead, D'Alonville is repelled by the incongruity of hearing a 'defence of the horrors that had stained with eternal disgrace, the annals of France as a nation' uttered from the 'beautiful mouth' of a French hostess (4, p. 6). D'Alonville's time in Paris, where tradesmen sit in empty shops and manufacturers have nothing to make, only compounds his conviction that the Revolution was no longer in tune with the 'real sentiments of the people' (4, p. 7). 'How,' he asked, 'could that government be established on the voice of the people, which the people were every where rising to oppose?' (4, p. 8). In the broader context of the novel, the force of D'Alonville's critique seems to be directed against the unrepresentative status of the British establishment as well as the French revolutionary order.

By focusing the political divide through the plight of the royalist and republican brothers D'Alonville and Du Bossé, Smith seems to suggest that the most significant impact of the Revolution and European war is the disintegration of the family and that the subordination of private family sentiment to the republican cause has destroyed the homes of Europe. The band of international wanderers who constitute D'Alonville's invented family (eventually relocated to Verona) seem again to emblematise a new order. As the novel draws to a close, Ellesmere is still in England, but is anxious to leave with his wife, the child of nature Alexina (a Polish replica of D'Alonville's Angelina) and her father Carlowitz, who still harbours 'too sanguine' hopes that his country might be restored. He hopes to join D'Alonville's invented community and to establish a home that is 'independent' but modest, stripped bare of the trappings which are deemed necessary to a man of his status in England. The pleasures of Alexina, he tells D'Alonville, will compensate for his reduced circumstances:

Ah, D'Alonville, with such a wife, how lightly the little disappointments and vexations of life may be passed over! As to our pecuniary circumstances, I now think it a weakness that I ever suffered reflections on them to depress me: we are above indigence; we are independent, though not rich; and well as I love England, I can be content to quit it, if the luxuries, that are here accounted among the necessaries of a man of family, cannot be enjoyed but at the expence [sic] of that independence.[18]

As the novel ends, the war in Europe still rages. The threat to paradise is evidenced by Ellesmere's injunction to D'Alonville on the dangers of returning to the emigrant counter-revolutionary army and the absence of de Touranges, who, D'Alonville notes, is gone to rejoin the army in Flanders, and whose absence alone, by rendering his newly redis-covered mother and his wife unhappy, 'detracts from the pleasure of our little society' (4, p. 328). The novel's grounding in Europe's immediate history, then, precludes a more Utopian projection and the tranquillity and autonomy of the small republic seems as fragile as Charlotte Denzil's dream of Prospero's island.

A NATION AT WAR WITH ITSELF: ''THE OLD MANOR HOUSE''
AND THE AMERICAN WAR OF INDEPENDENCE

Whilst *Desmond* and *The Banished Man* fictionalise contemporaneous events in France and Europe, the intervening novel, *The Old Manor House* looks back to the 1770s.[19] Such a move might suggest that Smith was distancing herself from the immediate political circumstances of 1793. If this was the case, she might have been advised not to focus on the period between September 1776 and September 1779, not to comment on the British military's mercenary employment of native Americans, nor to make recurrent comparisons between the violent turn of the French Revolution and the violence meted out by the British army against American subjects, all of which she does in *The Old Manor House*.

Like other revolutionary sympathisers in Britain, Smith had invoked the justice of the American rebellion as a vindication of the French cause in *Desmond*. In her 1793 novel, Smith reworked the analogy, asking only that the British look to themselves before condemning the internecine struggle of another country. When her protagonist, Orlando Somerive (surely a forerunner of Walter Scott's Waverley), is en route to fight in a war the origin of which he does not understand, he listens, unconvinced, to the arguments of his patriotic superior, Colonel Fleming. Fleming, like Desmond's mentor Bethel, is a man whose martial notions of duty to king and sword have been overtaken by modernity, by the 'privatisation' of public service and the rise of professional culture. In a typically dialogic moment in the narrative, Fleming rehearses the argument of his sword: 'I have sold that to my King, and therefore must use it in his service, whatever and wherever it may be pointed out to me' (p. 358). This is countered in part by Orlando's reflections that the war, carried out against part of the body of the British nation, contravened the will of the people 'who were taxed to support it' (p. 358). A more forceful indictment comes from the mouth of an American prisoner who recounts the brutality of 'the native American auxiliaries who had been called to the aid of the English' (p. 360). The American's account is supplemented by an extensive footnote, citing evidence of the brutality of the British army and American mercenaries from Ramsay's *History of the American Revolution* and the 'Annual Register' (p. 360). Recalling a violent expedition in Wyoming in which native Americans and 'British Americans' raided a number of settlements, Smith takes the opportunity to entreat her readers to 'recollect how much the exploits of this expedition . . . exceed any thing that happened on the 10th of August, the 2nd of September, or at any one period of the execrated Revolution in France' (p. 360).

By foregrounding the use of American Indians, Smith decries the mercenary tactics of modern warfare and debunks the myth of liberty-loving Britain. However, in this representation Smith succumbs to the colonial discourse that she critiques elsewhere; by depicting the 'savagery' of the Indians, she mediates the culpability of the British, making them complicit with brutality rather than its architects. The colonialist logic is reiterated in comparisons between the monstrous professionals of British institutions, caricatured in figures like Roker, and the 'savages' of North America, a trope that defuses the force of the anti-British commentary and makes corruption a symptom of universal brutality: 'there are savages of all countries – even our own!' (p. 360).[20] The optimistic binary of the universal brute, of course, is the noble savage, who Smith depicts here as the young Wolf-hunter, the native warrior who recognises in Orlando a common humanity, 'the secret sympathy between generous minds [which] seems to exist throughout the whole human kind' (p. 361). Wolf-hunter saves Orlando from certain death when a party of Indians turn viciously on the English troops who 'had not dealt fairly' with them (p. 378). For the rest of his time in North America, the young Englishman 'goes native', 'equipped like an Indian warrior' and conforming to 'the modes of his savage hosts' until he is secured a safe, if circuitous, passage back to England.

The episode of Orlando Somerive's transatlantic journey is a relatively brief passage in the context of the whole novel. Before obtaining his commission, under the aegis of a family acquaintance General Tracy, Orlando has spent two volumes waiting for something to happen, or rather, avoiding having something happen to him. Orlando is, of course, a second son, and thus in need of a profession. His redemption from a fate as a wine merchant, an assistant to his uncle Woodford, seems to lie precariously with the affections of an otherwise austere, but wealthy, paternal aunt. Grace Rayland, 'though like another Elizabeth, . . . could not bear openly to acknowledge her successor, . . . was as little proof as the royal ancient virgin, against the attraction of an amiable and handsome young man' (p. 228). Like some chivalric suitor, Orlando is granted audiences at Rayland Hall with the aunt who shares his distaste for trade, and is invited to make use of the library where he trains himself 'to enter one of the liberal professions', or 'as he heard much of the rapid fortunes made in India, and had never considered, or perhaps heard of the means by which they were acquired, he fancied that an appointment there would put him on the high road to happiness' (p. 138). His unworldly dreams of independence are fuelled by his desire to provide for the real charm of Rayland Hall, the orphan niece of the housekeeper, Monimia. Although forbidden to meet by the girl's aunt, Rachel Lennard, the two contrive nocturnal trysts, where Orlando shares with Monimia the fruits of his labours in the library.[21] Their meetings do not go unnoticed, however. This is, after all, a Gothic romance, and the way to true love is blocked by a network of schemers within the household: from Mrs Lennard, to the servant Betty Richards, described as a 'country coquette', and her secret amour, Pattenson the butler. Charged with running the household, the servants not only keep Orlando and Monimia under surveillance, but sustain their own black-market economies, with Lennard contriving to secure possession of the Hall after Mrs Rayland's death and Pattenson and Betty profiting from their dealings with Jonas Williams, a notorious smuggler who uses the house as a store for his contraband. 'In a great house,' the narrator notes, 'there are among the servants as many cabals, and as many schemes, as among the leaders of a great nation' (p. 52). Real power *within* the Hall lies with the domestics, and beyond the wall its land is encroached by the new owner of a neighbouring estate, Stockton, the son of a rich merchant, whose parties of dissolute young men roam the woods between Carloraine Castle and Rayland Hall. Here, then, is another national metonym: the notional power in the house is held by an antediluvian matriarch who invests her favours and patronage in a chivalric heir, whilst all the time real power lies with those administering and running the economy, cooking the books for their own ends, or with those with the capital to buy authority. Smith dialogises the effect of this 'underground economy' and the new-monied hegemony, however, by extending the analogy both to a corrupt public sphere and to the insurrection of lower ranks and colonised peoples. Thus, Betty justifies her small rebellions as a release from a life which otherwise would be no better than that of 'a slave . . . or a negur' (p. 82); domestic service under the Epicurean Stockton is evidently more free, as the prudent Mr Somerive is reluctant to let his servants visit Carloraine Castle for fear that they become dissatisfied with their lot. It is Mrs Rayland's discourse, however, which forges the more complex connection between the cultural capital of new money, as she rails against baronets who 'spring up like mushrooms' (p. 99), the increasing significance of colonial trade: 'Your Creoles and your East India people over-run every body – Money, money does everything' (p. 164), and the British nation's 'quarrel with people whom she considers as the descendants of the Regicides . . . whom she terms the Rebels of America' (p. 136). From Mrs Rayland's vantage point, the nation is giving way to a plethora of uppity subjects and Orlando has to learn the difference between one kind and another.

Orlando's shock when he learns that his commission as a 'safe soldier of peace' is to propel him into active service against the American rebels is symptomatic of the broader British complacency and indifference towards the developing conflict in the 1770s, at which Smith hints in the first two volumes of the novel. At the beginning of volume three, the narrator describes the British as '[e]late with national pride'. Success in the Seven Years War has left them 'to look with contempt on the inhabitants of every other part of the globe; and even on their colonists, men of their own country' (p. 246). Whilst Orlando is not guilty of contempt, nor brim with national pride, his insularity, epitomised in his ignorance of the means by which Indian traders amass their fortunes, has left him ill-prepared for a role in a war against his fellow nationals. In some respects, he seems to share in Mrs Rayland's chivalric fantasy, in which he is a 'Damoisell, now about to make his first essay in arms' (p. 249). As I have suggested, Orlando's American expedition rapidly disabuses him of this illusion, and confirms his doubts about the efficacy of the war. The conditions on board the ship recall the topos of slavery that figures earlier in the servants' discourse, and the scenes on his arrival demonstrate the brutality of territorial imperialism:

In a war so protracted, and carried on with such various success, these scenes of devastation had occurred so often that the country appeared almost de-populated, or the few stragglers, who yet lingered round the places most eagerly contended for, had been habituated to suffer till they had almost lost the semblance of humanity.[22]

Although Orlando cannot be sustained by the knowledge of the justness of his nation's cause, he can channel his chivalric energies into the cause of Monimia; the woman who comes to him in 'soothing and consolatory' dreams (p. 385). In a letter she describes how she is still pursued by Belgrave, and how Rayland Hall has been taken over by new managers, Roker and his nephew, whom Monimia suspects to be her aunt Lennard's lover. It seems that while the attention of the nation is turned to the defence of colonial order, a new régime is encroaching within. Driven by the need to return to establish his rightful status as heir to the Rayland estate, and to protect Monimia from Belgrave's designs, Orlando presents himself to the governor of Quebec, who furnishes him with the necessary documents to secure his passage back to England.

The precarious nature of wartime alliances sabotages Orlando's hopes for an easy return, however, when the sloop on which he sails from New York is intercepted by French frigates that are in the service of the colonial rebels. Luckily for Orlando, the captain holds the English nation in high esteem, and affords him a safe crossing to France, from where he eventually contrives passage to Southampton on board the ship of French smugglers. Having left England as an albeit reluctant defender of empire, Orlando returns as contraband goods, as Smith neatly reiterates the continuity of legitimate and black-market trade under imperial capitalism.

If Orlando, the 'Damoisell', was out-of-joint with the mores of modern England when he left, he returns as a stranger, to a place he no longer recognises as home. Catching sight of himself as he journeys toward Rayland Hall, he momentarily sees himself as others see him: a cultural hybrid, divested of the signs of his Englishness: '. . . his coat was French . . . He had no buckles in his shoes, for the fishermen had desired them; and his hair, which had not had time to grow long since his coiffure, was in the mode of the Iroquois, and now presented what is called a shock head' (p. 395). His alienation is complete when he approaches a desolate Rayland Hall, beckoned only by '[h]ideous spectres' (p. 395). Orlando is received as a spectre too, reputed to have been killed 'by the wild Ingines' (p. 414). With his father dead, his family on the brink of financial ruin, Monimia missing and Rayland Hall in the wrong hands, Orlando's task is to make himself at home again. As he gradually casts off the physical marks of his exile, and finds himself, after a fortnight in London 'no longer a stranger to the few acquaintances he had', he sets about unravelling the secrets of Mrs Rayland's missing will, and finding Monimia. The latter he traces to a woman consigned to debtor's prison, in whose service Monimia had been placed when the hall fell under new management. The woman is revealed as the widow of the patriotic Colonel Fleming, and whose circumstances – she is embroiled in a legal battle with her husband's villainous relatives – again recall Smith's own predicament.

Fleming's dying request to Orlando was that he should take care of his wife, so Mrs Rayland's young Damoisell must redouble his chivalric efforts to rescue *two* women wronged by the corruption of British property law and the legal system. He does so seamlessly, marrying Monimia and uncovering Mrs Rayland's final will, which makes him proprietor of the Hall. The Somerive family, that was scattered around London, is restored to the family home, Mrs Fleming is freed from debt, and the land on which Carloraine Castle stood is divided into farmland.

The wanderers in this novel all return to England: Fleming's son comes back from the East Indies to marry the younger Somerive daughter Selina, whilst Tracy's nephew Captain Warwick, who eloped with Isabella and is feared to be dead for a large part of the narrative, returns from a sojourn through America, Europe and Scotland.[23] Disguised as a Mr Lorrain, he courts favour as a playwright from a London literary assembly (an episode which seems designed to provide an opportunity for Smith to caricature Hannah More in the figure of Mrs Manby). Tracy's shame that his nephew should be reduced to the ignonimy of authorship prompts him to reinstate his inheritance.

With Orlando's dreams of independence now secure, he too is free from the patronage of the increasingly powerful Woodford. However, as always in her fictions of the 1790s, Smith provides a Janus-faced closure. The final image is of the mendicant soldier, who acted as a go-between for Orlando and Rachel Roker, whose reward for military service is to be instated as a tenant 'of a neat and comfortable lodge in his park – . . . an arrangement that gratified both the dependent and his protector. Orlando never passed through his own gate without being agreeably reminded, by the grateful alacrity of this contented servant, of his past afflictions, and his present felicity' (p. 533). The one-legged soldier, a victim of colonial war, is now the recipient of the patronage from which Orlando is freed by virtue of his inheritance. He is an abject reminder, and, for Orlando, a consoling talisman of the increasingly close relationship between property ownership and national subjectivity in a growing imperial Britain.

GOING WEST: "THE YOUNG PHILOSOPHER"

In *The Old Manor House*, America is a colonial space struggling for autonomy. The American War of Independence both throws into relief the French republican cause and explodes the myth that a benign English liberty underpins the British empire. Smith was to revive the North American references of the *Old Manor House*, in her final novel of the 1790s, *The Young Philosopher*, which was published in 1798.[24] Returning to a contemporaneous setting, America appears now as a confidently independent republic, and provides the setting, or at least the projected setting, for the most Utopian ending of any of Smith's novels.

The narrative opens in England. Smith introduces the protagonist using a plot device that is reminiscent of an episode in *The Banished Man*, where D'Alonville rescues the Rosenheim family after their carriage falls into a swollen river. On this occasion, the unfortunate travellers are an English clergyman, Dr Winslow and his family, his wife, son and niece, who are returning from a south-coast resort where Mrs Winslow was recovering from a nervous complaint. Caught in a storm, they prepare to spend the night on the road, although '[s]elf-preservation, which has been called the first law of nature, began to operate very forcibly' on the mind of young Winslow (again recalling *The Banished Man* and the primitive, misanthropic impulses of Heurthosen). When the curricle that is carrying young Winslow and Miss Goldthorp comes loose, the young man puts his principle into practice and leaves his cousin to meet her fate. Passing out with fear, she wakes to find herself 'supported by a stranger' (1, p. 17), who escorts her to a nearby house, Upwood. The chivalrous stranger is revealed as George Delmont, younger son of a Colonel Delmont, who died in the West Indies leaving two sons and two daughters in the care of an elderly and wealthy female relation, Mrs Crewkeherne (possibly another caricature of Hannah More). As she narrates Delmont's family history to the Winslows on their arrival at Upwood, we recognise a familiar formula: George is an idealist, who has somehow escaped the destiny of 'second branches of other noble families', to enter one of the professions or the army, while his elder brother Adolphous has his eye on an inheritance and its expenditure. George, we learn, has a mentor: not a Burkean like Desmond's Bethel, nor an old-school patriot like Orlando's Fleming, but a Painite republican, Armytage: a man whom Mrs Crewkeherne understands 'writes books – very bad books' (1, p. 39).

We meet Delmont when his principles are fully formed. He has been brought up under the tuition of his mother, who died when he was sixteen, and according to the tenets of Rousseau (the title of the novel is a reference to Rousseau's *La Nouvelle Héloïse*, in which Saint-Preux is described by Claire as Julie's 'young philosopher'). The manner of his upbringing is signalled from the outset by his rustic attire and the cut of his hair. The fashionable attire of Middletown Wilmslow, the 'Master Marmoset' of a very weak mother, offsets his appearance. *The Young Philosopher* is less a *bildungsroman*, in which the protagonists come to maturity after a series of trials, than a demonstration of the impact of educational principle, characterised in terms of the nature–art dichotomy that she used in all her fiction. In this respect the novel has much in common with contemporary fictions by Elizabeth Inchbald, Thomas Day and Mary Wollstonecraft.[25]

George Delmont, who according to Mrs Crewkeherne was made a 'Philosopher . . . in baby clothes' (1, p. 34), lives as a freehold farmer, much to the irritation of his more profligate elder brother, Adolphous. Delmont is introduced to the heroine of the story, Medora Glenmorris, by Armytage, who refers to her as the 'little wild Caledonia American' in light of her Scottish and Dutch parentage, Swiss birth and American education. Like George, she is the product of a liberal upbringing: a prototype, in fact, for George's ideal mate: 'entirely the child of nature . . . brought . . . up exactly as I should wish a woman to be educated for me' (1, p. 244).

George and Medora are second-generation republicans, incorruptible and, in narrative terms, thoroughly flat. As though acknowledging the lack of romance in having two characters prone neither to excessive emotion nor oppressed by the prejudicial values of their elders, Smith shifts our attention in the second volume to the prior generation, and recounts the history of Medora's parents, whose road to romance was suitably rocky. The story, which, much to the irritation of *The Critical Review*, takes up the whole of the second volume, is narrated to George by Medora's mother Laura.[26] She describes her upbringing as the youngest daughter of a Dutch merchant at the London exchange, whom 'having spent all his life in great cities, immersed in commercial pursuits, had no idea of any pleasure resulting from landed possessions and rural improvements' (2, p. 31) and a mother who believed herself to be a descendant of Geoffrey Plantagenet, whose most prized possession was a suit of armour believed to be that of her ancient English ancestor. Into this unpromising environment entered the heir to a Scottish lairdship, 'scholar, poet, . . . eccentric genius', Glenmorris, who had come to London after the death of his father, and 'soon learned to contemn the feudal pride with which his father's prejudices had fed him' (2, p. 7). In Glenmorris, then, the novel has its passionate hero, for having rejected the feudal lore of his inheritance, he finds himself unsuited to the mercantile lore of Laura's family. In the face of her parent's disapproval of this auld Scottish profligate, Laura elopes to Scotland with Glenmorris, who comically adopts the treasured costume of Geoffrey Plantagenet to confuse the household servants and ease their escape.

The highlands of Scotland prove an unwelcoming setting for the honeymoon. The landscape that greets Laura is marked by its emptiness: not the blank promise of a new land, but barren and depopulated, scarred by the ravages of American privateers. When one of these opportunists takes Glenmorris prisoner (an incident which provides another digression about Glenmorris's arrival in Boston, his journey to Jamaica and his discovery of the liberty of the New World) the by-then-pregnant Laura is left to be subjected to the jealousies of Glenmorris's great aunt, Ladie Kilbrodie. The aunt is locked into an ancient feud with

Glenmorris's branch of the family, and is intensely jealous of the inheritance of her two absent sons. Laura is carrying an heir to the Kilbrodie estate, so her status as national alien (which in itself arouses the fear of the superstitious local population and is anathema to the Catholic, Jacobite aunt) is exacerbated by the prospect of her bearing a competitor for the resources of the estate. The tyranny to which Laura is subjected produces conflicting responses to her pregnancy: '. . . at . . . times I wished only to give birth to my child – yet when I had reason enough to consider how unprotected and desolated a little wretch it would be, I desired rather that we might die together before it saw the light' (2, p. 95). These sentiments are similar to those of Mary Wollstonecraft who, in her *Scandinavian Letters* has visions of an overpopulated, under-resourced world (provoked paradoxically by the unpopulated scenes she was contemplating at the time) and announces her fears for children yet unborn. The echo is confirmed a little later when Smith has Laura refer to Wollstonecraft's *Letters*, drawing on the latter's haunting associations between the barren sublimity of the Norwegian coast (here redrawn as its nearest neighbour, the north-east coast of Scotland) and the desolation felt by a solitary woman, who fantasises about infanticide. The association is powerful as before her romantic reunion with Glenmorris and their escape to a new life in Switzerland, Laura loses the child.

Contemporary reviewers, and more recent commentators, were impatient with the digressive story of Laura and Glenmorris, its Gothic trappings and melodramatic twists of fate. However, the whole episode not only underlines the clash of old and new world values that inform the rest of the narrative but is also part of the novel's broader depiction of Britain's attenuated status as a promised land.

Each corner of Britain seems to have insufficient or unevenly distributed resources. The auld romance of Scotland has turned to a Gothic nightmare; its population is geographically and historically stagnant. Ireland features in a later episode when George Delmont travels in search of his dissolute brother Adolphous. There, he is hounded as a candidate for marriage by an overabundant supply of female suitors: a sign that the Anglo-Irish ascendancy is running out of heirs. England, meanwhile, is overcrowded and parasitic. The novel's opening, for instance, not only provides an opportunity for the hero to show his worth, but for Smith to depict the condition of the conventionally urban Winslow family, who are travelling back to London from a coastal resort where Mrs Winslow sought amelioration for her nervous condition, and who are haunted by the fear of hijack. Laura and Medora Glenmorris are at turns incarcerated and forced to keep moving. Laura has a spell in an asylum after Glenmorris is imprisoned for debt, and then runs mad through the streets. Medora, the child of nature and the New World, is evidently deracinated, a condition that is literalised by the fact that she carries a mobile garden with her whenever she flees from her parents' debtors. Again, there are the autobiographical parallels with Smith's condition, but the shadow of theft, debt and insanity in this narrative intimates a broader context of economic and emotional overspend in wartime Britain.

This was 1798: the year in which Malthus published his *Essay on the Principle of Population*, a querulous analysis of the relationship between the Earth's finite capacity to supply resources and the infinite increase in demand; the year of the Irish uprising, an attempt by Irish republicans to throw off the yoke of what they saw as a decadent, emasculated Anglo-Irish ascendancy; and the year of Wordsworth's Preface to the *Lyrical Ballads*, his fantasy of a remasculinsed, popular national poetry, overwhelming the miscegenating force of European and aristocratic influence in the literary arts. Smith shared the zeitgeist of crisis, preoc-cupied as she was throughout the 1790s by the need to find adequate resources to sustain her family and by finding constantly the existing resource – her children's estate – blocked by professionals who came to symbolise a corrupt public sphere. In 1798, the fantasy solution was to escape from debt and the wage-slavery of which Delmont talks and relocate to the New World. Hence, the 'young philosopher' takes his dream of a freehold to America, to live a life of companionate indepen-dence with the republican Glenmorrises.

Smith's fictions after and including *Desmond* are dark romances about literal and metaphorical exile, about populating and cultivating new spaces and leaving England – at least in the corrupt form that Smith envisaged it – behind. She transforms displaced wanderers into cosmo-politan communities living in New World freeholds. However, she leaves her readers haunted by signs of fracture: the surplus mother, Josephine de Boisbelle; the broken soldier at the threshold of Orlando's estate; the friends of D'Alonville who fight in the counter-revolutionary war. *The Young Philosopher* offers the most complete fantasy of spatial and historical relocation, of a new and equal community, of republican romance. The spectre that haunts the reader of this text, however, is Mary Wollstonecraft's fractured 'dystopia' *Maria; or the Wrongs of Woman*. In the preface to *The Young Philosopher*, Smith alludes to 'the untimely death I deeply regret' of Mary Wollstonecraft (p. v). She draws attention to the similarity between the scenes of Laura Glenmorris's incarceration and the asylum episodes in *The Wrongs of Woman*, but explains that she had drawn her own 'madhouse' before she had seen Wollstonecraft's version. Looked at together, these two fictions ironically comment upon one another, with *The Young Philosopher* fulfilling the Utopian promises – new forms of masculinity forged by republicanism – which are glimpsed, but never realised, in *The Wrongs of Woman*. Significantly, it is the uncertain plight of Maria and her daughter, rather than the escape of Laura and Medora, which has become an emblem of women's literary output in 1798 (a symptom, in part, of the poignant fact that Wollstonecraft did not finish the novel because of her death after the birth of her own daughter). However, the force of Wollstonecraft's unhappy legacy is consistent with Smith's own indictment of the state of the English nation in 1798, which she implies when she sends her young philosopher west, to live by the dictates of reason, not custom.

CHAPTER 5

Mary Wollstonecraft and the national body

> "'Behold your child!" exclaimed Jemima. Maria started off the
> bed, and fainted. – Violent vomiting followed.
> . . . She caught her to her bosom, and burst into a passion of tears
> – then, resting the child gently on the bed, as if afraid of killing it, –
> she put her hand to her eyes, to conceal as it were the agonizing
> struggle of her soul. She remained silent for five minutes, crossing
> her arms over her bosom and reclining her head, – then exclaimed:
> "The conflict is over! I will live for my child!"'[1]

The final scene that was appended to Mary Wollstonecraft's unfinished
novella, *Maria; or, The Wrongs of Woman*, in which the despairing Maria
swallows laudanum only to be immediately reunited with her daughter,
is a bathetic and painful coda to Wollstonecraft's embattled writing
career. The poignant biographical context is just one compelling aspect
of this representation of motherhood. In this scene, the physical retches
that are induced by the laudanum coincide with Maria's first sight of her
daughter; the reunion is followed by tears, a fear of unwilled infanticide
and spiritual torment, before Maria summons her reason and makes a
choice to live as a mother. As the rest of the text has already demonstrated, it is a choice to live as an object in a society that does not know
how to recognise mothers as subjects and citizens. For Wollstonecraft,
the fraught condition of mothers is intimately related to the objectified
condition of women under the sign of the modern nation in which
discourses of political economy determine the worth of its subjects'
participation. Despite the symbolic value of the mother in Romantic
nationalism, in the 1790s the matter of the maternal body had an
increasingly ambivalent status as a producer of national wealth.

The rationalist and idealist bases of Wollstonecraft's own perspectives
on citizenship to some extent reproduce the objectified state of the
maternal body in the discourse of political economy. She has become
renowned for her indifference to or outright hostility towards the female

body, and her commentary on the relationship between maternal fitness and national well being suggests that it is only the maternal body that has any significance in Wollstonecraft's approach to women's sensual life. She has thus been indicted for her 'masculinist', puritan and imperialist deployment of the maternal body.[2] To this degree, Wollstonecraft would seem to be collusive with what Michel Foucault famously termed the 'biopolitics' of eighteenth-century political economy, or the deployment of the discourse of sexuality for the production of docile, disciplined bodies:

Through the political economy of population there was formed a whole grid of observations regarding sex. There emerged the analysis of the modes of sexual conduct, their determinations and their effects, at the boundary line of the biological and economic domains. There also appeared those systematic campaigns which, going beyond the traditional means – moral and religious exhortations, fiscal measures – tried to transform the sexual conduct of couples into a concerted economic and political behavior.[3]

Wollstonecraft, I would argue, tried and failed to resist the objectification of the maternal body in contemporary political economy. She was an early critic of modern 'biopolitics', as she recognised and contested the means by which capitalism alienated men from women, women's minds from their bodies and valued those bodies as machines or as property, reproducer or commodity. Like other early critics of capitalism, including contemporary radicals such as William Godwin and Romantics like Wordsworth, Wollstonecraft's critique was based on the kind of mind-body dualism that is anathema to contemporary postmodern, corporeal feminism.[4] This foundation meant that she could only reproduce the logic of the system that she sought to eradicate. Her liberal philosophical inheritance, and her Christianity, meant that she conceptualised the body as separate from and subordinate to reason (that which in the Lockean tradition constitutes the subject as a right-bearing individual) and to the imagination (which, in the emerging Romantic tradition, was the sign of divine intelligence made human). In this order of things, maternal *re*production is a low form of creation, the simple production of matter. The social value of that matter depends not on its relation to the mother-machine who bears it, but on its cultural inscription (the child is a tabula rasa) or its realisation of divine gifts (creative genius). With this matrix as her philosophical foundation, Wollstonecraft could only ask for women to be recognised as reasonable beings with the potential for higher genius and that they be endowed with the rights of subjects – participating in and indeed representing a rational public sphere – despite and not because of their reproductive capacity.

Wollstonecraft's experience of and commentary on motherhood co-incided with a broader shift in political economists' attitude towards population. In the 1790s, social and political theorists in Britain and France turned with particularly anxious attention to the apparently growing and mobile populations of European nations. The theories that sought to give meaning to this numerical expansion and social and geographic movement of bodies bear out Foucault's account of the regulative effect of population discourse. The renowned 'exchange' between Condorcet, Godwin and Malthus in particular was inflected by fantasies of restrained and profligate sexual practice, by disciplined and desiring bodies. Condorcet's *Sketch for a Historical Picture of the Progress of the Human Mind* and Godwin's *Enquiry Concerning Political Justice* both outline rational schemes for social improvement.[5] They envisage the triumph of will over the body, which would, in a Utopian future, make humanity's desires commensurate with their rational needs, and eradicate the present causes of human suffering, including the most recalcitrant reminders of the body's presence: disease and death. Malthus's *Essay on Population*, which was published in 1798 and famously reversed the long-standing association between population increase and national well being, characterises a more intransigent body. He labelled Godwin and Condorcet's Utopian visions as little more than displaced religion: 'Both these gentlemen have rejected the light of human religion, which to the ablest intellects in all ages, has indicated the future existence of the soul. Yet so congenial is the idea of immortality to the mind of man that they cannot consent entirely to throw it out of their systems.'[6]

Mortality and disease, along with moral imperatives like marriage, are the natural checks to population growth, balancing resources with the numbers of those to be resourced. Both of these 'systems' assume a mind-body duality, as the rationalists claim the triumph of the will over the body, and Malthus asserts the dominant force of sexual passion and appetite. And in both, the reproductive body of the woman is figured as an object always in need of vigilance, to be checked naturally by famine, socially by marriage, or by the force of reason which renders sexual passion and its fruits unnecessary.[7] The interests served by these essays are those of bodies and minds which are implicitly male.

Wollstonecraft's writings of the 1790s consistently pursue the agenda that she initiated in 1792 with *A Vindication of the Rights of Woman*[8]: to write women into the class-based account of social inequalities that was being mapped out by her fellow radicals, including Godwin. Wollstonecraft measured her theoretical insights against empirical evidence, when, during journeys to France and Scandinavia in the 1790s, she observed the national differences in women's social status. She travelled first to France, going there at the end of 1792, in flight from a failed affair with Henry Fuesli. ('I intend no longer to struggle with a rational desire,' she wrote to Roscoe, 'so have determined to set out for Paris.'⁹) She was also, however, following her political conscience.

Like Helen Maria Williams and Charlotte Smith, Mary Wollstone-craft was a champion of the early Revolution, and had welcomed it as a harbinger of universal suffrage. She famously turned on Edmund Burke's Gothic fantasies in *Reflections*, claiming that he would reduce all women and men without property to the status of serfs, and begrudged the extension of British liberties to France.¹⁰ When the Revolution faltered, its vindicators needed to provide explanatory narratives that separated the cause of the terror from the cause for liberty. Wollstone-craft's first intervention in that cause took the form of a single letter 'on the present character of the French nation'.¹¹ Written from Paris in February 1793, it was intended to be an introduction to a series of letters that never came to fruition, but which may have evolved into her attempt at Enlightenment historical narrative: *An Historical and Moral View of the Origin and Progress of the French Revolution; and the Effect it has Produced in Europe.*¹² In the *Historical and Moral View*, Wollstonecraft tried to contextualise the Revolution in a broader historical trajectory, and to write off its failures as the symptoms of deterministic historical laws. Wollstonecraft brought various laws to bear as she struggled to absolve the revolutionary agents of absolute responsibility for its failures, and to project a more optimistic long-term outcome. Thus, at times she invokes a rationalist belief in human perfectibility, and argues that the progress of reason will gradually improve social relations; almost simultaneously, she evokes a primitivist indictment of the depraved trajectory of civilisation.

The unwieldy nature of these dialectical explanatory paradigms meant that Wollstonecraft failed to get much beyond the origins, or at least the events of the early months of the Revolution; the later volumes promised in the advertisement were never produced. The following account of the origin of national sentiment and social inequality – offered in part as an explanation of the 'vanity' of the 'pseudo-patriots' who dominated the National Assembly in the early months of the Revolution – is typical of Wollstonecraft's dialectical treatment of progress and degeneracy, improvement and decay:

Men in a savage state, without intellectual amusements, or even fields or vineyards to employ them, depending for subsistence on the casual supply of the chace [sic], seem continually to have made war, one with another, or nation with nation . . . But the social feelings of man, after having been exercised by a perilous life, flow over in long stories . . . [h]is soul also warmed by sympathy, feeling for the distresses of his fellow creatures, and particularly for the helpless state of decrepit age; he begins to contemplate, as desirable, associations of men . . . Hence little communities living together in the bonds of friendship, securing to them the accumulated powers of man, mark the origin of society: and tribes growing into nations, spreading themselves over the globe . . .

The invention of the arts now affords him employment; and it is proportion to their extension that he becomes domestic, and attached to his home . . . and we shall find, if we look back to the first improvement of man, that as his ferocity wore away, the right of property grew sacred. The prowess or abilities of the leaders of barbarians gave them likewise an ascendancy in their respective dynasties; which . . . produced the distinctions of men, from which the great inequality of conditions has originated; and they have been preserved long since the necessity has ceased to exist.[13]

In this account, the formation of nations is an early stage of civilisation, a primitive sign of man's domestication that brings with it an attachment to property and the hierarchical social arrangements that secure that property. Wollstonecraft thus rewrites Burke's account of the sentimental evolution of national belonging, which grows from an attachment to 'the little platoon', as a throwback to a less evolved moment in civilisation. In an earlier passage, she subjects patriotism to a similar critique. 'What is patriotism,' she asks, 'but the expansion of domestic sympathy, rendered permanent by principle?' (6, p. 54). Whilst Burke celebrated the sentimental foundations of national belonging, Wollstonecraft was arguing for a redefinition of patriotism through the prism of political science. Nations, she suggested, must be led away from the habits of nature, and from the contingencies of passion, if they are to sustain more complex and disinterested forms of human community:

Unfortunately, almost every thing human, however beautiful or splendid the superstructure, has, hitherto, been built on the vile foundation of selfishness; virtue has been the watchword, patriotism the trumpet, and glory the banner of enterprise; but pay and plunder have been the real motives. I do not mean to assert, that there were not any real patriots in the assembly. – I know there were many. By real patriots, I mean men who have studied politics, and whose ideas and opinions on the subject are reduced to principles; men who make that science so much their principal object, as to be willing to give up time, personal safety, and whatever society comprehends in the phrase, personal interest, to secure the adoption of their plans of reform, and the diffusion of knowledge.[14]

Wollstonecraft's 'real patriot' is reminiscent of an earlier incarnation of a professional spectator: Adam Smith's political economist (one of 'those few, who, being attached to no particular occupation themselves, have leisure and inclination to examine the occupations of other people'[15]). Wollstonecraft aspires to this professional disinterest in her account of the Revolution, guarding against the 'inferences of sensibility' to contemplate 'these stupendous events with the cool eye of observation' (6, p. 6). Thus, in the *Historical and Moral View* and the publication which followed it – *Letters Written During a Short Residence in Sweden, Denmark and Norway*[16] – Wollstonecraft adopts the tone of the Enlightenment historian, scientifically measuring the progress of the French and the Scandinavians towards civilisation, and charting the relative wealth of nations.

'ALL HIGHER KNOWLEDGE IN HER PRESENCE FALLS'

Wollstonecraft followed the example of stadial theory by measuring the degree of a culture's civilisation by the treatment of women. In much of Wollstonecraft's analysis of the effects of social inequality, women, the most abused, are, consequently, first to reach the level of the brute, the first to lose their powers of reflection, the most alienated from their labours and from their bodies. If dependence is the root of corruption, then women, of all classes, are the most corrupt elements of a nation. Working with such logic in the *Historical and Moral View*, Wollstonecraft offers some unfortunate but telling analogies between sexual and national character, whilst trying hard to establish corruption as a social effect rather than a natural disposition. Wollstonecraft characterises pre-revolutionary France as 'a nation of women' (6, p. 121). A Frenchman, she writes, by occupation and habits of living (not from 'occult causes') 'like most women, may be said to have no character distinguishable from that of the nation' (6, p. 230). Whilst sounding like Pope, she is recalling here her own argument in a chapter of the *Vindication of the Rights of Woman*, 'Observations on the State of Degradation to Which Woman is Reduced by Various Causes'. There she draws on Adam Smith's portrait of the character of people of rank and fortune, to extend an analogy with the condition of women:

. . . if, excepting warriors, no great men, of any denomination, have ever appeared amongst the nobility, may it not be fairly inferred that their local situation swallowed up the man, and produced a character similar to that of women, who are *localized*, if I may be allowed the word, by the rank they are placed in, by courtesy?[17]

She goes on from this premise to make her case for women's rational education, and compounds her 'masculinist' sins by quoting Milton on the dangerous social power of the characterless woman. The woman who is equipped with 'frivolous accomplishments' so changes the nature of things:

> 'That what she wills to do or say
> Seems wisest, virtuousest, discreetest, best;
> All higher knowledge in her presence falls
> Degraded. Wisdom in discourse with her
> Loses discountenanc'd, and, like Folly, shows;
> Authority and Reason on her wait.'[18]

The woman who is 'in herself complete' by virtue of accomplishments, measures the world by her localised, yet imperial, sense of worth. Most valued in a fallen society, the accomplished woman distorts the real value of things in paradise. Wollstonecraft's recourse to this version of the fallen woman is significant in its characterisation of that fall; her fault is not her distance from nature, but from the 'higher knowledge' of reason. To be fully human, to be most herself, she must be differently socialised; socialised, that is, as professional men are. With 'a broader survey', she will be taken away from nature to become more natural and reasonable. Again recalling Smith, she says:

A man when he enters any profession has his eye steadily fixed on some future advantage (and the mind gains great strength by having all its efforts directed to one point) and, full of his business, pleasure is considered as mere relaxation; whilst women seek for pleasure as the main purpose of existence. In fact, from the education they receive from society, the love of pleasure may be said to govern them all; but does this prove that there is a sex in souls? It would be just as rational to declare that the courtiers in France, when a destructive system or despotism had formed their character, were not men, because liberty, virtue and humanity, were sacrificed to pleasure and vanity. – Fatal passions, which have ever domineered over the whole race![19]

Her gendered descriptions of pre-revolutionary France in the *Historical and Moral View* thus differ in emphasis from Helen Maria Williams's celebration of a feminised public sphere. Wollstonecraft sketches a critical analogy between women of leisure and the French court: socially empowered to pursue pleasure, they are morally enfeebled by their myopic endeavours. The impact of their 'fatal passions' is felt by an underclass, alienated by the baseness of their labours:

Whilst it was the sole object of living among the higher orders of society, it was the business of the lower to give life to their joys, and convenience to their luxury. This cast-like division, by destroying all strength of character in the former, and debasing the latter to machines, taught frenchmen to be more ingenious in their contrivance for pleasure and show, than the men of any other country; whilst, with more respect to the abridgement of labour in the mechanic arts, or to promote the comfort of common life, they were far behind.[20]

The French, that is, lacked a professional class of political scientists to wrench them from a cycle of depravity and broaden their horizons; the Revolution failed because it was not put in place by such a class.

Wollstonecraft's advocacy of Smithian spectatorship, both as a model for a professional, rational middle class for France, and for the 'cool eye of observation' to guide her own sketch, competes in the *Historical and Moral View* with the more compelling Swiftean perspectives on corruption. Her rationalist attempt to diagnose the origins of the Revolution in the context of an overview of the uneven progress of nations towards Enlightenment (plotting France along a continuum somewhere between America, England and the countries of northern Europe), gives way to a close-up of corruptions of the French court; the narrative of the ideal progress of universal reason loses its way in the recalcitrant and particular matter of the degenerate body of France. The court is both the nation's rotten core and a metonymic sign of the whole nation's sexual degeneracy. Straining to place this state of things in a historical perspective, and to contain the portrait of corruption in her depiction of the court, Wollstonecraft traces a genealogy of debased monarchs and *manqués*, from Louis XIV, the regent, Phillipe the duc d'Orléans, Louis XV, through to Marie Antoinette and 'Egalité' (the progressive duc d'Orléans of the revolutionary years). Repeatedly, however, she finds broader, more complex and debased economies of sexual dependence and sustenance which permeate *beyond* the court. The regent '[d]evoted to pleasure . . . so soon exhausted the intoxicating cup of all it's sweets, that his life was spent in searching amongst the dregs, for the novelty that could give a gasp of life to enjoyment'. A drain on the sexual and fiscal national economies, his only return was the patronage of 'a few debauched artists and men of letters' (6, p. 27). Louis XV, she writes, was rendered 'the slave of his mistresses' by impotence of body and indolence of mind (6, p. 28). In turn, his mistresses:

fought to forget his nauseous embraces in the arms of knaves, who found their account in caressing them: Every corner of the kingdom was ransacked to satiate these cormorants, who wring the very bowels of industry, to give a new edge to sickly appetites; corrupting the morals whilst breaking the spirit of the nation.[21]

The mistresses, not the king, are the agents of destruction here, generating desire in the hapless monarch, pillaging the nation to dull the taste of his embraces and renew their own craving. It is an unsustainable economy, in which the most dependent are most ready to be sold: 'Kings have been the dupes of ministers, of mistresses, and secretaries, not to notice the sly valets and cunning waiting-maids, who are seldom idle; and these are most venal, because they have least independence of character to support' (6, p. 34).

In her representation of Marie Antoinette, Wollstonecraft offers a risky counter to Edmund Burke's encomium of the French queen in *Reflections*. She has Marie Antoinette arrive at court as a relatively innocent young woman, who soon learns the habit of the coquette, and prostitutes herself to the monarch: 'Over the king she had unbounded sway, when, managing the disgust she had for his person, she made him pay the kingly price for her favours' (6, pp. 73–4). The queen, like other women of the court, gains in power what she loses in moral character. According to Wollstonecraft's version of October 5, the women's march on Versailles and the assault on Marie Antoinette's chamber, the 'arch dissembler' herself falls victim of another kind of unsexed female.[22] Wollstonecraft, that is, goes on to follow conservative accounts of the multitude of women who marched from the Hôtel de Ville, forcing others to join them along the route, to Versailles. She describes how the 'mob' was joined by a number of men, some disguised in women's clothes, and led by market women 'and the lowest refuse of the streets, women who had thrown off the virtues of one sex without having power to assume more than the vices of the other' (p. 197). Arriving at Versailles, the ambiguously gendered rabble 'prowl about' the hall and galleries, and find their way to the queen's chamber. The queen flees, wrapped only in a gown, to the king's apartment.

The episode takes on yet another direction, however, when, Wollstonecraft seems unable to countenance the idea that these women acted on their own, and shifts the responsibility onto the notoriously permissive duc d'Orléans. She thus disrupts the broader historical explanation with the sketch of an extraordinarily debased individual. Like the women of the court who have no essence, these women are no more than pawns of 'designing men' who: '. . . lurk behind them as a kind of safeguard, working them up to some desperate act, and then terming it a folly, because merely the rage of women, who were supposed to be actuated only by the emotions of the moment' (6, p. 196).

As Vivien Jones has argued, this climactic moment, like others in the *Historical and Moral View*, disrupts the 'linear rationalist narrative' with a novelistic paradigm: here 'Wollstonecraft writes history as Richardsonian Gothic fiction.'[23] The description of the duke which follows, as Jones notes, reworks Richardson's version of the seraglio, 'Lovelace among the prostitutes at Mrs Sinclair's', where he is 'partly the instrument of the prostitutes' vicarious revenge on innocence' (p. 186):

To a disposition for low intrigue was added also a decided preference for the grossest libertinism, seasoned with vulgarity, highly congenial with the manners of the heroines, who composed the singular army of the females. Having taken up his abode in the centre of the palais royal, a very superb square yet the last in which a person of any delicacy, not to mention decorum, or morality, would choose to reside; because, excepting the people in trade, who found it convenient, it was entirely occupied by the most shameless girls of the town, their hectoring protectors, gamesters, and sharpers of every denomination. In short, by the vilest of women; by wretches, who lived in houses from which the stript bodies, often found in the Seine, were supposed to be thrown – and he was considered as the grand sultan of this den of iniquity. Living thus in the lap of crime, his heart was as tainted as the foul atmosphere he breathed. Incapable of affection, his amours were the jaundiced caprices of satiety.[24]

Again, Wollstonecraft is intent on counteracting Burke's version of the event, where responsibility lies squarely with the lower-class mob. More striking perhaps in this portrait of the interdependence of aristocratic excess and lower-class depravity is the matter-of-fact presence in the lap of crime of 'the people of trade, who found it convenient' (6, p. 207). The apparently amoral tolerance of another kind of business and of the human detritus of prostitution, is a stark indictment of commercial culture, the complicity of the legitimate trade in goods with the underground trade in female bodies; and of the respectable bourgeois in the heart of pandemonium. Trade in female bodies – be it prostitution or marriage – is just another kind of business.

BARTERING THE INTERESTS OF NATIONS

Overall in the *Historical and Moral View*, the critique of the French *ancien régime* is haunted by a proto-Malthusian pessimism about the potential of reason to transform social relations. The barbarity of commercial culture and the violent turn of the Revolution, she suggests, is a sign of humanity's 'biological' intransigence, and, as though citing some new-found rule of nature, Wollstonecraft punctuates her narrative with the maxim that reason progresses more slowly than passion: '. . . the strongest conviction of reason cannot quickly change a habit of body;

much less the manners that have been gradually produced by certain modes of thinking and acting' (6, p. 53).

Wollstonecraft is alert to the drives of appetite and passion which exceed a rational régime, and to the intractable power of the body, which, for women, more often leads to destruction than to glory. This conviction underpins some of Wollstonecraft's most repressive statements about sensual pleasures, such as the attacks on promiscuity, physical inertia, 'luxury', over-refined or excessive eating, which so trouble later generations living with the legacy of early feminist puritanism. In her *Vindication of the Rights of Woman*, for instance, she uses a commonplace association between luxury and female infertility:

Luxury has often introduced a refinement in eating, that destroys the constitution . . . The depravity of the appetite which brings the sexes together, has had a still more fatal effect. Nature must ever be the standard of taste, the gauge of appetite – yet how grossly is nature insulted by the voluptuary . . . Women becoming . . . weaker, in mind and body, than they ought to be, were one of the grand ends of their being taken into the account, that of bearing and nursing children, have not sufficient strength to discharge the first duty of a mother.[25]

Wollstonecraft is certainly unable or unwilling to countenance non-productive sexual pleasure as a form of satisfaction (and certainly not as sustenance) for women. Here is the censorious voice noted by Kaplan and which seems to make the case for bourgeois domesticity and maternity as the guarantor of national well-being. However, such attacks come in the context of a critique on a culture that consumes more than it reproduces, and weakens the social body in the process: a commercial culture.

The destructive force of commerce is implicit in Wollstonecraft's account of the Revolution's failure. Whilst Helen Maria Williams explained the anti-democratic turn in terms of the Jacobins' resistance to commercial freedom, the oil which had greased the wheel of English liberty, Wollstonecraft provided a less optimistic gloss on Smithian economics. In the *Historical and Moral View*, her only direct reference to Smith is an explicit critique of the theory of the division of labour as promulgated in his *Wealth of Nations*. The critique comes as the culmination of Wollstonecraft's scathing assessment of the spirit of aspiration which leads 'every order of men, from the beggar to the king' to live beyond their means (6, p. 233). Commercial society, she suggests, is an infrastructure that legitimises the tendency for individual extravagance; its rewards are inherently unevenly distributed and its impact on national well-being is devastating:

The destructive impact of commerce, it is true, carried on by men who are eager by overgrown riches to partake of the respect paid to nobility, is felt in a variety of ways. The most pernicious, perhaps, is it's [sic] producing an aristocracy of wealth, which degrades mankind, by making them only exchange savageness for tame servility, instead of acquiring the urbanity of improved reason. Commerce also, overstocking a country with people, obliges the majority to become manufacturers rather than husbandmen; and then the division of labour, solely to enrich the proprietor, render the mind entirely inactive. The time which, a celebrated writer says, is sauntered away, in going from one part of an employment to another, is the very time that preserves the man from degenerating into a brute . . . The very gait of the man, who is his own master, is so much more steady than the slouching step of the servant of a servant, that it is unnecessary to ask which proves by his actions he has the most independence of character.[26]

Significantly, Wollstonecraft invests 'commerce' with an independent power as it 'overstock[s] the country with people'. Commerce has the power of population, driving people from their non-industrial subsistence to the only system that can now sustain them: the divided labours of manufacturing. It is a self-perpetuating economy, supplying its own demand, and is free from the check of moral discourse. The miraculously multiplying workers are doubly alienated: with no time for reflection, their minds lose contact with their bodies. Remunerated for labour which supplies only part of the final product, the value of their industry is contingent on a system which they do not determine: a system of exchange.

Like many other commentators of the 1790s who were attentive to the means that were being used to support the war effort, Wollstonecraft was anxious about the production of paper money. In the *Historical and Moral View* she issued a warning about its inflationary effects and its potential to erode the sovereignty of national economies. Paper notes are empty signs, she suggests, heralds of the arbitrary relation between commodity and its exchange value:

The precious metals have been considered as the best of all possible signs of value, to facilitate the exchange of commodities, to supply our reciprocal wants; and they will ever be necessary to our comfort, whilst by the common consent of mankind they are the standards of exchange. Gold and silver have specific value, because it is not easy to accumulate them beyond a certain quantity. Paper, on the contrary, is a dangerous expedient, except under a well-established government: and even then the business ought to be conducted with great moderation and sagacity. – Perhaps it would be wise, that its extent should be consistent with the commerce of the country, and the quantity of species actually in it. – But it is the spirit of commerce to stretch credit too far.

The Notes, also, which are issued by a state before it's [sic] government is well established, will certainly be depreciated; and in proportion as they grow precarious, the gold and silver, which was formerly in circulation will vanish, and every article of trade, and all the comforts of life, will bear a higher price.[27]

The attack on the demise of the gold standard and her critique of Smith's arguments in the *Wealth of Nations* for the division of labour are typical of Wollstonecraft's attempt in the *Historical and Moral View*, and elsewhere, to reinscribe ethical relations into the operations of the market. It is an intervention into nascent political economy that, like those of other men and women of the 1790s, of various ideological persuasions, sought to keep alive the link between the scientific and moral discourses of economic theory. Godwin's *Political Justice*, for instance, famously aligned the proto-industrial arguments for the division of labour with capitalist avarice:

It has been found that ten persons can make two hundred and forty times as many pins a day as one person. This refinement is the growth of monopoly. The object is to see how vast a surface the industry of the lower classes may be beaten, the more completely to gild over the indolent and the proud.[28]

The precious commodity in this portrait is labour: it is the industry of the many, beaten fine to mask (hide and protect) the leisure and luxury of the few. From an opposing ideological perspective, and embodying an extensive critique of Godwin's indictment of socially institutionalised inequality, Malthus's *Essay on Population* also criticised Smith's conflation of value and 'exchange value'. For Malthus, the only valuable commodity is that which directly sustains the labourer, just as the only valuable labour is that which produces the sustaining commodity, food:

The fine silks and cottons, the laces, and other ornamental luxuries, of a rich country, may contribute to augment the exchangeable value of its annual produce; yet they contribute but in a very small degree, to augment the mass of happiness in the society . . .

A capital employed upon land, may be unproductive to the individual that employs it, and yet be highly productive to the society. A capital employed in trade on the contrary, may be highly productive to the individual, and yet be almost entirely unproductive to the society: and this is the reason why I should call manufacturing unproductive, in comparison of that which is employed in agriculture.[29]

He imagines a pre-capitalist, purely agrarian economy, short-circuiting mechanisms of exchange and the abstractions on which they depend. Crucially for the anti-reformist Malthus, such an economy counteracts the need for poor laws and channels an increasingly self-conscious working class back into feudal subservience.

Other responses to Smith in the 1790s came from a number of women who, as Kathryn Sutherland has argued, were the first to disseminate and popularise Smith's economic theories even as they modified his narrative by foregrounding the contribution of women to the economy.[30] Sutherland cites Priscilla Wakefield, Mary Ann Radcliffe, Hannah More and their nineteenth-century 'descendants', Jane Marcet and Harriet Martineau, as participants in an explicitly economic debate, arguing for women's involvement in the national production of value. I have suggested in earlier chapters that other women like Ann Radcliffe, Charlotte Smith and Helen Maria Williams participated in this debate in a more oblique form, by extending the meaning of 'value' and 'belonging', often in gendered terms. Wollstonecraft's intervention into political economy in her various writings of the 1790s is a complex and often indirect account of the contribution of women to the wealth of nations, and a gendered critique of prevailing models of 'value' which produce not only sexual and class-based inequality but which place a distorted premium on the body, particularly the female body. She suggests that with the satisfaction of the 'wants' of the body as its rationale, consumer culture simultaneously devalues and almost erases it. Wollstonecraft, on the other hand, gives a body to the gendered contradiction of capitalism. She demonstrates that whilst the fantasy female body is central to the capitalist imaginary (both as generator of desire and in its capacity for 'infinite' reproduction) the woman who inhabits its real domain is its most degraded subject.

The disciplined subject that is the corollary of Wollstonecraft's attacks on consumption is not, as some of her critics have suggested, the neatly reproductive mother, who fulfils her duty as the woman-machine of capitalism, for Wollstonecraft indicts the unreflective maternal body too. The barely disguised contempt for 'child-begetters', part of the 'common herd of eaters and drinkers' of whom she wrote several years later in a letter to Gilbert Imlay suffuses her work (6, p. 41). Unpalatable as it is, this contempt is to be understood not simply as an attack on female pleasure, but as part of a gendered contribution to nascent political economy, as a rationalist's call for conscious self-reflection and a proto-Romantic response to the tyranny of matter: a tyranny which is particularly imprisoning for women.

The critique of Wollstonecraft as an advocate of the restriction of female sexuality to productive maternity, then, tells only a partial story. Frequently, bourgeois motherhood is figured as a flytrap, the inevitable but fatal destiny for women like Wollstonecraft. At one point in

Vindication, Wollstonecraft acknowledges her inability to think outside of the discourse of marital if not maternal female subjectivity. In what could be read either as a pious plea for women to be prepared for an after-life, or a demand for the single woman's right to survive in this one, she complains: 'How are women to exist in a state where there is to be neither marrying nor giving in marriage, we are not told' (5, p. 102). As a woman undoubtedly struggling to register her own consciousness and that of other women, to seek out happiness as well as survival, she is alert to the fragile border between plenitude and deprivation, delight and abjection: a border marked most strongly in the maternal body itself, that productive object of the power of sex.

This is a case she makes most vociferously in her later writing from Scandinavia: a perspective that may be overdetermined by her own predicament during her time there. Having fled to France to escape Fuesli, Wollstonecraft met Gilbert Imlay, an American entrepreneur. In the course of their relationship she became pregnant and when he left France on business she found herself abandoned. Despite their estrangement, or because of it, she agreed to act as his agent for a business deal in Scandinavia. There are two sets of published letters from this period: *Letters Written During a Short Residence in Sweden, Denmark and Norway* (abbreviated here to the *Scandinavian Letters*) and her private *Letters to Imlay.*[31] The former amount both to a reprimand to her erstwhile lover Imlay for involving himself in business to the detriment of their relationship, and a gendered critique of Smithian free enterprise, as she extends her criticism to the opportunistic traders who thrive on the wartime black market:[32]

You may think me too severe on commerce; but from the manner it is at present carried on, little can be advanced in favour of a pursuit that wears out the most sacred principles of humanity and rectitude. What is speculation, but a species of gambling, I might have said fraud, in which address generally gains the prize? I was led into these reflections when I heard of some tricks practised by merchants, mis-called reputable, and certainly men of property, during the present war, in which common honesty was violated.[33]

The particular needs of local and national economies, she observes, are disregarded in the rush to capitalise on the insecurities of war: 'The interests of nations are bartered by speculating merchants. My God! with what sang froid artful trains of corruption bring lucrative commissions into particular hands, disregarding the relative situation of different countries' (6, p. 343). As the wealth of nations is eroded by unregulated enterprise, so the fabric of social and domestic life is withering through the neglect of men driven by commercial gain. Just as the hedonism of French court culture engendered a chain of sexual amorality, a debased national trade in bodies, so the hegemony of commerce in Scandinavia weakened the civilised ties of marriage, affection and domestic life. The case against commerce is crystallised for Wollstonecraft when she encounters the parochialism of the Copenhagen bourgeoisie:

The men of business are domestic tyrants, coldly immersed in their own affairs, and so ignorant of the state of other countries, that they dogmatically assert that Denmark is the happiest country in the world; the prince royal the best of all princes; and count Bernstorff the wisest of ministers.

As for the women, they are simply notable housewives; without accomplishments, or any of the charms that adorn more advanced social life. This total ignorance may enable them to save something in their kitchens; but it is far from rendering them better parents. On the contrary, the children are spoilt; as they usually are, when left to the care of weak, indulgent mothers, who having no principle of action to regulate their feelings, become the slaves of infants, enfeebling both body and mind by false tenderness.[34]

If the status – and consequently the behaviour – of a nation's women is an index of its state of civilisation, then commercial society in Denmark is yielding retrograde effects. Danish bourgeois women may be reasonable domestic economists (able to 'save something in their kitchens') but they contribute nothing to political economy. Lacking the accomplishments of French courtesans and the power to distort the value of things, they expose their minimal worth. Maternity, which might in other contexts redeem them for Wollstonecraft, only enslaves them in a cycle of tyranny, draining them of value, 'enfeebling both body and mind'.

In her letters to Imlay, she figures herself at times like the Scandinavian bourgeois mother, enslaved to the tyrant child. When she asks for him to take part in her upbringing she uses language she expects him to understand: 'My little one . . . wants you to bear your part in the nursing business, for I am fatigued with dancing with her, and yet she is not satisfied' (6, p. 394). Her playful conflation of private and public business, metaphors of debt and satisfaction, turns to bitter invective as Imlay proves to be impervious to her persuasions. In one of many letters that claims (probably unnecessarily) to put an end to their relationship, she argues for the right of possession of their child. Hers, she writes, have been the greater labours, hers the higher, more committed investment:

Considering the care and anxiety a woman must have about her child before it comes into the world, it seems to me, by a natural right, to belong to her. When men get immersed in the world, they seem to lose all sensations, excepting those necessary to continue or produce life! – Are these the privileges of reason? Amongst the feathered race, whilst the hen keeps the young warm, her mate stays by to cheer her; but it is sufficient for man to condescend to get a child, in order to claim it.[35]

Throughout these letters, she threatens to make herself independent, to divest herself of 'want', to pursue her 'own project' and to give up the hope of 'being necessary' to him (5, p. 395). Again, these threats are evidently superfluous, as Imlay does not appear to contest them.

In her letters to Imlay, Wollstonecraft's Malthusian strain over-whelms her Godwinian optimism. However, whilst she anticipates Mal-thus in his inducements to sexual and reproductive restraint, she directs her arguments away from the line which he was to take in favour of women's sexual and economic dependence. Wollstonecraft argues in-stead for women's access to a life of the mind; a life that can only be achieved when they are liberated from their bodies. It is capitalism, she suggests, that keeps them tethered and she reiterates this point in sketches of women impoverished by excessive sexual and economic spending, who produce too many children and have too little to support them. She attacks a society in which men are encouraged to 'spend' more than they can afford, where women are not equipped to control their sexual and financial economies but are frequently left to pick up the bill of caring for children inside and outside marriage. In Scandina-via, for instance, she is moved by the sight of a young woman whose predicament struck a chord with her own. Working as a wet nurse, the woman earned twelve dollars a year, and paid out ten 'for the nursing of her own child; the father had run away to get clear of the expence [sic]'. This 'most painful state of widowhood' demonstrates 'the instability of the most flattering plans of happiness', none more flattering nor un-stable than domestic security (6, p. 283).

What often appear to be conservative calls for the regulation of domestic and national economies through the control of sexuality and social miscibility, inducements to companionate, adequately resourced domesticity, are also portraits of women already made miserable through marriage or motherhood, and for whom middle-class domestic-ity yields as much risk as profit. For instance, as a counter to Rousseau's portrait of woman 'formed to please and be subjected to man', she imagines the same woman widowed and responsible for a large family:

. . . encumbered with children, how is she to obtain another protector – a husband to supply the place of reason? A rational man, for we are not treading on romantic ground, though he may think her a pleasing docile creature, will not choose to marry a family for love, when the world contains many more pretty creatures. What is then to become of her? She either falls an easy prey to some mean fortune-hunter, who defrauds her children of their parental inheritance, and renders her miserable; or becomes the victim of discontent and blind indulgence. Unable to educate her sons, or impress them with respect; for it is not a play on words to assert, that people are never respected, though filling an important station, who are not respectable; she pines under the anguish of unavailing impotent regret. The serpent's tooth enters into her very soul, and the vices of licentious youth bring her with sorrow, if not with poverty also, to the grave.[36]

Sketched in defence of a rational education and economic independence for women, this portrait of the 'mother . . . lost in the coquette', tells of the downward mobility of the maternal body, and anticipates the destiny of those childless 'pretty creatures'. Valued most for their reproductive potential, they are lost to fortune the moment that they embrace motherhood, or motherhood embraces them.

In the *Scandinavian Letters*, another claim for women's education in the duties of motherhood conceals an insight into one of the solutions for population control that Malthus could not bring himself to name: the practise of infanticide. Describing the women's tendency to bundle up babies in flannels to protect them against the severity of the Swedish winters and the 'natural antipathy to cold water', Wollstonecraft finds an explanation for a mysterious absence on her travels:

. . . the squalid appearance of the poor babes, not to speak of the noxious smell which flannel and rugs retain, seems a reply to a question I had often asked – Why I did not see more children in the villages I passed through? Indeed the children appear to be nipt in the bud, having neither the graces nor charms of their age. And this, I am persuaded, is much more owing to the ignorance of the mothers than to the rudeness of the climate.[37]

Ignorance, not cruelty, leads these children to die at the hands of their mothers; unable to be sustained through the winter, they are passively 'nipt in the bud'. Wollstonecraft's ambivalently liberal attitude towards infanticide is expressed in another anecdote premised on demonstrating the leniency of the Danish prince royal in his pardoning a girl 'condemned to die for murdering an illegitimate child, a crime seldom committed in this country'. Characterising a pardon as extraordinary as the crime, Wollstonecraft goes on to vindicate the judgement by the reassurance that '[s]he is since married, and become the careful mother of a family' (6, p. 274); her crime, that is, was induced by lack of marital resource rather than lack of maternal feeling.

Descriptions of the infertile rich, of the idle, fertile, 'voluptuous' women unfit for maternal duty and the degraded state of the abandoned or widowed mother, are accumulative evidence against a culture that has devalued the maternal body, and fears its powers of reproduction. In this respect she negatively anticipates the 'matriphobic' content of Malthus's *Essay*, its dreadful fantasy of woman's prolific reproductive potential, which is only barely containable by companionate marriage. Thus, in a single passage in the *Scandinavian Letters*, her perfectibilist optimism ('The increasing population of the earth must necessarily tend to its improvement') gives way to anxiety for a world in which increase of supplies is outstripped by the geometrical increase of bodies. She imagines a population that has not been 'checked' by the Godwinian will of reason:

I anticipated the future improvement of the world, and observed how much man had still to do, to obtain of the earth all it could yield. I even carried my speculations so far as to advance a million or two years to the moment when the earth would perhaps be so perfectly cultivated, and so completely peopled, as to render it necessary to inhabit every spot; yes, these bleak shores. Imagination went still further, and pictured the state of man when the earth could no longer support him. Where was he to fly to from universal famine? . . . I really became distressed for these fellow creatures, yet unborn. The images fastened on me, and the world appeared a vast prison.[38]

Wollstonecraft's distress for 'these fellow creatures, yet unborn' is underscored perhaps by the more immediate spectre of children abandoned by fathers, and mothers imprisoned by insufficient resources. However, another reproductive economy controls this passage too: the economy of Wollstonecraft's productive imagination and its powers of generation. Like the maternal body, the imagination is figured pathologically, beyond the control of reason. She is unable to stop her speculations, to stem her fantasies of reproduction, and thus peoples the earth beyond its capacity to provide; her imaginary children 'fasten' on and overwhelm her, and she mourns them before they are born. This over-fertile imagination is perhaps the Gothic, feminine underside of a masculine model of Romantic creativity. The latter is a model to which Wollstonecraft undoubtedly aspires in her pursuit of independence from her body and from other bodies, but which she can never quite achieve, or at least conceptualise. As she notes in a letter that describes the fatigue and melancholy she experiences on her travels: 'My imagination has never yet severed me from my griefs – and my mind has seldom been so free as to allow my body to be delicate' (6, p. 310). By delicacy,

Wollstonecraft infers lightness not fragility and suggests that her present frame of mind weighs upon her body.

IMPERIOUS SYMPATHIES

The imaginative transcendence that eludes Wollstonecraft is underpinned by the sublime aesthetic that, for her Romantic contemporaries, provided a fantasy of autogenesis, and not only negates the need for other people (both their minds and bodies) but also demands their elimination from the imagined scene, until matter becomes a figment of the mind's eye. The operation of the sublime is epitomised in Wordsworth's solitary contemplations of the scene of nature in 'Tintern Abbey', in which the poet's imagination empties out the land, eventually eliminating all matter. As Frances Ferguson has argued so cogently in *Solitude and the Sublime*, this Romantic dematerialisation is a fantasy retreat from the pressure of other bodies and other minds, symptomatic both of the perception of population growth, urban crowding and of demands in the 1790s for political franchise from those who had not previously 'counted'.

Wollstonecraft certainly seems to desire this state of transcendence, but never records Wordsworthian moments of epiphany.[39] The closest she comes to this is to a state of solitude. In a letter from Scandinavia, for instance, she recalls a night she spent looking out on to the sea and the rocks of the shoreline and writes 'I was alone'. Romantic solitude lasts for only one clause of a sentence, however: 'I was alone till some involuntary sympathetic emotion, like the attraction of adhesion, made me feel that I was still a part of a mighty whole, from which I could not sever myself' (6, p. 249). Wollstonecraft's attachment to the mighty whole is figured here less as a choice than as a corporeal compulsion. It is a discursive compulsion, symptomatic of the fact that Wollstonecraft's conception of the imagination is still grounded in eighteenth-century sentimentalism and associationism. In such discourse, the imagination functions as an extension of the body, closely related to the concept of sympathy. Its operation is always figured therefore as a material relation: a relation to the vibrations of the body and mind, responding to other things and other bodies exerting the pressure of other wills. It is precisely this sense of interrelation between bodies and minds that overwhelms Wollstonecraft and leaves her feeling body-bound. In the scene to which I have just referred it is significantly the sight of her sleeping child that prompts Wollstonecraft's train of thought and that takes her from solitude to connection: from the 'rosy cheek I had just kissed' to 'the idea of home', to 'the state of society'. As she sheds a tear on her daughter's face she is lost for an explanation of this pull towards community and asks 'What are these imperious sympathies?' (6, p. 249).

That Wollstonecraft's sympathies produce tears is a sign of the abjection that she associates with her body, a body that is here explicitly maternal. If at times Wollstonecraft exhibits no more than a rational indifference to the demands of her body (especially, as Vivien Jones has noted, to the demands of her pregnant body[40]), at other moments she rails at the power it exerts over her, a power which she identifies as sympathy. Imagination and sympathy were of course central in Adam Smith's explanation, and vindication, of the mechanisms of the marketplace; far from engaging in the cut-throat competition which dominated Hobbesian versions of the social world, Smith's commercial world, he argued, is regulated by the benign operations of sympathy, a correspondence of like minds. The aspirational, upwardly mobile entrepreneur is driven by a desire to emulate the successes of his 'correspondents' and the sign of true sympathetic connection, of the operation of imagination, is social and economic success.

For Wollstonecraft, when imagination is in the service of capitalism, it is degraded and libidinous, bound to the body. As she writes in her 1793 *Letter on the Present Character of the French Nation*, imagination is an artful coquette 'who lures us forward, and makes us run over a rough road, pushing aside every obstacle merely to catch a disappointment'. To disrupt the cycle of commercial economy, imagination should be subdued by reason, for the 'wants of reason are very few,' and, 'were we to consider dispassionately the real value of things, we should probably rest satisfied with the simple gratification of our physical necessities, and be content with negative goodness' (6, p. 444).

Wollstonecraft's fantasy of a pared-down economy, a world where we consider 'the real value of things' ungilded by imagination, is apparently attainable in the northern reaches of Scandinavia, where, she is told, there are communities which are untouched by the debauch of commerce. Descriptions of these places carry her back to 'the fables of the golden age: independence and virtue; affluence without vice; cultivation of mind, without depravity of heart'. Oddly she stops herself from journeying to these Utopian spaces on the grounds that she is 'hurrie[d] . . . forward to seek an asylum in such a retreat' by that wanton 'imagination': a guide that she cannot trust. She feels herself obliged to follow reason, figured as a kind of reality principle, as it 'drags [her] back, whispering that the world is still the world, and man the same compound of weakness and folly, who must occasionally excite love and disgust, admiration and contempt' (6, pp. 308–9). Her own need to live by reason is subordinate, then, to the responsibility she feels to live in an unreasonable world. This is the same responsibility that Maria assumes when she 'chooses life' at the end of *The Wrongs of Woman*.

The world shows its Janus face to Wollstonecraft when she is forced to make an unplanned stop at an inn in Quistram. There she meets a concourse of people from a neighbourhood fair, a group who excite disgust and contempt more than love and admiration. Amidst 'clouds of tobacco', fumes of brandy, 'a rude tumult of the sense', she fails to find a bed, or 'even a quiet corner . . . – all was lost in noise, riot, confusion' (6, p. 313) Like Wordsworth in London, she fails to see signs of her own humanity in these 'stupid, obstina[te] . . . half alive beings, who seem to have been made by Prometheus, when the fire he stole from Heaven was so exhausted, that he could only spare a spark to give life, not animation, to the inert clay' (6, p. 314). Here is the Romantic Wollstonecraft, figuring herself as the index of full humanity, able to distinguish herself from merely material beings. She possesses that genius, which she wrote to Imlay is 'the foundation of taste, and of that exquisite relish for the beauties of nature, of which the common herd of eaters and drinkers and child-begetters, certainly have no idea' (6, p. 41).

Like other Romantics, Wollstonecraft is desiring and unsatisfied, wishing to empty the world through the power of imagination, and longing to live according to the wants of reason. That she fails to do so is a symptom of an imagination that is grounded in the body: a body that is an object of a materialistic culture. Wollstonecraft doubles the 'exclusion' of the feminine in population discourse when she retreats to metaphysics, and what we now call Romantic individualism, in order to bypass the unintelligible condition of the maternal body in capitalist culture. Her perspective on other mothers is marked by her inability to reconcile fallen female sexuality and wasted reproduction with her Enlightenment vision of a rational species. She can make her own maternal body intelligible not as matter but as an outward, if lesser, sign of her higher consciousness. In her happiest moments, she describes her reproductive capacity as an extension of her Promethean creativity, evidenced in numerous references to her first child Fanny as a small, dancing child, a matter-less 'sprite'. In more conventionally Christian terms, she suggests that the body is no more than a casement for her soul: 'I feel a conviction that we have some perfectible principle in our present vestment, which will not be destroyed just as we begin to be sensible of improvement; and I care not what habit it next puts on, sure that it will be wisely formed to suit a higher state of existence' (6, p. 279).

Undoubtedly, Wollstonecraft's nascent feminism is stymied by mind–body binarism. She offers a powerful cultural critique of the material effects of capitalism on women, which could be paraphrased as the rejoinder she issues to Imlay: 'You would render mothers unnatural and there would be no such thing as a father' (6, p. 435). When she tries to resist the distorted premium that commerce places on the wants of the body, and indeed the demand of love that is 'a want of the heart', she resorts to idealism; or, at least, she gropes towards it, bound as she is by the 'imperious sympathies' of her own maternal body. Freedom from that melancholy weight is achieved only at the expense the body itself, as Wollstonecraft repeats the matriphobia of her male contemporaries, figuring the body as abject and alienated.

THE WOMAN WHO WOULD BE KING

Wollstonecraft recommends a Romantic régime, the exercise of the imagination to liberate the body, in particular the female body, from a cycle of deprivation and satiety. Her texts are complexly driven by a wish to make the individual body matter less and the social body matter more. Wollstonecraft's critique of the prevailing method of calculating value is evidently directed to the production of a future when all subjects will be fit to be considered as reflective beings. As she conceded in the *Historical and Moral View*: 'To consult the public mind in a perfect state of civilization, will not only be necessary, but it will be productive of the happiest consequences, generating a government emanating from the sense of the nation, from which alone it can legally exist' (6, p. 212).

However, on the evidence of the Revolution's collapse and of the prevailing degradations, 'the public mind' is not yet ready for sovereignty. Whilst her critique of court and commercial hegemony implies historical answers (a redistribution of wealth will liberate the public mind), the laws of historical or divine necessity that Wollstonecraft invokes make it seem impossible that such a state could ever come about. Her social commentary becomes fixated on the difference between unreflective objects and the rational subjects of society. Thus, in Wollstonecraft's anti-capitalist narrative, the wealth of nations is still dependent on a division of labour: dependent on the patient labours of

those 'just above the brute creation' and the refining minds of those alive
to nature's perfections. The underlying fear of granting sovereignty to
those patient labourers, a Romantic, unconscious fear of democracy, is
evidenced in the spectral visions that spring unbidden from Wollstonecraft's rational mind. In Scandinavia she imagines once empty spaces
crowded by children, who ask for more than the world can provide. In
her first days in France, she is haunted by the spectre of a revolutionary
mob, shaking their bloodied fists at her. The latter nightmare is recorded in a letter to Joseph Johnson in 1792, and it throws into relief the
personal and political underside of Wollstonecraft's idealism and rationalism. She describes how she watched, from behind a casement in a
Paris salon, the procession that led Louis XVI towards his trial for
treason. Although Wollstonecraft emphasises her physical and emotional detachment from the scene, the image of Louis leaves a deep
impression. '[A]n association of ideas made the tears flow insensibly
from my eyes', she writes, as she figures him as the last of a triumphant
race going to meet his death, as her mind moves from the 'sunshine' of
Louis XIV's entry into the capital, to the 'sublime gloom of misery' of
the procession before her. Wollstonecraft oddly implicates herself in the
imagined scene:

I have been alone ever since; and, though my mind is calm, I cannot dismiss the
lively images that have filled my imagination all the day . . . I have seen eyes
glare through a glass-door opposite my chair, and bloody hands shook at me . . .
I want to see something alive; death in so many frightful shapes has taken hold
of my fancy. – I am going to bed – and, for the first time in my life, I cannot put
out the candle.[41]

The glaring eyes and bloody hands are reminiscent of the mob that
turned on Helen Maria Williams, when she watched a Parisian procession from the window of the salon in the Palais de Bourbon. This was a
moment that brought her to understand that the people regarded
neither the monarch nor her as '*la natie*'. Wollstonecraft's mob, however,
are spectral, fashioned from a fancy that is gripped by images of death
rather than illusions of liberty. By 'an association of ideas', Wollstonecraft had traced a line of French monarchs, a metonymic nation, from
glory to extinction. In a moment of Romantic reversal, with her fancy
and imagination in thrall to the images they have created, the asso-
ciative process runs out of her control. With the death march of Louis
XVI before her, the pomp of Louis XIV in her head, Wollstonecraft
regenerates herself as the monarch, taunted for her solipsism by imaginary assassins, who intimate her own mortality.

On this slight evidence, it seems clear that Mary Wollstonecraft was less at home in France than was Helen Maria Williams. She was not, however, at home in Scandinavia or England either. Wollstonecraft is a detached observer, a solitary outsider who is as likely to people her scenes with imaginary as real figures, and to fashion images which take hold of her fancy and make her the subject of her own phantasmatic scenes. The alienated affect of these letters is, of course, characteristic of Wollstonecraft's best-known writing: the embattled polemic of her two *Vindications*, and the bathos of her novella *Mary* and of her unfinished experimental novel *Maria; or the Wrongs of Woman*. Her alienation, that is, was not merely symptomatic of her being 'abroad'. Conceptualising herself as forced to inhabit a body that betrayed her reason, and living in a culture that depended on the alienation of mind from matter, for Wollstonecraft, home was hard to put a name to.

Wollstonecraft's matriphobic legacy may be undergoing revision under the aegis of post-modern 'corporeal' feminism, with its drive to collapse mind–body dualism and to grant subjectivity to matter. Still, while the philosophical ground is being prepared, the redistribution of resources that would mean that women can afford maternity, and could experience the pleasures and pains of the maternal body continuously with other forms of subject performance, is a slow and uneven process. If Wollstonecraft's melancholy reflections have any historical value, it is surely that her descendants should continue to attend both to the material and ideal constituents of women's subjectivity, so that our social sympathies and forms of belonging are less 'imperious' than radically transformative.

CHAPTER 6

Patrician, populist and patriot: Hannah More's counter-revolutionary nationalism

For a while, in accounts of the wave of political self-analysis which swept Britain in the 1790s, Hannah More conveniently represented the reactionary 'other' to Mary Wollstonecraft's democratic radical. One need only look at accounts of her fraught patronage of Ann Yearsley, her vociferous critique of Wollstonecraft's sexual character, her self-confessed desire to use education to manage an increasingly self-conscious working-class mob, and the imperialist rhetoric of her anti-slavery poetry, to demonstrate the 'disciplinary' dynamic that underpinned her various public campaigns. More's explicit distrust of democracy, which culminated in her refusal to sign a petition for reform in 1832, consolidated an image that recent feminist appraisal of More's work has begun to contest.[1] As I have suggested in my analyses of Wollstonecraft's fraught vindications of 'the public mind' in the previous chapter, and of the work of Radcliffe, Williams and Smith before that, the radical–reactionary binary is an inadequate framework with which to approach the discursive complexities of national belonging in the 1790s. With respect to More, it is not difficult to find a liberal, if not a radical voice in her texts, to contest the image of the reactionary: in her commitment to the campaign for the abolition of slavery; in her material contribution to the reform and extension of the education franchise; in her re-evaluation of women's contribution to the national economy; and in the 'anti-establishment' character of her religious practices from the 1790s. Rather than resolve the tension between the disciplinary and libertarian impulses in More's work, this chapter considers them as effects of More's patrician populism, and of her ambitious attempt to rouse and pacify the spirit of a nation.

In the 1790s, More devoted much of her considerable energy to keeping up with British 'public opinion', which was constituted in and by the wide range of print media, corresponding societies and *ad hoc* associations that often threatened to overwhelm the established channels of political opinion throughout the decade. For many British commentators, fear of the speed with which changes in France had taken hold and with which revolutionary events were being represented to a British readership, merged into an anxiety that a popular appetite for news and the spectacle of sensation, heroism and tragedy in France would lead the public to play out such scenes in Britain. The crude response to this kind of revolutionary panic was censorship. Hannah More, however, had a more sophisticated grasp of the difference between medium and event and saw the potential to mobilise the power of print for the counter-revolutionary and national cause. More was a canny manipulator not only of the Press, but of social connection and of economic patronage. This political aptitude meant that More could respond more rapidly, widely and powerfully than many of her counter-revolutionary contemporaries (including Edmund Burke) to a public that was quickly redefining itself, its relationship with the British establishment and with politics. More was willing to engage with the 'popular imagination'. If her motivation was to harness and discipline the productive powers of that imagination, the discursive effects of her counter-revolutionary campaigns would have unforeseen consequences, for the patrician nationalism of the 1790s generated a new breed of patriot reformers in the decades that followed.

'A NEW SIMILITUDE WHEREWITH TO COMPARE MY WICKEDNESS'

I have been an arrant stroller – amusing myself by sailing down the beautiful river Wye, looking at abbeys and castles, with Mr Gilpin in my hand to teach me to criticize, and talk of foregrounds, and distances, and perspectives, and prominences, with all the cant of connoisseurship, and then subdue my imagination, which had not been a little disordered with this enchanting scenery. I have been living in sober magnificence with the Plantagenet Dowager Duchess at Stoke, where a little more discretion, and a little less fancy was proper and decorous.[2]

This wry correspondent, writing to Horace Walpole in 1789 to recount the overheated effects of a picturesque stroll, is neither the 'great enchantress' Ann Radcliffe, nor the 'solitary walker' Mary Wollstonecraft, who were both famed for their meditations on landscape, but the pious blue stocking, Hannah More. This letter to Walpole is part of a correspondence that began in the 1780s and lasted until his death in 1796, and is the sign of a friendship that grew out of More's involvement in London and Bristol literary circles. The pastiche is significant not just as an illustration of the socialite side of 'the bishop in petticoats'.[3] It also demonstrates her ability to mimic the 'popular', or here at least, the fashionable pursuits of her contemporaries whilst signalling her critical distance from them. The letter begins in a similar vein, as she parodically anticipates Walpole's rebuke to her for not writing sooner, and provokes him to find new terms in which to describe her neglect:

I have been so brutally negligent of your last favour, that you might once have taunted me with the proverbial reproach, that 'ingratitude is worse than the sin of witchcraft'; but now that demonology, and miracles, and witchcraft are become fashionable and approved things, you must endeavour to find out a new similitude wherewith to compare my wickedness.[4]

This taunt at her friend's petulance (and at his taste for the Gothic) spells out More's sensitivity to the speed with which novelty becomes orthodoxy, and the sacrilegious seems acceptable. She echoes, of course, a charge that had become fairly commonplace in the field of literary criticism, and that was frequently levelled at eighteenth-century novelists who were simultaneously attacked for feeding, and feeding on, the morally dubious public appetite for new matter, newly told, and for failing to produce anything novel at all. More later participated in this kind of critique when, in her *Strictures on Female Education* of 1799, she described the means by which popular fiction proliferates without the will of an author.[5] The 'glutted imagination' of the reader, she proclaims:

. . . soon overflows with the redundance of cheap sentiment and plentiful incident, and by a sort of arithmetical proposition, is enabled by the perusal of any three novels, to produce a fourth; till every fresh production, like the prolific progeny of Banquo, is followed by
    'Another, and another, and another!'[6]

It was the public that read, and imitated, these fictions, and that was voracious and restless in its taste, which alarmed counter-revolutionary political commentators in the 1790s. The fear of a newly literate public was registered in Burke's *Reflections on the Revolution in France in a Letter Intended to Have Been Sent to a Young Gentleman in Paris*. Burke's 'letter' is a querulous fantasy of political discourse as an urbane exchange between men of a certain class, and was a crucial discursive intervention at a moment when such upper-class, masculine intimacy was under severe pressure from a new constituency of politicians. Whilst More might have been reluctant to celebrate the fact, she understood that 'public opinion' far outreached the 400,000 political citizens that Burke was ready to acknowledge in 1796, and that these unknown people had to be addressed.[7] Whilst Burke, at least superficially, eschewed the popular media that addressed this new public, More apparently immersed herself in it. Whilst in Bath recovering from a chest complaint in February 1793, she wrote to Walpole, ironically figuring herself as a pulp-junkie, the boredom of her illness having produced an addiction to the quick fixes of expurgated texts:

I wonder if I shall ever live to read a book again that shall cost a shilling. I have lived so long on halfpenny papers, penny cautions, twopenny warnings, and threepenny sermons, that I shall never be able to stretch my capacity even to a duodecimo! I shall try though, for I find my present studies very harassing to the nerves, and although like dramdrinking, they invigorate for a moment, yet like that too, they add to the depression afterwards.[8]

The intoxicating power of these rapidly produced and disseminated texts is the theme of much of her correspondence with Walpole, and, in the privacy of their virtual literary salon, the two exchange jokes about the merits of the latest publications. Although More is addicted to pulp fiction, she determines not to keep up with some of the latest print fashions:

I have been much pestered to read the *Rights of Women* [sic], but am invincibly resolved not to do it. Of all jargon, I hate metaphysical jargon; besides there is something fantastic and absurd in the very title. How many ways there are of being ridiculous! I am sure I have as much liberty as I can make a good use of, now I am an old maid, and when I was a young one, I had, I dare say, more than was good for me.[9]

More's apparently complacent, post-feminist posture conceals a much sharper anxiety about the 'ridiculous metaphysical jargon' of Wollstone-craft's *Vindication*; jargon that was saturating all kinds of discourse, and which, at least from some perspectives, had been wrenched from British political tradition, appropriated by the French and reimported across the Channel. Walpole joined More in exiling Wollstonecraft's tract, unread, from his library, preferring to give thanks for 'the tranquillity and happiness we enjoy in this country':

... in spite of the philosophizing serpents we have in our bosom, the Paines, the Tookes, and the Woolstoncrafts [sic]; I am glad you have not read the tract of the last-mentioned writer: I would not look at it, though assured it contains neither metaphysics nor politics; but as she entered the lists in the latter, and borrowed her title from the demon's book, which aimed at spreading the wrongs of men, she is excommunicated from the pale of my library. We have had enough of new systems, and the world a great deal too much already.[10]

The distaste for new systems that More shared with Walpole is expressed in her brand of 'politics', and in her tendency to privilege the local and particular over the abstract cause.[11] Paradoxically, but not unusually in British political and philosophical tradition, her impatience with metaphysics stems from her own metaphysical logic and her faith in religion as the basis of all social action. More's is a 'practical piety', however, and she is less given to speculative theology than the perform-ance of faith through humanitarian relief of suffering and Christian conversion of 'the godless'.

PRACTICAL PIETY

More's attitude to the Revolution, particularly as she expresses it in her correspondence with Walpole, demonstrates her apparent antipathy towards political abstraction. Like most liberal commentators, More welcomed the destruction of the Bastille. In a letter to Walpole she wrote that with the 'extinction of the Inquisition' and the 'redemption of Africa', the demise of the notorious prison amounted to the demolition of 'three great engines of the Devil' (p. 321). However, More was quick to express her regret at the transfer of power in France, which she regarded as the triumph of 'the lawless' and the godless: this was to be the tenor of the rest of her commentary on the Revolution.

During July of 1790, while Paris was celebrating its new order with the Fête de la Fédération, More was taking refuge in Cowslip Green, the house in the Mendips that she shared with her sister Martha. The rural isolation of the house suited her antagonistic posture to the universalist sentiments issuing from France, and in a letter to Walpole, she dramatises herself in geographical and historical exile. 'I live here in so much quiet and ignorance, that I know no more of what is passing among mankind,' she writes, 'than of what is going on in the planet Saturn' (p. 340). Her Walpolean claim that she thinks of 'anything but politics' does not bear scrutiny.[12] From her little corner of the world, she is quick to comment on the most current events, if only to dismiss their significance. Comparing the feast in the Champs de Mars, with which she supposes (sardonically paraphrasing Milton) "All Europe rings from side to side", with the Champs du Drap d'or (the meeting near Calais between Francis I and Henry VIII in 1520) she finds in the latter 'the remnants of chivalry, and old grandeur, of which modern festivity gives me no idea' (p. 340). Here, like Burke, she mocks the drabness of revolutionary spectacle and laments the passing of the age of chivalry. Three years later, commenting on the execution of the king, she again echoes *Reflections*, as she writes as the shocked surveyor of the incomprehensible scene: 'the iniquity of today furnishes you with no data to conjecture of what sort will be the iniquity of tomorrow' (pp. 375–6). Unwilling or unable to make sense of the disordered epic in France, she turns in her letters to singular episodes of her own charitable actions, relating them in all their quotidian detail. When she *does* write of the Revolution, she reserves her sympathy for the anthropomorphised country, 'poor France', victim of the anarchic mob and for monarchy, about whom she colludes with Walpole in his portrait of wronged goodness, and depicts herself 'weeping at the picture of the Queen carrying her little bundle into her narrow and squalid prison' (p. 388).

Walpole expresses ironic surprise at her reaction against the Revolution, and claims it is at odds with her charitable bent and her penchant for a good cause. More's attention to suffering is frequently the subject of their letters, and Walpole regularly rails at the disproportionate relation between her concern for a passing charity case and her neglect of their friendship. Provoking her to respond to him if only in anger, Walpole writes in July 1790:

One must be found stark under a hedge, or be sold for a slave, or be a cripple, to put you in mind of one. You have no feelings but in your virtues, nor friendship upon a less occasion than one's being in danger of one's life. You would not give a straw for a friend upon whose misfortunes you could not go to Heaven.[13]

When not berating More for ignoring him, Walpole sketches an astute, and more interesting, characterisation of the paradoxical posture of retired sensibility that More adopts in her correspondence from Cowslip Green. When he writes in August 1792, with details of the Paris massacres, he demands a *political* response from More insofar as he pushes her to contemplate an epic scene in which a 'whole nation', rather than an individual, is in need of salvation. 'What must your tenderness not feel now,' he asks 'when a whole nation of monsters is burst forth?' Recounting details of the massacre, he taunts:

. . . why do I wound your thrilling nerves with the relation of such horrible scenes! Your blackmanity must allot some of its tears to these poor victims. For my part, I have an abhorrence of politics, if one can so term these tragedies, which make one harbour sentiments one naturally abhors; but can one refrain without difficulty from exclaiming, such a nation should be exterminated?[14]

More was eventually to find less apocalyptic means of dealing with the August massacres by channelling her counter-revolutionary activism into a humanitarian cause: that of the French émigré priests who were exiled from France by the revolutionary government in August

1792 and who were portrayed with ambivalent sympathy by Charlotte Smith in *The Emigrants*. Their plight was brought to public attention by Edmund Burke, an acquaintance of More's on whose behalf she had campaigned in his election to parliament as member for Bristol in 1774. Burke's plea for the recusants had led to a series of subscription appeals throughout Britain, and More was prompted by Charles Burney to invite some of the refugees into her home in Bath and to lend her services to a campaign addressed to the 'Ladies of Great Britain'. To this end, she wrote a tract, *Remarks on the Speech of M. Dupont*, which was published by Cadell, and the proceeds of which were donated to the priests' relief fund.[15]

Here, as she was quick to point out, was a local cause, that was counter-revolutionary in a broad sense, but 'of no party' (p. ix). Partyless politics was, of course, the hallmark of radical opposition, that multifaceted groundswell of opinion set against party political division and motivated by a desire to expose and overturn a corrupt political system.[16] More never turned her attention to the corruption within British party politics, willing as she was to accept the patronage of both Whig and Tory benefactors. Unlike William Cobbett, who saw the nation as a chain of dependence cultivated by an all-consuming centre, she conceived of corruption as a kind of local weakness. One side effect of More's diagnosis of corruption, and her prescriptions for its localised treatment, is the discursive production of female authority: an authority that radical opposition rarely imagined. More understood that the fate of national economy, patriotism, pedagogy, as well as the more conventionally feminine responsibility for moral and spiritual welfare lay in the hands of Britain's women, the *doyennes* of households and local community.

It is in the guise of 'a private individual', then, that More banishes 'lesser motives of delicacy', and makes a robust appeal to 'the Ladies, etc. of Great Britain' for their charitable donations to the émigrés' relief fund. The subject of the pamphlet was another cause close to More's heart: national education. It was prompted by a speech made in the National Convention at Paris in December 1792 by Jacob Dupont, in a debate on the establishment of secular public schools in France. Dupont, a professed atheist, called for the overthrow of religious idolatry, the propagation of the nature-worship and the cultivation of reason in primary schools. The speech, which was published in the French paper *Le Moniteur*, was translated and reproduced in More's pamphlet. She did this in the face of criticism from 'many good men' who believed that the speech 'ought not to be made familiar to the minds of Englishmen, for there are crimes with which even the imagination should never come in contact' (p. 10). On the contrary, More argued that the speech was already so widely known in Britain that there was little point in shielding her readers from its pernicious policy. More chose rather to adopt the principles of 'an ancient nation' that 'intoxicated their slaves, and then exposed them before their children, in order to increase their horror of intemperance', in the belief that such impiety would strengthen rather than shake the faith of the Christian reader (p. 11). Further, she included in the transcription references to the behaviour of the Assembly during Dupont's address, and reproduced the dramatic scene as a combination of tragedy and blasphemous farce. So, as Dupont proclaims 'Nature and Reason, these ought to be the gods of men! These are my gods!', More parenthetically describes the reaction in the Assembly: 'Here the Abbé Audrein cried out, "There is no bearing this;" and rushed out of the Assembly. – A great laugh' (p. 9).

Having set and deflated the scene of Dupont's rhetorical impiety, More's commentary goes on to rail against the prospect of a system of secular education spreading to Britain. As she explained to Walpole, she was moved to comment on the speech in lieu of an intervention by the Anglican establishment. Their silence on the matter, she argued, would allow atheism to take hold of the British populace by virtue of familiarity:

Dupont's and Manuel's atheistical speeches have stuck in my throat all the winter, and I have been waiting for our bishops and our clergy to take some notice of them, but blasphemy and atheism have been allowed to become familiar to the minds of our common people, without any attempt being made to counteract the poison.[17]

More evidently had little faith in the Enlightenment principles of rational education as the route to civil society. Her pedagogical regimen is strictly metaphysical, based on absolute not relative truth:

no degree of wit and learning; no progress in commerce; no advances in the knowledge of nature, or in the embellishments of art, can ever thoroughly tame that savage, the natural human heart, without RELIGION. The arts of social life may give a sweetness to the manners and language, and induce in some degree, a love of justice, truth, and humanity; but attainments derived from such inferior causes are no more than the semblance and shadow of the qualities derived from pure Christianity.[18]

Given that More is writing this pamphlet on behalf of Catholic émigré priests, it seems that any Christian religion will do. She anticipates the hostility to her appeal on these grounds: 'Christian charity is of no party. We plead not for their faith, but for their wants' (p. ix). This did not prevent the most immediate criticism of *Remarks*, turning on More not only in defence of Dupont, but also in objection to her support of 'popery'. Of three 'answers' to her pamphlet cited by More in a letter to Walpole, the only identifiable author is Michael Nash, who, she complains, 'declares, that I am a favourer of the old popish massacres'. In *Gideon's Cake of Barley Meal: a Letter to the Rev. William Romaine . . . with Some Strictures on Mrs Hannah More's Remarks,* Nash moots the possibility that Hannah 'may be a descendant of that bitter persecutor Sir Thomas More', and that 'she would have made an excellent maid of honour to that bloody queen [Mary]'.[19]

Edmund Burke, who initiated the campaign for the émigrés, came in for similar kinds of criticism from various quarters during his career, partly because of the Catholicism of his maternal family, the Nagles, and because of his advocacy of Catholic emancipation; like all counter-revolutionaries who based their opposition partly on religious grounds, Burke and More were bound to face ridicule from those who saw the irony of launching a defence of the British establishment through the cause of the Catholics of the French *ancien régime*. More than this, however, More's religious principles, though not Catholic, were not representative of the Anglican establishment. Indeed, as I shall suggest, the Evangelical circle in which More moved in the 1790s, the so-called Clapham Sect, which included William Wilberforce, the Tory Member of Parliament for Hull, and his cousin, the banker Henry Thornton, were more subversive than supportive of many facets of the established order in Britain.

The anti-establishment character of the Clapham Sect is apparent in a number of pamphlets written by More herself during the period she was involved with them, including *Thoughts on the Manners of the Great* of 1788 and *An Estimate of the Religion of the Fashionable World* of 1790. *Remarks* too, whilst written to counteract the poison in the minds of the 'common people', are addressed to their betters, with a mind to their reformation. More appealed to those in a position to afford the subscription to the priests' fund, and petitioned them to use their social authority in the vigilant watch against the invasion of revolutionary doctrine. It is they, of course, who are most susceptible to infection. Addressing herself in particular to women of 'luxurious habits', who have little to spare, she pleads the case for sacrificing 'one costly dish . . . one expensive desert [sic] . . . one evening's public amusement' to furnish 'at least a week's subsistence to more than one person as liberally bred as herself' (p. 4). She is careful, then, not to argue against luxurious habits but flatters her readers through appeals to their domestic acumen, and to their empathy for their social equals. The support of these priests, she argues, is not downward benevolence, but relief of those of similar social standing, victims of 'the revolution of human affairs . . . thrown from equal heights of gaiety and prosperity' (p. 5). If one of the most resonant symbols of the cultural revolution in France was the women of the court donating their goods to the nation, then this welcoming gesture to the exiled clergy, 'without a home – without a country!' has an equally powerful counter-revolutionary and English national resonance (p. 5).

More dwells less on the abstract power of empathy or on the symbolic value of the donations than on more immediate interests for the maternal and patriotic reader: the promotion of domestic discipline and national wealth. She illustrates the bonus of 'the lesson of economy' that the charitable mother can bestow on her daughter through her contribution. If the daughter as yet has no money of her own to bestow (which, More suggests, no daughter of a prudent mother would) she can learn to hold back on feathers, ribbons and 'idle diversions': '. . . if they are thus instructed, that there is no true charity without self-denial, they will gain more than they are called upon to give: For the suppression of one luxury for a charitable purpose, is the exercise of two virtues, and this without any pecuniary expense' (p. 4).

To those with less means, and to whom lessons in personal accumulation through restraint may be insufficient argument, More evokes the cause of national wealth. The small contribution of 'the industrious tradesman' will bring relief with interest: 'The money raised is neither carried out of our country, nor dissipated in luxuries, but returns again to the community; to our shops and to our markets, to procure the bare necessaries of life' (p. 5).

HOME ECONOMICS

More was to revive her arguments for national Christian pedagogy and domestic economy a few years later in her *Strictures on Female Education*. The Revolution having given way to war, More turned her attention to the education of female patriots, who would 'come forward, without departing from the refinement of their character, without derogating from the dignity of their rank . . . to raise the depressed tone of public morals, and to awaken the drowsy spirit of religious principle' (1, pp. 4–5). Her emphasis is now less on the sound management of expenditure, on the visible and local returns of money spent, but on the well-regulated household as the model and foundation of the British way of life:

Oeconomy, such as a woman of fortune is called on to practise, is not merely the petty detail of small daily expenses, the shabby curtailments and stinted parsimony of a little mind, operating in little concerns; but it is the exercise of a sound judgement exerted in the comprehensive line of order, of arrangement, of distribution; of regulations by which alone well-governed societies, great and small, subsists. She who has the best regulated mind will, other things being equal, have the best regulated family . . . A sound economy is a sound understanding brought into action; it is calculation realised; it is the doctrine of proportion reduced to practice; it is foreseeing consequences, and guarding against them; it is expecting contingencies and being prepared for them.[20]

In this anti-speculative, and implicitly anti-Gallic vision, the economy of the household is not simply analogous to the economy of the nation. For More, domestic and national economy exist on a material continuum; moreover, the line from home to nation begins with the well-regulated mind of the woman, which can bring 'understanding' into 'action', which can realise a calculation and reduce 'doctrine' to 'practice'. The well-regulated woman of More's patriotic household carries on her tasks unseen; she exerts her influence without ostentation and with no expectation of reward. She is thus to be distinguished from the 'narrow minded vulgar economist', to whom the details of the household are 'continually present', and who is: '. . . overwhelmed by their weight, and is perpetually bespeaking your pity for her labours and your praise for her exertions; she is afraid you will not see how much she is harassed. She is not satisfied that the machine moves harmoniously, unless she is perpetually exposing every secret spring of observation' (2, p. 7).

More's vilification of the woman who visibly labours under the burden of domesticity can be understood in the context of More's gendered intervention into a discourse of political economy that, she implies, has long assumed but not articulated or protected the role of the domestic economist. Whilst, as Kathryn Sutherland has argued, Adam Smith had established the value of 'a feminised space . . . as generative of long-term economic good', the worth of 'the enclosed family groups' as 'the nursery of some of the best characteristics of modern commercial man' and the significance of 'the household's capacity for consumption' as a 'vital stimulus to large-scale production', his economic vision of the wealth of nations paid scant attention to the actual running of households.[21] Smith was, in fact, largely responsible for severing the primary semantic link between the term 'oeconomy' and the running of households, a move that gave rise to the qualifying term 'home economics'. More, on the other hand, not only followed Smith's contemporaries like James Steuart and Josiah Tucker in assuming the domestic referent, but she placed women at the centre of economic regulation, as the 'invisible hand' of domestic and national organisation. Following an earlier tradition of domestic manuals on household management, More sketched in her *Tracts* and her *Strictures* models of domestic regulation for her female readers to emulate. Further, as Sutherland suggests, More stands along with Sarah Trimmer, Priscilla Wakefield, Jane Marcet and Harriet Martineau within an 'enlarged female tradition' that consciously feminises 'the public representation of the moral and political economy' and attributes a national importance to her models of household management (p. 59).

More departed from Smith not only in the gendering of 'oeconomy' but in her conception of the relationship between sound economy and virtuous community. Smith's models were based on secular fantasies of self-regulated exchange, and promulgated the idea of the marketplace as a series of sympathetic correspondences between people of common constitutions, which provided the possibility (if not the reality) that the sexes and the ranks could engage in mutual trade. More, again following Tucker, argues for a more providentially organised scheme of commerce, in which freedom of exchange is compatible with difference in rank and gender.[22] More's conception of a moral commercial society depends on the *acquisition* of sympathy rather than the reliance on the natural compassion of one being for another. She articulates this position in a discussion 'On Sensibility' in her *Strictures*, where, typically, her economic model is embedded in a sketch of the woman of charity. The 'tender-hearted woman', she writes, 'whose hand . . . is "Open as day to melting charity"; nevertheless may utterly fail in the . . . duty of christian love'. As her feelings are 'acted upon solely by local circumstance' her sympathies lack the principle to survive in 'another scene, distant from the wants she has been relieving' (2, p. 118). Proper sympathy must be cultivated if it is to resemble Christian compassion and not disappear at the first distraction. This apparent departure from More's own penchant for a local cause is, in fact, a critique of the logic of the self-regulating relations of the Smithian market and its secular conception of sympathy. Only a systematic and regulated flow of sympathies, which does not disrupt the providentially ordained distinction between ranks, will guarantee the efficient operation of the national body. The poor and women must be kept content but encouraged to keep their wants in check. An economy that encourages aspiration cannot guarantee the passive acquiescence of one part of its population to a lesser share of the nation's resources. From More's perspective, there is no more chastening example of the effects of an unregulated economy than France, and no more dangerous economy than the unmonitored circulation of ideas.

IMAGINATIVE LABOUR

With the example of France before her, then, More offers a scheme for the regulation of Britain's 'sympathetic economy', which amounts to a programme of emotional and mental discipline. Significantly, this programme, at least as it is defined in the *Strictures*, is based less on indoctrination in moral precept than on exposing would-be citizens to 'works of the imagination'. 'When moderately used,' she argues 'works of the imagination' can 'serve to stretch the faculties and expand the mind' (1, p. 206). This 'expansion of mind' comes to sound surprisingly like orientalist abandon, when More argues for the pedagogical merits of the 'bold fictions of the east'. More, of course, recommends oriental tales as mental discipline: as cultural histories, they afford 'some tincture of real local information . . . which will not be without its uses in aiding the future associations of the mind in all that relates to eastern history and literature'. Read alongside 'accurate and simple facts' these 'original and acknowledged fictions' help to cultivate in the reader the distinction between 'truth and fable' (1, pp. 206–7). The 'true metaphors' of the literature of the east return unexpectedly in More's defence of the 'hyperbolical style' of the Old Testament:

The lofty style of the Eastern, and other rhetoric poetry, does not . . . mislead; for the metaphor, and the imagery is understood to be ornamental. The style of the Scriptures of the Old Testament is not, it is true, plain in opposition to figurative; nor simple in opposition to florid; but it is plain and simple in the best sense, as opposed to false principles and false taste; it raises no wrong ideas; it gives an exact impression of the thing it means to convey; and its very tropes and figures, though bold, are never unnatural and affected.[23]

This defence of literary ornament, albeit a moral defence, does not sit easily with the prevailing image of More, who is better known for her dire warnings about the effects of pernicious reading matter on those morally susceptible orders: 'the sex' and the lower ranks. This censoriousness is reserved largely, though not exclusively, for the publications associated with the French Enlightenment, which, as she suggests in her

Remarks, have put More's faith in the freedom of the Press under pressure:

. . . is the cheapness of poison, or the facility with which it may be obtained, to be reckoned among the real advantages of medicinal repositories? And can the easiness of access to seditious or atheistical writings, be numbered among the substantial blessings of any country? Would France, at this day, have had much solid cause of regret, if many of the writings of Voltaire, Rousseau, and d'Alembert, (the prolific seed of their wide-spreading tree), had found more difficulty in getting into the world, or been less profusely circulated when in it? And might not England at this moment have been just as happy in her ignorance, if the famous orations of Citizen Dupont and Citizen Manuel had been confined to their own enlightened and philosophical countries?[24]

Whilst her liberal contemporaries, in particular Helen Maria Williams, put their hopes for progress in increased Press freedom, easier access of information, ease of circulation, within and across national borders, More here called for the channels to be stemmed or at least monitored. As in her commentary on national and domestic economy, More argues for controlled circulation of the Press and print and has little faith either in the internally regulating force of market principle or freedom of information.

Perhaps unsurprisingly, whilst More gave to women a symbolic authority in the regulation of economic circulation, she characterised them as most vulnerable to the free circulations of Enlightenment thinkers and a host of other corrupting forces. She warned in the *Strictures* that the 'attacks of infidelity in Great Britain are at this moment principally directed against the female breast':

Conscious of the influence of women in civil society, conscious of the effect which female infidelity produced in France, they attribute the ill-success of their attempts in this country to their having been hitherto chiefly addressed to the male sex. They are now sedulously labouring to destroy the religious principles of women, and in too many instances have fatally succeeded. For this purpose, not only novels and romances have been made vehicles of vice and infidelity, but the same allurement has been held out to the women of our first country, which was employed by the first philosophist to the first sinner – Knowledge.[25]

Echoing Mary Wollstonecraft, More rails against a system of female education that has left women 'susceptible', particularly the tendency to educate aristocratic and middle-class women in accomplishments that fit them for nothing but domestic decoration, and the sedentary occupations that render their bodies delicate. Whilst for the perfectibilist Wollstonecraft, the prevailing mode of female education violates women's natural capacity for reason, for More, it exacerbates their 'corrupt nature and evil dispositions'; those very evils 'which it should be the main end and objective of Christian instruction to remove' (1, pp. 67–8). This distinction is illustrated in their mutual denigration of Rousseau as an author of female ills. Whilst Wollstonecraft condemns the legacy of Sophie, a woman educated to please, More points to Julie, that 'victim, not of temptation, but of reason' (1, p. 34). More worries less about sexual promiscuity than the plethora of distractions that erode women's '[p]atience, diligence, quiet, and unfatigued perseverance, industry, regularity, and oeconomy of time' (1, p. 182) . It is not just the seductive fantasies of Rousseauan fantasy that distract women's atten-tion. In fact, a greater threat lies in 'that sober and unsuspected mass of mischief, which, by assuming the plausible names of Science, of Philos-ophy, of Arts, of Belles Lettres', have found their way into young ladies' dressing rooms (1, p. 33). They are subtle toxins, packaged as sober and improving fare:

Avowed attacks upon revelation are most easily resisted, because the malignity is advertised: but who suspects the destruction which lurks under the harmless or instructive names of General History, Natural History, Travels, Voyages, Lives, Encyclopedias, Criticism, and Romance? Who will deny that many of these works contain much admirable matter; brilliant passages, important facts, just descriptions, faithful pictures of nature, and valuable illustrations of science? But while 'the dead fly lies at the bottom,' the whole will exhale a corrupt and pestilential stench.[26]

The 'corrupt and pestilential stench' of French Enlightenment that More claims was banished once already in the century by 'the plain sense and good principles of the far greater part of our countrymen' (1, p. 43) is seeping back through the cracks and weak points in British society. Britain's women are Eves and Julies, who succumb to the philosophy of rights and reason and, through their power of 'influence' drag their country down with them. Such women, More claims, are seduced less by the heat of passion than by the 'benumbing touch', the 'cool, calculating, intellectual wickedness' of this 'most destructive class in the whole range of modern corrupters' who:

. . . effect the most desperate work of the passions without so much as pretending to urge their violence in extenuation of the guilt of indulging them. They solicit this very indulgence with a sort of cold blooded speculation, and invite the reader to the most unbounded gratifications, with all the saturnine coolness of a geometrical calculation.[27]

This philosophic vampirism is 'the iniquity of phlegm rather than spirit' (1, p. 51). The spirit is all More's as she concocts her antidote to the pernicious recipe of 'English Sentiment, French Philosophy, Italian

Love-Songs, and fantastic German imagery and magic wonders'. Noting that the 'corruption occasioned by these books has spread so wide, and descended so low, as to have become one of the most universal, as well as most pernicious, sources of corruption among us' she recommends a 'preparatory course' of reading for middle-class girls and for the 'milliners, mantua-makers' (I, pp. 221–2). Her regimen is for 'strong meat' to 'act upon the constitution of the mind . . . and . . . help to brace the intellectual stamina': Watt's or Duncan's 'little book of Logic, some parts of Mr Locke's Essay on Human Understanding, and Bishop Butler's Analogy' (I, p. 214). It is a recipe for productivity as well as salvation, for in 'trades where numbers work together, the labour of one girl is frequently sacrificed that she may be spared to read those mischievous books to the others' (I, pp. 221–2).

As I have suggested, her utilitarian pronouncements on the benefits of literacy belie another kind of fascination with the power of imaginative arts and indirectly with the power of revolutionary thought (the recommendation of Locke as reading matter for milliners and mantua-makers exemplifies the ambivalence of More's conservatism). This power cannot be entirely accounted for in the disciplinary logic of More's imaginative economy, which is premised on the release of female productivity and the constraint of non-remunerative mental energy. This uncontainable imaginative power can be better understood in relation to More's pedagogical and religious practices. These not only had revolutionary potential but provoked a public debate about the revolutionary character of her 'missionary' activities in the rural communities of the southwest. The so-called 'Blagdon persecution' of 1800–4, in which More was vilified for her suspected Methodism, brings to light the fear of the performance of new class and gender relations in the emerging Sunday school movement and its 'religion of the heart', and exposes the transgressive nature of the social practices that were initiated by More's 'regulative' régimes.

THE RELIGION OF THE HEART

More was an evangelist. Evangelicalism is a broad-ranging term used to describe a range of doctrinal positions embraced by members of the Anglican church, but in its early years could be characterised as a movement designed to reinvigorate a lethargic established church. More was a member of the Clapham Sect, a group largely made up of business and professional men who doubled as crusaders for revitalised religion in England. The Clapham Sect were undoubtedly inspired by the zealous preachings of Wesley and the Methodists, who had led a new wave of religious enthusiasm among the lower classes, and which took hold strongly during the 1790s, partly because of the inadequacy of the established church to offer solace in the face of the radical social upheavals that were taking place so close to home.[28] The utilitarianism of the orthodox church, it seems, was an inadequate source of consolation to a nation in need of conviction. Although the Church of England was equipped to denounce French infidelity, it could offer little in terms of belief or credible doctrine in the wake of a new modernity. As the social historian V. Kiernan argues, 'dust lay on the Thirty-nine Articles . . . what had seemed modern before 1789 was now antediluvian'. The broader character of 'the public', too, called for a new public creed. 'If high and low were to join in worship,' Kiernan argues, ' it must be the worship of the poor' (p. 47).

More, and other evangelicals, espoused their unequivocal attachment to the Established Church and, as her first biographer Thompson suggests, were committed to the promotion of 'loyalty, good morals, and an attachment to Church and State'.[29] It is apparent, however, that Evangelicalism was in many respects a 'progressive' bearer of middle-class dissent, initiating demands for state reform based on a wide-reaching critique of aristocratic value. Under the respectable guise of the 'Anglican saints', the Clapham Sect (who one of More's biographers, Mary Alden Hopkins, describes as leading 'a sort of pruned and quieted Methodism within the Church of England'[30]) seized the opportunity that was given them by the French Revolution to undertake a radical critique of the British establishment. As demonstrated in More's *Remarks*, her first public commentary on the Revolution, the evangelical call for reformation was carried out in part on the back of anti-Gallic and anti-aristocratic nationalism. Inevitably, evangelical 'patriots' were to find unlikely bedfellows not only in French Catholic priests but also in English radicals. This was an association that brought More into conflict not only with the Established Church but also with the conservative Press with which she had allied herself at the beginning of the 1790s. The fact that More was a woman did not, of course, help to assuage doubts about her dangerous enthusiasms, as is evident in Polwhele's caricature of the bishop in petticoats, an image of female authority usurping the role of an established church. The conflict that haunted More during the early part of the 1800s was precipitated in part, then, by the spectre of a woman engaging with the lower orders.

More had begun to court controversy with her social peers in 1793, when she addressed herself to a less than polite constituency of readers in her contribution to a series of tracts distributed by the Association for Preserving Liberty and Property against Republicans and Levellers: a counter-revolutionary pamphlet called 'Village Politics'.[31] She had been asked to write the pamphlet by the Bishop of London, Beilby Porteus. Porteus, who was afraid the French Revolution was encouraging British factory and farm workers to consider the inequity of their own condition, asked More to write a simple tract to explain the terms 'liberty' and 'equality' to readers who might come across them in other, more incendiary, contexts. More responded to the request with a departure from her usual polite idiom and produced 'Village Politics'. Written under the name of Will Chip, 'a country carpenter', and 'addressed to all the mechanics, journeymen, and labourers in Great Britain', it takes the form of a dialogue between Jack Anvil, the blacksmith, and Tom Hod, the mason. As Olivia Smith suggests, More writes in 'Village Politics' as though 'righteously seducing people who have no control over their passions'.[32] Tom has read *The Rights of Man* and has discovered that he is 'very unhappy, and very miserable', which he should never have known 'if I had not had the good luck to meet with this book' (1, p. 346). It is up to Jack to disabuse him of his ideal miseries and to restore his faith in the blessings of the British constitution, the benefits of class organisation, the dividends of high taxation and the merit of public credit. Jack's trump card is Tom's taste for ale:

Tom, I don't care for drink myself, but thou dost, and I'll argue with thee, not in the way of principle, but in thy own way; when there's all equality there will be no superfluity: when there's no wages there'll be no drink: and levelling will rob thee of thy ale more than malt tax does.[33]

Two years after the publication of 'Village Politics', More again seized on the methods of the *Liberty and Property* series and began to publish her monthly tracts, *Cheap Repository*. These exemplary tales and parables for a virtuous and industrious life, aimed principally at a newly literate readership, circulated in large numbers in England and Ireland between March 1795 and November 1797.[34] Like Wordsworth in the Preface to the *Lyrical Ballads*, More sought not to woo a new class of readers, but to instruct a known constituency in a new aesthetic. Of course, Wordsworth's manifesto couched its social purpose (the production of a manly middle-class English readership to counteract the effects of an effete aristocracy) as a poetics (the cultivation of a taste for a native

ballad tradition in the place of neo-classicism and sickly German sensation). More, on the other hand, explicitly advertised her *Tracts* as a
means to shape a public along particular national and class lines. In
1818, when she reflected on her motivation for publishing the *Tracts* in
1795 (a year of poor harvests and economic hardship in Britain), she
claims she had judged it 'expedient at this critical moment to supply
such wholesome aliment as might give a new direction to the public
taste' to counteract the 'relish for those corrupt and impious publications which the consequences of the French Revolution had been fatally
pouring in upon us.'[35]

The titles of the stories speak for themselves: the 'histories' of Mr
Fantom, the New-Fashioned Philosopher and Mr Bragwell, or, the Two
Wealthy Farmers; of Betty Brown, with 'some account of Mrs Sponge
the Money Lender', and Black Giles the Poacher, 'containing some
account of a family who had [sic] rather live by their wits than their
work'. As well as the moral fables, More included a number of ballads,
reviving her early interest in a form with which she had experimented in
the 1770s when she produced 'The Ballad of Bleeding Rock' and 'Sir
Eldred and the Bower'. These early ballads were part of a broader
revival of interest in old English legends and a national ballad tradition
that More shared with Percy, Beattie and Chatterton, amongst others.
More's return to the ballad in the 1790s, best exemplified in 'The Riot:
or Half a Loaf is Better than No Bread' of 1795 ,was a less 'literary' but
more politically effective intervention in the shaping of the nation.
Based on the unrest about scarcity in that year, More's 'The Riot' used
dialogue, rhyme and the tune of 'A Cobbler There Was' to convince
'the people' that the famine conditions to which they were subject were
not the effect of misgovernment. This was a common refrain in More's
Tracts. According to Hopkins, one of More's sympathetic biographers, it
proved convincing, and More's jaunty ballad was reported to have
stopped a food riot near Bath (p. 211).

As I have suggested, the apparent utilitarianism of the *Tracts*, the
allegorical method that subordinates medium to message, disguises
More's interest in the power of the imaginative arts. It is a fascination
which, from a deconstructive point-of-view, is endemic to a utilitarian
view of culture. Her view of the corruptibility of human nature, of life as
a disciplinary struggle and of an imaginative economy dedicated to
curbing the expenditure of mind which exhausts rather than sustains the
body produces, of course, a textual preoccupation with excess, with
luxury and with decadence. In a more empirical sense, however, the

ambivalence that More displays with respect, in particular, to the powers of the imagination is a legacy of her connections with London literary society, with the Della Cruscans and with the emerging 'Romantic' circle of Coleridge, Southey and Robert Hall.[36]

By the 1790s, More's interest in the literary was explicitly focused on its didactic potential. In her letters to Horace Walpole, More reflexively connects literary trends to social mores, and predominantly characterises the imagination as an instrument that simply moulds material in response to local circumstance. This is, of course, a much more strategic, and empirical, understanding of the imagination than that which was being formulated by her Romantic contemporaries, for whom the work of imagination would transcend the local and particular demands of mere social occasion.

More translates the empirical character of imagination into a utilitarian programme for the use of imaginative 'works', paying as much attention to the medium as the message of her reading regimen, in particular the figurative language of the Old Testament and the fancy of tales of the Orient. More's own didactic fictions do not display her interest in ornament. Her *Tracts* 'for the common people' are allegorical tales that leave little gap between figure and maxim, and no room for speculation. They are addressed to a readership who, More assumes, lack the mental discipline that produces the difference between east and west, fable and truth, theory and practice, and, most crucially between the English and French meanings of liberty. More orchestrates this discipline with the anti-relativist confidence that is borne of metaphysical faith, and the utilitarian belief in her own control of her imaginative libido. Knowing her own poison, she dispenses it with evangelical abandon; not just in print, but in the pedagogical practice of her Sunday schools. Inevitably, the repressed returned, and More found herself vilified for her own enthusiasms and for the pernicious doctrine she preached in her classrooms and meeting houses.

IRREGULAR THINGS

In 1789, More had the opportunity to put her pedagogical principles into practice outside the confines of the Bristol girls' school she ran with her sisters, when she opened her first Sunday school in Cheddar. When William Wilberforce 'discovered' a community living in caves in the Cheddar gorge and was appalled by their poverty, illiteracy and lack of religious conviction, he called on the Mores to intervene. He had already made Hannah's acquaintance through anti-slavery campaigns and through their mutual involvement in the Society for the Reformation of Manners, a movement established in 1787 to curb the 'excesses' of the poor. With the financial backing of Wilberforce (whom Elizabeth Montagu dubbed 'The Red Cross Knight') and Henry Thornton, the Mores went on in 1791 to open further schools in Conglesbury, Yatton and Axbridge and, a year later, in Nailsea. The Mendips schools, undoubtedly a laudable humanitarian scheme in an area where local grandees had neglected and abused their 'charges', were inevitably to be an extension of the Wilberforce's 'management project', with the emphasis on spiritual recovery before social reformation.

An account of the Mores' experiences as 'missionaries' in the southwest of England appears in *The Mendip Annals*: the journal of Hannah's sister Martha, a selection of their correspondence and fulsome editorial commentary by Arthur Roberts.[37] The Mores' familiarity with contemporary travel writing and orientalist fantasy is evident in *The Annals*, which are littered with tropes of racial difference and encounters with 'savages' in which the sisters assert their own moral and biological superiority. The Mores' moral purpose seems unswerving from beginning to end and, rationally, the narrative of *The Annals* bears out their mastery of a hostile environment, of Godless 'barbarians' and sparse or apathetic clergy. '[T]here is as much knowledge of Christ in the interior of Africa as there is to be met with in this wretched, miserable place' Hannah laments (p. 160). Like De Quincey's Malay, the robustness of the Mendips' miner is a sign of his moral degeneracy; unlike the English opium eater, however, the Mores do not allow themselves to succumb to the power of the 'other'. On the contrary, their mission is to transform, to make an impression without being inscribed by their surroundings. According to Roberts, their imperviousness forced their subjects to yield: '. . . the astonishing impression was wrought on the adults. The most hard and rugged natures were melted into tenderness. Rough workers in the coal-pits became the gentle-hearted, philanthropic Christians. Instead of the grossest immorality, a high standard of modesty and decency, became everywhere apparent' (p. 4).

There are, of course, discursive echoes in the Mores' account of their Mendips mission of Hannah's abolitionist rhetoric, exemplified in her verse polemic 'On Slavery', which she wrote on behalf of the Abolition Society in 1788, to coincide with a proposed parliamentary debate early that year.[38] As various commentators have noted, 'On Slavery' is a gendered as well as a class-marked and nationalistic response to colonialism and the slave trade.[39] 'On Slavery' is in part a paean to English liberty, as More distinguishes between the 'pure daughter of the skies', the light of 'fair Freedom', the 'Bright intellectual sun' and the ungovernable, irrational 'monster', who is the creature and the creator of the mob of the Gordon Riots in 1780:

> To thee alone, pure daughter of the skies,
> The hallow'd incense of the bard should rise!
> Not that mad liberty, in whose wild praise
> Too oft he trims his prostituted bays;
> Not that unlicens'd monster of the crowd,
> Whose roar terrific bursts in peals so loud,
> Deaf'ning the ear of Peace; fierce Faction's tool,
> Of rash Sedition born, and mad Misrule;
> Whose stubborn mouth, rejecting Reason's reign,
> No strength can govern, and no skill restrain;[40]

The poem does not dwell on the distinction between the 'pure daughter' and the 'unlicens'd monster'; for it has another didactic purpose. The poetic burden lies in the plea to the intellectual sun to distribute its rays more equally, to irradiate 'sad Afric quench'd in total night'. However, the memory of Faction, Sedition and Misrule, now 'past' (l. 47) disrupts the controlling distinction between dark, enslaved Africa and Britain, basking in Liberty's 'full blaze of light'. It is this kind of slippage that raised suspicions about the association between abolitionists and social radicalism. With this in mind, perhaps, More distances herself from 'the mob' by constructing her campaigning role as an extension of, rather than a threat to, feminine decorum (at least insofar as the sentimental philanthropy of the bluestocking circle was ever understood as feminine). The female narrator of the 'Slave Trade' sympathises, chides and 'civilises', exerting the 'influence' proper to the female politician.

As recorded in *The Annals*, the Mores extend this civilising programme to England. The project is fuelled by the 'acquired' sympathy of which More speaks in her *Strictures*: that which is based on Christian female duty and independent of the effects of local circumstances, furnished by 'self-denial' and 'a regular provision for miseries' (2, p. 118). Her mission to convert the locals has first to overcome the atheism of the farmers, whose wealth, like that of the slave trader, supports and controls the region. In a letter to Wilberforce, reproduced in *The Mendip*

Annals, More recounts an encounter with one of them, in terms of a colonial adventurer confronting a native chief:

Dear Sir, – Though this is but a romantic place, as my friend Matthew well observed, yet you would laugh to see the bustle I am in. I was told we should meet with great opposition if I did not try to propitiate the chief despot of the village, who is very rich, and very brutal; so I ventured to the den of this monster, in a country as savage as himself, near Bridgewater. He begged I would not think of bringing any religion into the country; it was the worst thing in the world for the poor, for it made them lazy and useless. In vain did I represent to him that they would be more industrious, as they were better principled; and that, for my part, I had no selfish views in what I was doing.[41]

In this colonial fantasy, More is the disinterested missionary, bargaining for souls in return for productive bodies. It is a position that each sister takes up as they comment on the amoral and 'irregular' working practices in the glasshouses and mines in Nailsea, so 'abounding in sin and wickedness' that 'we could not help thinking it would become our little Sierra Leone' (pp. 42–3). It is the glasshouses in particular that shock the sisters, as Hannah recalls:

Whatever we had seen before, was of a different nature, and though we had encountered savages, hard-hearted farmers, little cold country gentry, a super-cilious and ignorant corporation, yet this was still new, and unlike all other things – not only differing from all we had seen, but greatly transcending all we had imagined. Both sexes and all ages herding together; voluptuous beyond belief. The work of a glass-house is an irregular thing, uncertain whether by day or night; not only by infringing upon man's rest, but constantly intruding upon the privileges of the Sabbath. The wages high, the eating and drinking luxur-ious – the body scarcely covered, but fed with the dainties of a shocking description. The high buildings of the glass-house ranged before the doors of the cottages – these great furnaces roaring – the swearing, eating, and drinking of these half-dressed, black-looking beings, gave it an almost infernal and horrible appearance.[42]

This demonic site that could have been drawn from Milton's descrip-tion of pandemonium defies the laws of industrial organisation and divided labour. The half-clothed, savage bodies, 'both sexes and all ages' fed incongruously on 'dainties of a shocking description' are tuned neither to the rhythms of the clock nor the Christian calendar. With cottages lit by the glare of the furnace, the 'voluptuousness' of the workplace must extend to the home. The 'irregularity', 'infringement' and 'intrusion' are other to the productive industrial scene that controls the passage: male day workers giving way to night workers; the working week giving way to the replenishment of the Sabbath; a home sustained by a subsistence wage and run by the female domestic economist. It is this kind of regularity that the Mores tried to establish through their work in the Mendips.

THE BLAGDON PERSECUTION

As in the rest of the Sunday school movement in which the Mores played a founding role, the principles of industrial labour were inculcated in their schoolrooms.[43] Their pedagogical strategies were an extension of the maternal regulation of the household, instilling respect for hygiene and sexual decorum. The relationship between religious pedagogy and the industrial workplace was also literal, with the attachment of 'schools of industry', offering rudimentary training in skills such as spinning, to some of the Cheddar schools. Perhaps most surprisingly, given Hannah's antipathy to the autonomy of women and the lower classes, the Mores established a series of women's clubs modelled on men's friendly societies, to which members paid a subscription and could draw on the capital to support them through sickness, childbirth or the cost of a funeral. The official logic of these clubs and schools was the maintenance of the status quo, the pacification of the lower orders and the provision of training, particularly to women, in the regulation of households and moral management. However, it was not the regulative agenda but the seeds of female and working-class self-organisation that drew most attention to the Mores' schools.

For about five years from 1799, two of More's Sunday schools became the focus of attack from conservative members of the Established Church, who suspected them of spreading Methodist propaganda. The ostensible problem was the nature and location of the evening prayer meetings that the Mores held for the parents of children in the parish of Wedmore and later in Blagdon: meetings which, their conservative antagonists suggested, contravened the 1664 Conventicle Act, which decreed that religious meetings for more than five persons worshipping in any other than the established forms of the Church of England would be punishable by imprisonment or transportation. The Act was, of course, no longer enforceable but was still invoked as a sign of the Established Church's intolerance of dissent. It is less the origins of the controversy which interest me here than the terms in which it was conducted in editorials and letters to magazines and in twenty-three pamphlets which were published on the subject in 1802.[44] Some of these were written in the Mores' defence, but most were aggressive in their attack not only on the impropriety of the prayer meetings, but on the sisters' 'enthusiasm' and their suspected Methodism. One of the best known of the pamphlets, *Truths, Respecting Mrs Hannah More's Meeting-Houses, and the Conduct of her Followers; Addressed to the Curate of Blagdon*, written by Edward Spencer, has for an epigraph a quotation from *Ward's Reformation*, which crystallises the fear of feminine influence that underpins much of the criticism they received:

> O! Tom, . . .
> Put not the Women into Pulpits,
> For they'll deride our Sex for Dull-pates;
> They'll murder with eternal din.[45]

Spencer's pamphlet continues to make this commonplace misogynist connection between the elevation of female authority and the demise of hegemonic masculinity. Addressed to the curate of Blagdon, who had from Spencer's perspective been the victim of the More's 'savage' practices, it extends into a fantasy about men ensnared by the Mores' uncontrollable sexuality. Thus, as evidence of Hannah's Methodism, he depicts her 'drawing within the vortex of her petticoats, numerous bodies of the regular Clergy of the land, who are made subservient to her views and accessory to her designs by the liberty of issuing her bulls and promulgating her mandates' (p. 48). A dissimulating woman who 'indulges in fish with the Catholic, and in the company of a Jew will not touch pork', this 'Pope Joan' cast her wide spell over 'simple honest peasantry', dignitaries of the Established Church, and the monarch (p. 50; p. 52; p. 64).[46] Spencer appropriates some of More's own discourse when he calls for vigilance against the revolutionary potential of 'puritanic fanaticism'. To this, and 'its concomitant levelling principles' are to be attributed:

. . . most of the horrors of revolution, blood, and carnage, which mankind have so grievously mourned, since the unfortunate days of Charles I, and from which, to the discredit of our nation, as can be regularly traced from that period to the present, in this country, all modern mischiefs took their origin; this has been the seed bed from which the whole have sprung.[47]

For Spencer, then, More and her sectarian enthusiasts are a reanimated puritan faction. Whilst Hannah preached against the influence of foreign infidels, she was vilified as an orchestrator of native insurrection. Perhaps the greatest irony is that More was maligned in terms that were similar to those used by Edmund Burke a decade earlier to describe the monstrous women who took to the streets during the

French Revolution, and stood as symbols both of a degraded femininity and the overturning of natural authority.

Perhaps unsurprisingly, Hannah More suffered what her biographers refer to euphemistically as 'a great illness' in the years following the Blagdon controversy, although she continued to produce works of Christian dogma from her home, Barley Wood in Wrington, until several years before her death in 1833. More's loyalty to church and state from the period when she became an active campaigner until her death never publicly swerved. The means that she chose to demonstrate that loyalty and to instil it in others produced more disruptive effects than she could have anticipated, however. Even though More's name would never appear on any petition in support of reform or the extension of the political franchise, her 'influence' is evident both in a female literary tradition that stood against public corruption – nineteenth-century domestic realism – and in the self-determination of a generation of newly literate political activists who would write their own petitions and organise their own fund-raising campaigns.[48] This new generation of 'patriots' – Chartists and organisers of the movement for reform – were dedicated to rooting out the corruptions of state from which More and her fellow propagandists had hoped to distract them by promoting their loyalty to the nation.

Afterword

Let me make the novels of a country, and let who will make the systems.[1]

Anna Laetitia Barbauld's closing thought in the prefatorial essay to the 1820 edition of *The British Novelists* – evidence if it were needed that women did and continue to participate in canon-building – encapsulates her simultaneously Romantic and utilitarian view of the novel and its relation to national culture. Adding another gloss on the well-documented 'origin and progress of novel-writing', Barbauld finds the significance of the genre lies in its ubiquity: 'Books of this description are condemned by the grave, and despised by the fastidious; but their leaves are seldom found unopened, and they occupy the parlour and the dressing-room while productions of higher name are often gathering dust upon the shelf.'[2] Whilst Hannah More was so alarmed by the easy circulation of these pernicious fictions that she took it upon herself to concoct a corrective diet, Barbauld finds in novels a benign, unsystematic form of cultural cohesion, which reflects and arbitrates the national character. As for the effects of their ready availability, Barbauld argues that whilst English novels have neither 'flavour nor nourishment' they are not 'vicious' nor 'poisoned', so the 'chief harm done by a circulating library is occasioned by the frivolity of its furnishings, and the loss of time incurred' (p. 55). It was precisely this loss of time to literary consumption that worried More, but Barbauld shared her fellow dissenter Ann Radcliffe's sense of the productive effects of a 'liberal' reading régime. Indeed, she includes Radcliffe in her vindication of a range of British novelists, classifying her along with D'Arblay, Edgeworth and Inchbald amongst the women of whom 'it will not be said that either taste or morals have been losers by their taking the pen in hand' (p. 56).

As a poet, a pedagogue and pamphleteer, Barbauld provides another

159

example of a woman who contributed in multiple ways to English letters and to the discursive shaping of the nation. Barbauld belonged and was exiled in similar ways to the women I have considered in this study and made public her own sense of the rights and responsibilities pertaining to membership of the national community in the 1790s.[3] I introduce Barbauld here not as another variation on a theme, however, but to draw attention to a line of continuity and to reflect on the legacy of these middle-class women who occupied a particular role in English 'civil society': the role of educator. Barbauld's preface is penned by the hand of a teacher as she compares, contrasts, summarises and reviews the novels, novelists, literary techniques and moral sensibilities of nations. Having been brought up in a dissenting academy, Barbauld's primary route to the public was pedagogy, and, like Mary Wollstonecraft and Hannah More, she spent a large part of her life teaching, writing educational tracts and reflecting on the process of national education. Whilst Radcliffe, Williams and Smith were not teachers, I have charac- terised their work – more by accident than design – as kinds of peda- gogical practice. Radcliffe's educational tours, Williams's sentimental guides to the French republic of letters, and Smith's satirical sketches of the English professional classes, all share an Enlightenment faith in the power of knowledge to transform social relations. Perhaps this emphasis is endemic in a study which seeks to contextualise literature in a social milieu – in this case national identity – and thus is primarily interested in the analysis of its instrumental rather than its aesthetic qualities. It is also symptomatic, however, of the oddly detached role that women often occupied – and continue to occupy – in civil society.

In my introduction, I provided a positive version of the sense of possibility offered to women by the prevailing metaphors of the public sphere – mediation, conversation, exchange – as opposed to the con- straints and contradictions embedded in the image of the mother in the discourse of the Romantic nation. However, as I have suggested, women's participation in the public sphere is marked by its vicarious- ness. While the pains of literal maternity are all too evident in the work of Smith and Wollstonecraft, as educators and disseminators of culture all of these women seem to act in *loco parentis*, at one remove from the messy business of mothering and, by analogy, the production of national culture as it comes to be represented in the canons of English literature. They belong yet are detached and detachable from national tradition, a condition that makes them intellectually free but culturally homeless.

What of the legacy of these wandering women? I am thinking here less of a literary tradition than the legacy for those who have taken up the role of observation, commentary and often education in the literary domain: literary critics. Is there a gendered, national critical style, a discourse of feminine English civility that has survived since the 1790s? Obviously, part of my argument is predicated on the historicity of national belonging and to argue for some transhistorical, monolithic national style of criticism would contradict this view. However, the instrumentality, the sense of 'purpose' – variously defined, but ethically inflected – that I have addressed here is evident in certain kinds of literary historical work, which seeks to 'recover' something, even if what is recovered provides more questions than answers about that past. Works of archival recovery in literary studies are after all premised less on the promise of new aesthetic pleasure than the communication of concealed knowledge (although for most of us this is a difficult distinction to make). Whilst archival scholarship is by no means an exclusively 'English' practice, British historical and political traditions, with their respectively empirical and pragmatic bases do impact on the kind of criticism practised by British scholars, including feminist literary critics. Despite the impact of deconstruction and the various kinds of new historicism in the 1970s and 1980s, the literary historical criticism that emanates from British presses is still predominantly characterised by biographical and teleological historicism. The impulse to locate origins, to trace continuities and, implicitly, to project futures, that informs such criticism is an impulse born of the eighteenth-century public sphere, to build as well as to understand culture through rational critique. Similarly, the motivation for feminist critics to recover and contextualise women's writing is surely to come to an understanding of women's conditions in the present in the hope of changing the future. This study shares that Utopian sense of purpose.

To draw an analogy between these cultural commentators of the 1790s and those of the 1990s might be more meaningful in a study which addressed the institutional frameworks which produce critical practices: for us, the universities; for the middle-class women of the late eighteenth century the loose, *ad hoc* assemblies afforded by literary salons and private connection. We share with them the virtual communities of print culture: publishers, critics and readers. Institutional frameworks vary within and across national boundaries, and the academic contexts in which women disseminate and arbitrate national cultures in the 1990s are as various as those of the 1790s. Perhaps what has changed insufficiently in the English and British context is the level of institutional 'misrecognition' of women's place in civil society and the contradictory status of mothers in the discourse of nationhood. One need only look to the status of women employed in higher education to understand that access to civil society is uneven.[4] For the many women employed on temporary or part-time contracts, who continue to earn less than their male peers and who struggle to return to the workplace after a period of maternity leave, their sense of belonging to an intellectual community, to English civil society and of themselves as disseminators, mediators or critics of 'national' culture is partial at best. The political economy of higher education as it is presently constituted means that time to research and write is a luxury afforded to few, and to fewer women than to men. This is not the legacy that the wandering women of the 1790s would have wished to pass on to later generations of female intellectuals. It is, however, a testament to the enduring power of Romantic nation-hood as I have sketched it here that the feminisation of the workplace (which includes a flexible, multi-skilled and temporary workforce), which is much lauded in managerial discourse as the key to the maxi-misation of national wealth, reinforces the material inhibitions on women's full entry into civil society and their participation in the production of national culture.

Notes

I INTRODUCTION: ROMANTIC BELONGINGS

1 *The Poems of Charlotte Smith*, ed. by Stuart Curran (Oxford University Press, 1993). Selections of Smith's poetry are also included in the various anthologies of Romantic women's poetry which have been published in recent years, including those published by Jennifer Breen, Andrew Ashfield, Jerome McGann and Duncan Wu, and which reflect the impact of feminist scholarship and criticism on the field of literary study.

2 The availability of the material I refer to in this book is mixed. The novels of Ann Radcliffe and Charlotte Smith's *The Old Manor House* have been available in World's Classics editions for some time, Smith's *Desmond* has recently been edited by Janet Todd and Antje Blank, and published by Pickering. Todd and Marilyn Butler are editors of the seven-volume Pickering edition of the *Works of Mary Wollstonecraft*, which was published in 1989. Apart from facsimile of Helen Maria Williams *Letters from France* and a Woodstock edition of the first volume, the *Letters* remain out of print, as do Smith's *The Banished Man, The Young Philosopher* and Radcliffe's travel writing (available on ESTC microfilm) and almost the entire works of Hannah More (the most recent collection of her work is the 1818 edition).

3 For a broader historical approach to the links between 'English Romanticism' and the operation of Empire, see Alan Richardson and Sonia Hofkosh (eds.), *Romanticism, Race, and Imperial Culture, 1780–1834* (Bloomington and Indianapolis: Indiana University Press, 1996).

4 Carole Pateman, *The Sexual Contract* (Cambridge: Polity Press, 1988); Susan Staves, *Married Women's Property in England, 1660–1833* (Cambridge, Mass.: Harvard University Press, 1990).

5 I am drawing here on Nancy Fraser's model of insitutional misrecognition, in which she refers to capitalism's material (i.e. economic *and* cultural) restrictions on female subjectivity. Her recent response to and critique of Judith Butler's ahistorical understanding of 'materialism' in 'Heterosexism, Misrecognition and Capitalism: A Response to Judith Butler', *New Left Review* 228 (1998), 141–9, trenchantly underlines the significance of this model for contemporary feminists trying to approach questions of female identity and citizenship.

6 See J. Armstrong, *Nations Before Nationalism* (Chapel Hill: University of North Carolina Press, 1982); J. Breuilly, *Nationalism and the State* (Manchester University Press, 1982); J. Fishman (ed.), *Language Problems of Devoloping Nations*, (New York: Wiley, 1968); Ernest Gellner, *Nations and Nationalism* (Oxford: Blackwell, 1983); Eric Hobsbawm, *Nations and Nationalism Since 1780: Programme, Myth, Reality* (Cambridge University Press, 1991); Tom Nairn, *The Break-up of Britain* (London: Verso, 1981); Elie Kedourie, *Nationalism* (Oxford: Blackwell Press, 1960; 1993); Anthony Smith, *The Ethnic Origin of Nations* (Oxford: Blackwell Press, 1986) and *Nations and Nationalism in a Global Era* (Cambridge: Polity Press, 1995). As Nira Yuval-Davis has suggested in *Gender and Nation* (London: Sage, 1997) the gender-blindness of these studies is all the more remarkable because 'a major school of national-ism scholars, the "primordialists" ... have seen in nations a natural and universal phenomenon which is an "automatic" extension of kinship rela-tions' (p. 1). Amongst the primordialist approaches to nation is Clifford Geertz's *Old Societies and New States* (New York: Free Press, 1963).

7 This conceptualisation of the civil domain of economic exchange as the mediator between nation and state also draws upon the influential work of the political scientist J. G. A. Pocock. See in particular *Politics, Language and Time: Essays on Political Thought and History* (London: Methuen, 1971) and *Virtue, Commerce and History* (Cambridge University Press, 1985).

8 See Rita Felski, *Beyond Feminist Aesthetics: Feminist Literature and Social Change* (London: Hutchinson Radius, 1989); Nancy Fraser, 'What's Critical about Critical Theory: The case of Habermas and Gender', in *Feminist Interpreta-tions and Political Theory*, ed. by Mary Lyndon Shanley and Carole Pateman (Cambridge: Polity Press, 1991); Nancy Fraser, *Unruly Practices: Power, Dis-course and Gender in Contemporary Social Theory* (Cambridge: Polity Press, 1989); Nancy Fraser and Paul James (eds.), *Critical Politics: From the Personal to the Global* (Melbourne: Arena, 1994); Joan Landes, 'The Public and the Private Sphere: A Feminist Reconsideration', in *Feminists Read Habermas: Gendering the Subject of Discourse*, ed. by Johanna Meehan (London: Routledge, 1995).

9 'The sexual contract ... is not associated only with the private sphere. Patriarchy is not merely familial or located in the private sphere. The original contract creates the modern social whole of patriarchal civil society. Men pass back and forth between the private and public spheres and the writ of the law of male sex-right runs in both realms. Civil society is bifurcated but the unity of the social order is maintained, in large part, through the structure of patriarchal relations' (Pateman, *Sexual*, p. 12).

10 Marlon Ross, 'Romancing the Nation-State: The Poetics of Romantic Nationalism', in *Macropolitics of Nineteenth-Century Literature: Nationalism, Exoti-cism, Imperialism*, ed. by Jonathan Arac and Harriet Ritvo (Philadelphia: University of Pennsylvania Press, 1991), pp. 56–85, esp. p. 56. For an analy-sis of the traditions that emerged in this period attached to national identity see Eric Hobsbawm and Terrence Ranger, *The Invention of Tradition* (Cam-bridge University Press, 1983). Katie Trumpener's *Bardic Nationalism: The*

Romantic Novel and the British Empire (Princeton University Press, 1997) provides a comprehensive survey of the appropriation of antiquarian and nationalist literary developments in Scotland, Wales and Ireland by 'English literature' in the late eighteenth and early nineteenth centuries.

11 Edmund Burke, *Reflections on the Revolution in France in a Letter Intended to Have Been Sent to a Young Gentleman in Paris*, ed. by Conor Cruise O'Brien (1790; Harmondsworth: Penguin, 1989).

12 See Nicholas Phillipson, 'The Scottish Enlightenment', in *The Enlightenment in National Context*, ed. by Roy Porter and Mikulas Teich (Cambridge University Press, 1981), pp. 19–40, for an exploration of the Scottish philosophers' contribution to the construction of the 'privatized citizen'.

13 See in particular David Hume, *A Treatise of Human Nature*, ed. by L. A. Selby-Bigge (1739–40; Oxford: Clarendon Press, 1965) and Adam Smith, *The Theory of Moral Sentiments*, ed. by D. D. Raphael and A. L. Macfie (1759; Oxford: Clarendon Press, 1976).

14 Kathleen Wilson, 'Citizenship, Empire, and Modernity in the English Provinces, c. 1720–1790', *Eighteenth-Century Studies*, Special Issue, 'The Public and the Nation' 29:1 (Fall, 1995), 69–96, esp. p. 76.

15 See Hugh Cunningham, 'The Language of Patriotism', in *Patriotism: the Making and Unmaking of British National Identity*, ed. by Raphael Samuel, 3 vols. (London: Routledge, 1989), vol. 1, pp. 57–89.

16 See Linda Colley, *Britons: Forging the Nation 1707–1837* (New Haven: Yale University Press, 1992). E. P. Thompson, *The Making of the English Working Class* (1963; Harmondsworth: Penguin, 1968), pp. 84–110, and Wilson, 'Citizenship, Empire, and Modernity', pp. 71–8, for analyses of the impact of Wilkes on the English national idea. Wilson, in particular, focuses on the gendered aspect of his influence: 'The aftermath of war and massive imperial expansion saw these identities renewed and reworked by other means. The political and debating clubs of the Wilkite period, for example, not only articulated an overtly radicalized vision of the polity, but also an ideal of citizenship that recovered androcentric patriotism for new purposes. Wilkite journalism, street theater, prints and plays retailed to a wide audience the ideology of independence and deals of resistance and "manly patriotism" that made explicit a hostility to intrusions of the feminine as well as effeminate in the political sphere' (p. 77).

17 See Seamus Deane, *The French Revolution and Enlightenment in England, 1789–1831* (Cambridge, Mass.: Harvard University Press, 1988), for an analysis of the impact of Enlightenment philosophy on English Dissent.

18 *The Works of Mary Wollstonecraft, (WMW)*, ed. by Janet Todd and Marilyn Butler, 7 vols. (London: Pickering and Chatto, 1989), vol. 5.

19 *Ibid.*, vol. 6. References will be to this edition, abbreviated to *Scandinavian Letters*.

20 Helen Maria Williams, *Letters from France, (LFF)*, ed. by Janet Todd, 8 vols. (Delmar, New York: Scholars Facsimiles and Reprints, 1975).

21 I am concerned principally with four of Smith's novels of the 1790s:

Desmond, ed. by Antje Blank and Janet Todd (1792; London: Pickering and Chatto, 1997); *The Old Manor House*, ed. by Anne Henry Ehrenpreis, The World's Classics (1793; Oxford University Press, 1989); *The Banished Man*, 4 vols. (London: Cadell, 1794); *The Young Philosopher*, 4 vols. (London: Cadell, 1798).

22 My discussion of Radcliffe focuses on three of her best-known romances: *The Romance of the Forest*, ed. by Chloe Chard, The World's Classics (1791; Oxford University Press, 1986); *The Mysteries of Udolpho*, ed. by Bonamy Dobrée, The World's Classics (1794; Oxford University Press, 1966; repr. 1980); *The Italian, or the Confessional of the Black Penitents*, ed. by Frederick Garber (1797; Oxford University Press, 1968) and her travel memoir, *A Journey Made in the Summer of 1794, Through Holland and the Western Frontier of Germany: to which are added Observations During a Tour of the Lakes of Lancashire, Westmoreland, and Cumberland* (London, 1795).

23 *The Works of Hannah More*, (*WHM*), 18 vols. (1793; London: Cadell, 1818), vol. 1, p. 364.

24 More, *Strictures on the Modern System of Education with a View of the Principles and Conduct Prevalent Among Women of Rank and Fortune*, *WHM*, vol. 7, pp. 4–5. Subsequent references will be to this edition, abbreviated to *Strictures* 1 and 2.

25 Nancy Armstrong and Lennard Tennenhouse, *Imaginary Puritan: Literature, Intellectual Labor, and the Origins of Personal Life* (Berkeley: University of California Press, 1992).

26 See Benedict Anderson, *Imagined Communities: Reflections on the Origin and Spread of Nationalism* (London: Verso, 1991); Lennard J. Davis, *Factual Fictions: The Origins of the English Novel* (New York: Columbia University Press, 1983); Simon During, 'Literature: Nationalism's Other? The Case for Revision', in *Nation and Narration*, ed. by Homi K. Bhabha (London: Routledge, 1990), pp. 138–53.

27 See Nancy Armstrong, *Desire and Domestic Fiction: A Political History of the Novel* (Oxford University Press, 1987); Catherine Gallagher, *Nobody's Story: The Vanishing Acts of Women Writers in the Marketplace, 1670–1820* (Oxford: Clarendon Press, 1994); John Mullan, *Sentiment and Sociability: The Language of Feeling in the Eighteenth Century* (Oxford: Clarendon Press, 1988).

28 Greg Laugero, 'Infrastructures of Enlightenment: Road-Making, the Public Sphere, and the Emergence of Literature', *Eighteenth-Century Studies*, Special Issue, 'The Public and the Nation' 29:1 (Fall 1995), 45–68.

29 More, *Stories for the Middle Ranks*, *WHM*, vol. 4, pp. iii–iv.

30 David Simpson, *Romanticism, Nationalism and the Revolt Against Theory*, (Chicago University Press, 1993), p. 135.

31 Samuel Taylor Coleridge, *Biographia Literaria*, ed. by George Watson (London: J. M. Dent, 1975; repr.1984), p. 174.

32 Burke, *Reflections*, p. 131.

33 Simpson, *Romanticism*, p. 138.

34 Ross, 'Romancing', p. 58.
35 *WHM*, vol.1, p. 214.

2 DOMESTICATING THE SUBLIME: ANN RADCLIFFE AND GOTHIC DISSENT

1 Robert Miles, *Ann Radcliffe: The Great Enchantress* (Manchester University Press, 1995), makes a particularly enthusiastic case for a new understanding of Radcliffe's literary and cultural significance.
2 See, for instance, Kate Ferguson Ellis, *The Contested Castle: Gothic Novels and the Subversion of Domestic Ideology* (Urbana and Chicago: University of Illinois Press, 1989); Claire Kahane, 'The Gothic Mirror', in *The (M)other Tongue: Essays in Feminist Psychoanalytic Interpretation*, ed. by Shirley Nelson Garner, *et al.* (Ithaca and New York: Cornell University Press, 1985), pp. 334–52; Carol Ann Howells, 'The Pleasure of the Woman's Text: Ann Radcliffe's Subtle Transgressions', in *Gothic Fictions: Prohibition/Transgression*, ed. by Kenneth W. Graham (New York: AMS Press, 1989); Cynthia Griffin Wolff, 'The Radcliffean Gothic Novel: A Form for Feminine Sexuality', *Modern Language Studies* 9 (1979), 98–113.
3 In *The Great Enchantress*, Miles suggests that the author's dissenting roots – her connections with the liberal intellectual circle of Thomas Bentley and Josiah Wedgewood – and the signs of her strong liberal political beliefs have been overlooked in readings that have emphasised her conservatism.
4 Ann Radcliffe, *The Mysteries of Udolpho*, ed. by Bonamy Dobrée, The World's Classics (1794; Oxford University Press, 1966), p. 421.
5 Associationism – a model of the mind responding mechanically and predictably to the stimulus of external impressions – had its roots in Lockean empiricism and had close analogues in the culture of sensibility, which also informs Radcliffe's portraits of human potential for education.
6 *The Romance of the Forest*, ed. by Chloe Chard, The World's Classics (1791; Oxford University Press, 1986), p. 222.
7 *The Romance of the Forest*, p. 261.
8 William Wordsworth, Preface to *Lyrical Ballads, Selected Prose*, ed. by John O. Hayden (1798; Harmondsworth: Penguin, 1988), p. 283.
9 See Ioan Williams (ed.), *Novel and Romance 1700–1800: A Documentary Record* (London: Routledge, 1970) for an anthologised version of the debate. Recent books which, from a variety of perspectives, include analyses of the 'novel/romance' distinction and its wide-ranging implications include: Nancy Armstrong, *Desire and Domestic Fiction: A Political History of the Novel* (Oxford University Press, 1987); Ros Ballaster, *Seductive Forms: Women's Amatory Fiction from 1684 to 1740* (Oxford: Clarendon Press, 1992); Catherine Gallagher, *Nobody's Story: The Vanishing Acts of Women Writers in the Marketplace, 1670–1820* (Oxford: Clarendon Press, 1994); Laurie Langbauer, *Women and Romance: The Consolations of Gender in the English Novel* (Ithaca: Cornell Univer-

sity Press, 1990): Michael McKeon, *The Origins of the English Novel 1600–1740* (Baltimore: Johns Hopkins University Press, 1987); Robert Miles, *Gothic Writing: A Genealogy* (London: Routledge, 1993).

10 The most celebrated genealogy is Thomas Warton, *The History of English Poetry, from the Close of the Eleventh to the Commencement of the Eighteenth Century* (London, 1779–81). Interest in Shakespeare, Spenser and Milton was expressed in the context of the romance revival, led by James Beattie, 'On Fable and Romance', *Dissertations Moral and Critical* (London, 1783); Richard Hurd, *Letters on Chivalry and Romance: Serving to Illustrate Some Passages in the Third Dialogue* (London, 1762); Elizabeth Montagu, *An Essay on the Writings and Genius of Shakespear . . . To Which are Now First Added, Three Dialogues of the Dead* (London, 1777); Clara Reeve, *The Progress of Romance Through Times, Countries and Manners* (Colchester, 1785). Interest in popular folklore was increasingly expressed in 'literary culture' towards the end of the eighteenth century. This was symptomatic of both post-Enlightenment reaction to the global perspectives of cosmopolitan culture, and a compulsion to assert local, regional and national difference in the face of imperial expansion.

11 Richard Helgerson, *Forms of Nationhood: The Elizabethan Writing of England* (Chicago and London: University of Chicago Press, 1992), p. 41.

12 For readings of the political, cultural and literary significance of the late eighteenth-century interest in romance see particularly: Ian Duncan, *Modern Romance and Transformations of the Novel: The Gothic, Scott, Dickens* (Cambridge University Press, 1992); Harriet Guest, 'The Wanton Muse: Politics and Gender in Gothic Theory after 1760,' in *Beyond Romanticism: New Approaches to Texts and Contexts 1780–1832*, ed. by Stephen Copley and John Whale (London: Routledge, 1992), pp. 118–39; Robert Miles, 'The Gothic Aesthetic: The Gothic as Discourse', *The Eighteenth Century* 32 (1991), 39–57; Gerald Newman, *The Rise of English Nationalism, a Cultural History 1740–1830* (London: Weidenfeld and Nicolson, 1987), esp. pp. 87–120.

13 George Canning, *The Microcosm* 26 (Monday, May 14, 1787).

14 *A Journey Made in the Summer of 1794, Through Holland, and the Western Frontier of Germany, With a Return Down the Rhine: To Which Are Added Observations During a Tour of the Lakes of Lancashire, Westmoreland, and Cumberland* (London, 1795), p. 12.

15 *Ibid.*, p. 92.

16 *Ibid.*, p. 33.

17 *Ibid.*, p. 443.

18 Samuel Taylor Coleridge, *Biographia Literaria*, ed. by George Watson (London: Dent, 1975), p. 190.

19 The description of the La Luc house in *The Romance of the Forest*, with its combination of simple decor, utility, communal centrality and signs of Enlightened and improving recreation is typical: 'The chateau was not large, but it was convenient, and was characterised by an air of elegant simplicity and good order. The entrance was a small hall, which opening by

a glass door into the garden, afforded a view of the lake, with the magnificent scenery exhibited on its borders. On the left of the hall was La Luc's study, where he usually passed his mornings; and adjoining was a small room fitted up with chymical apparatus, astronomical instruments, and other implements of science. On the right was the family parlour, and behind it a room which belonged exclusively to Madame La Luc. Here were deposited various medicines and botanical distillations, together with the apparatus for preparing them. From this room the whole village was liberally supplied with comfort; for it was the pride of Madame to believe herself skilful in relieving the disorders of her neighbours' (p. 248).

In *The Italian*, the house which Ellena shares with her aunt, Signora Bianchi, conceals from Vivaldi the labours of its inhabitants: labours which, significantly, furnish the residence of his wealthy family: 'From the style of their residence, he imagined that they were persons of honourable, but moderate independence. The house was small, but exhibited an air of comfort, and even of taste. It stood on an eminence, surrounded by a garden and vineyards, which commanded the city and bay of Naples, an ever-moving picture, and was canopied by a thick grove of pines and majestic date-trees; and, though the little portico and colonnade in front were of common marble, the style of architecture was elegant.' *The Italian, or The Confessional of the Black Penitents*, ed. by Frederick Garber, The World's Classics (1797; Oxford University Press, 1968), p. 6.

'He was ignorant of what was very true, though very secret, that she [Ellena] assisted to support this aged relative, whose sole property was the small estate on which they lived, and that she passed whole days in embroidering silks, which were disposed of to the nuns of a neighbouring convent, who sold them to the Neooplitan ladies, that visited their grate, at a very high advantage. He little thought, that a beautiful robe, which he had often seen his mother wear, was worked by Ellena; nor that some copies from the antique, which ornamented a cabinet of the Vivaldi palace, were drawn by her hand' (p. 9).

20 *The Romance of the Forest*, p. 163.

21 E. P. Thomson, *The Making of the English Working Class* (1963; Harmondsworth: Penguin, 1979), p. 77.

22 *The Romance of the Forest*, p. 36.

23 Terry Castle, 'The Spectralization of the Other in *The Mysteries of Udolpho*', in *The New Eighteenth Century: Theory, Politics, English Literature*, ed. by Felicity Nussbaum and Laura Brown (New York: Methuen, 1987), pp. 231–53.

24 Sigmund Freud, 'The Uncanny' (1919), in *The Standard Edition of the Complete Psychological Works*, ed. and trans. by James Strachey (London: Hogarth Press, 1955), vol. 17, pp. 218–52; Tzvetan Todorov, *The Fantastic: a Structural Approach to a Literary Genre*, trans. by Richard Howard (Ithaca: Cornell Unversity Press, 1975).

25 Castle follows the work of Phillipe Ariés (*The Hour of Our Death*, trans. by Helen Weaver (New York: Alfred A. Knopf, 1981)) to argue that these

fantasies of the breakdown between the real and the ideal, mind and matter, speak of a historical moment when attitudes shift towards that most compelling boundary between life and death. Death, like all other aspects of modern experience, was coming to be understood in increasingly private, subjective terms, less fathomable by those left behind. The idealisation of the dead which such a shift produces is accompanied by the mourner's acute sense of isolation – a pathological tendency to repress the image of the lost object, only for it to resurface in the form of a phantom. This repression spills over into other aspects of experience, expressed in that 'romantic individualism' where things exist only as a screen image on the subject's consciousness, where the corporeality of the other is rendered 'insubstantial and indistinct' and what matters is 'the mental picture, the ghost, the haunting image' (p. 237). The modern subject is constitutionally melancholic.

26　*The Mysteries of Udolpho*, p. 662.

27　'The confession was, and still remains, the general standard governing the production of the true discourse on sex. It has undergone a considerable transformation, however. For a long time, it remained firmly entrenched in the practice of penance. But with the rise of Protestantism, the Counter-Reformation, eighteenth-century pedagogy, and nineteenth-century medicine, it gradually lost its ritualistic and exclusive location; it spread; it has been employed in a whole series of relationships: children and parents, students and educators, patients and psychiatrists, delinquents and experts . . . the confession lends itself, if not to other domains, at least to new ways of exploring the existing ones. It is no longer a question of simply saying what was done – the sexual act – and how it was done; but of reconstructing, in and around the act, the thoughts that recapitulated it, the obsessions that accompanied it, the images, desires, modulations, and quality of the pleasure that animated it. For the first time no doubt, a society has taken upon itself to solicit and hear the imparting of individual pleasures.' Michel Foucault, *The History of Sexuality: Volume One, an Introduction*, trans. by Robert Hurley (London: Allen Lane, 1978), p. 63.

28　James Clarke, *Survey of the Lakes* (1787); William Gilpin, *Observations of the Western Parts of England* (1786); William Hutchinson, *Excursion to the Lakes in Westmoreland and Cumberland* (1774); Thomas West, *Guide to the Lakes* (1778); William Wordsworth, *Topographical Description of the Country of the Lakes in the North of England* (1820), later revised as *A Guide Through the District of the Lakes* (1835).

29　Hurd, *Letters on Chivalry and Romance*.

30　Alan Liu, *Wordsworth, the Sense of History* (Stanford University Press, 1989).

31　*Ibid.*, p. 87.

32　In this context, his argument turns partly on the emergence of new tourist 'zones' of picturesque property, such as parts of the Lake District, which were neither occupied by freeholders, tenants or leaseholders, nor owned by the Tory landed gentry. Tourists of the intelligentsia and, later, middle-class tourists from the urban centres imaginatively appropriated land that was relatively free from enclosure. Although the picturesque journey was recreational, and the arts which commemorated such journey privileged repose and avoided images of labour and cultivation, tourists and artists alike, Liu argues, were 'in love with productivity' (p. 93). That is, they invested in the unowned property of the Lakes with 'imaginary' capital from industrial centres. These tourist zones, which were to be designated as everybody's property with the establishment of national parks, were thus, despite their freedom from ownership, a symbol of new property relations, and of the consolidation of the cultural dominance of the new monied élites of the Whig state. These signs of liberty and national community, then, belie the 'disciplining' procedures of the picturesque, which, Liu suggests, were analogous to the new Whig bureaucratic administrative practices of rural districts which were replacing the rule of the Tory squire.

33 Humphrey Repton's attack on Price's *Essays on the Picturesque* and Knight's *The Landscape* accuses them of promoting 'untried theoretical improvement' to gardens, derived from the principles of painting 'Letter to Mr Price', in Uvedale Price, *Essays on the Picturesque*, vol. 3 (London, 1810). For Repton, this is the aesthetic equivalent of the theoretical principles of government which were being put into practice by the French revolutionary régime and, implicitly, is antithetical to the British constitutional spirit. Price's counter-attack justifies his principles – political and aesthetic – by invoking his belief in that mainstay of constitutional liberty and picturesque theory: variety within unity.

34 Anne Janowitz, *England's Ruins: Poetic Purpose and the National Landscape* (Oxford: Blackwell, 1990), p. 3.

35 *The Romance of the Forest*, p. 16.

36 *The Mysteries of Udolpho*, p. 296.

37 *Ibid.*, p. 294.

38 *Ibid.*, p. 164.

39 *Ibid.*, p. 456.

40 *The Italian*, p. 222.

41 *Ibid.*, p. 223.

42 Uvedale Price, *An Essay on the Picturesque as Compared with the Sublime and the Beautiful; And, on the Use of Studying Pictures, for the Purpose of Improving Real Landscape* (London, 1796–8), pp. 105–6.

43 William Gilpin, *Three Essays: on Picturesque Beauty; on Picturesque Travel; and on Sketching Landscape*, 2nd edn. (London, 1794), pp. 47–8.

44 *The Mysteries of Udolpho*, p. 160.

45 *The Italian*, p. 414.

3 FORGOTTEN SENTIMENTS: HELEN MARIA WILLIAMS'S *LETTERS FROM FRANCE*

1 I am grateful to Simon Bainbridge for bringing my attention to this sonnet:

> She wept.– Life's purple tide began to flow
> In languid streams through every thrilling vein;
> Dim were my swimming eyes – my pulse beat slow,
> And my full heart was swelled to dear delicious pain.
> Life left my loaded heart, and closing eye;
> A sigh recalled the wanderer to my breast;
> Dear was the pause of life, and dear the sigh
> That called the wanderer home, and home to rest.
> That tear proclaims – in thee each virtue dwells,
> And bright will shine in misery's midnight hour;
> As the soft star of dewy evening tells
> What radiant fires were drowned by day's malignant power,
> That only wait the darkness of the night
> To cheer the wandering wretch with hospitable light.

William Wordsworth, 'Sonnet on Seeing Miss Helen Maria Williams Weep at a Tale of Distress', in *The Poetical Works of William Wordsworth*, ed. by Ernest De Selincourt (Oxford: Clarendon Press, 1940), p. 269.

George McLean Harper provides a speculative history of the poem's composition and publication in his biography, *William Wordsworth: His Life, Works, and Influence*, 2 vols. (London: Murray, 1916). Harper notes that: 'In April, 1787, Wordsworth was only sixteen. Miss Williams was eight years older, and already known as an author. As a composition, the sonnet is packed full of almost all the faults supposed to be characteristic of pre-Wordsworthian verse. "Axiologus" is a Greek compound that may be translated "Wordsworth", and was used by Coleridge as an appellation for him. Where the boy Wordsworth could have seen Miss Williams weep, in 1787, is a mystery to me' (vol. 1, pp. 148–9).

The young Wordsworth would not have been exceptional in having his juvenilia published in *The European Magazine*, for, as Harper continues, 'its poetry department contained a large quantity of verse by children' and 'effusions upon living authors were a favourite feature' (p. 149).

2 Letter to Walter Savage Landor, 20 April 1822, *The Letters of William and Dorothy Wordsworth*, ed. by Alan G. Hill, 2nd edn, vol. 3, Part 1, 1821–8 (Oxford: Clarendon Press, 1978), pp. 125–6.

3 For approaches to the gendering of poetry in the Romantic period see Philip Cox, *Gender, Genre and the Romantic Poets* (Manchester University Press, 1996) and Marlon B. Ross, *The Contours of Masculine Desire: Romanticism and the Rise of Women's Poetry* (Oxford University Press, 1989).

4 Helen Maria Williams, *Letters from France*, ed. by Janet Todd, 8 vols (Delmar, New York: Scholars Facsimiles and Reprints, 1975). I have added volume numbers 5–8 to correspond with Todd's Part Two, volumes 1–4. The following simplifies the complex bibliographical details of the *Letters*:

1: *Letters from France, in the Summer of 1790, to a Friend in England Containing Anecdotes Relative to the French Revolution and Memoirs of M. and Mme. du F-*, 5th edn (London, 1796), vol. 1.

2: *Letters from France: Containing Many New Anecdotes Relative to the French Revolution, and the Present State of French Manners*, 2nd edn (London, 1792), vol. 2.

3 and 4: *Letters from France: Containing a Great Variety of Interesting and Original Information Concerning the Most Important Events that have Lately Occurred in that Country, and Particularly Respecting the Campaign of 1792*, 2nd edn (London, 1796), vols. 3 and 4.

5 and 6: *Letters Containing a Sketch of the Politics of France from the Thirty-first of May 1793, Till the Twenty-eight of July 1794, and of the Scenes which have Passed in the Prisons of Paris* (London, 1795), vols. 1 and 2.

7: *Letters Containing a Sketch of the Scenes which Passed in Various Departments of France During the Tyranny of Robespierre, and of the Events which Took Place in Paris on the 28th July 1794* (London, 1795), vol. 3.

8: *Letters Containing a Sketch of the Politics of France, from the Twenty-eighth of July 1794, to the Establishment of the Constitution in 1795, and of the Scenes which have Passed in the Prisons of Paris* (London, 1796), vol. 4.

One of the fullest recent accounts of the *Letters from France* is Mary Favret's in *Romantic Correspondence: Women, Politics and the Fiction of Letters* (Cambridge University Press, 1993), pp. 53–95.

5 In letters to Alexander Dyce in the 1830s, Wordsworth recommends Williams's sonnets for inclusion in Dyce's production of two anthologies of British poetry, *Specimens of English Sonnets* and *Specimens of British Poetesses*. See *Letters of William and Dorothy Wordsworth*, ed. by Alan G. Hill, 2nd edn, vol. 5, Part 2, pp. 259–60; pp. 603–5.

6 *Ibid.*, p. 260.

7 In a letter to his brother Richard from Orléans, dated December 1791, Wordsworth writes: 'Mrs Smith who was so good as to give me Letters for Paris furnished me with one for Miss Williams, an English Lady who resided here lately, but was gone before I arrived. This circumstance was a considerable disappointment to me, however I have in some respects remedied it by introducing myself to a Mr Foxlow an Englishman who has set up a Cotton manufactory here' (*Letters of William and Dorothy Wordsworth*, ed. by Chester L. Shaver, 2nd edn, vol. 1, 1787–1805 (Oxford: Clarendon Press, 1967)).

8 Cited in Harper, *William Wordsworth*, p. 149.

9 Andrew Ashfield (ed.), *Romantic Women Poets, 1770–1838: An Anthology* (Manchester University Press), p. 67.

10 *The Monthly Review* 2, (September 1790), p. 429; 9 (September 1792), p. 94.

11 *The Anti-Jacobin Review* 3 (May 1799), p. 30.

12 Laetitia Matilda Hawkins, *Letters on the Female Mind, its Powers and Pursuits; Addressed to Miss H. M. Williams, with Particular Reference to her Letters from France*, 2 vols. (London, 1793).

13 A review of Mary Hays's *Emma Courtney* in *The Anti-Jacobin Review and Magazine*, for instance, quotes an extract from the novel in which the heroine refers to her 'republican ardour' and 'high-toned philosophy'. The reviewer comments archly: 'Does this not out-Helen even the wife or mistress of Stone? Not less alive does she appear to have been to the softer affections...' (3 (May 1799), p. 56). Stone, an English entrepreneur who was committed to establishing commercial outlets in France, was a member of the English Revolution Society and a leader of the British and American revolutionary sympathisers who met at White's Hotel in Paris in the early 1790s. In *Women, Writing, and Revolution, 1790–1827* (Oxford: Clarendon Press, 1993), Gary Kelly reads Stone's extra-marital relationship with Williams as typical of 'avant-garde Revolutionary culture, a rejection of both the court "mistress system" and petty bourgeois respectability' (p. 47).

14 M. Ray Adams, in an essay that sets out to make up for the lack of notice given to Williams in the early twentieth century – 'Helen Maria Williams and the French Revolution', *Wordsworth and Coleridge, Studies in Honour of George McLean Harper*, ed. by Earl Leslie Griggs (Princeton University Press, 1939) – sees her as a 'political sentimentalist' who 'probably wore her heart on her sleeve too much' (p. 90). W. N. Hargreaves-Mawdsley, placing Williams in the context of the *English Della Cruscans and Their Time, 1783–1828* (The Hague: Martinus Nijhoff, 1967), is perhaps afflicted with a touch of the Robert Merrys, when he refers to Williams as 'the vivacious republican, the auburn-haired Scot', who charmed the Tuscan patriot poet Pindemonte. It was Williams of all the Della Cruscan circle, he says, who 'would wholeheartedly share the Italian's views, and for whom he seems for a time to have entertained a little more than mere admiration' (p. 205). Ralph M. Wardle, the editor of the *Collected Letters of Mary Wollstonecraft* (Ithaca and London: Cornell University Press, 1979) speculates that Williams is the unnamed, 'unworthy' mistress of Gilbert Imlay, to whom Wollstonecraft refers in two letters to her lover (pp. 261, 281). Wardle perhaps takes his cue from Wollstonecraft's own rather mealy mouthed praise of Williams in a letter to Everina Wollstonecraft, after Mary's arrival in Paris in December 1792: 'Miss Williams has behaved very civilly to me and I shall visit her frequently, because I *rather* like her, and I meet french company at her house. Her manners are affected, yet the *simple* goodness of her heart continually breaks through the varnish, so that one would be more inclined, at least I should, to love than admire her. – Authorship is a heavy weight for female shoulders especially in the sunshine of prosperity' (p. 225).

15 The circle was international and culturally and politically diverse and included various Italian writers, Benjamin Franklin, the Burneys, the blue stocking Elizabeth Montagu, Anna Seward, the circles of William Godwin and Robert Merry, Scottish 'sentimentalist' Henry Mackenzie, actress Sarah Siddons and Edmund Burke. As Gary Kelly suggests, '[a]fter the

outbreak of the Revolution debate in Britain it would be difficult for one person to circulate in such varied companies' (*Women, Writing, and Revolution*, p. 31).

16 Williams's main poetic output of the 1780s and 1790s includes: *Edwin and Eltruda: a Legendary Tale* (London: Cadell, 1782); *An Ode on the Peace* (London: Cadell, 1784); *Peru: a Poem; in Six Cantos* (London: Cadell, 1784); *Poems*, 2 vols. (London: Cadell, 1786); *A Poem on the Bill Lately Passed for Regulating the Slave Trade* (London: Cadell, 1788); *A Farewell, for Two Years, to England: a Poem* (London: Cadell, 1791). Her two-volume collection was revised in 1823, published as *Poems on Various Subjects; with Introductory Remarks on the Present State of Science and Literature in France* (London: Whittaker, 1823). Her novel, *Julia* (London: Cadell, 1790) and numerous collections of letters and sketches of the French republic, and of Switzerland, which she continued to produce until 1819, included 'poetical pieces' which were also reproduced independently in magazines.

17 Letter from Hester Thrale to Miss Weston, October, 1791, *Letters of William and Dorothy Wordsworth*, ed. by Shaver, vol. 1, p. 68.

18 Apart from a brief return to England in 1790, and a compulsory excursion to Switzerland in 1794 (which she later recorded as *A Tour in Switzerland*, 2 vols. (London: Robinson, 1798)) Williams settled in Paris, where she lived with Stone until his death in 1818. After a brief and depressing spell in Amsterdam, she returned to Paris, and was financially supported by her nephew until her death in 1827.

19 For an analysis of the role of women in the French republic of letters see Dena Goodman, *The Republic of Letters: a Cultural History of the French Enlightenment* (Ithaca and London: Cornell University Press, 1994) and Joan Landes, *Women and the Public Sphere in the Age of Revolution* (Ithaca and London: Cornell University Press, 1988). Both engage with and critique Jürgen Habermas, *The Structural Transformation of the Public Sphere: an Inquiry into a Category of Bourgeois Society*, trans. by Thomas Burger with Frederick Lawrence (Cambridge: Polity Press, 1989). See also Chapter 1, note 8.

20 See Kathleen Wilson, 'Citizenship, Empire, and Modernity in the English Provinces, c. 1720–1790', *Eighteenth-Century Studies*, 'The Public and the Nation' 29: 1 (Fall 1995) , 69–96, esp. pp. 76–7.

21 David Hume, *Essays Moral, Political, and Literary*, ed. by Eugene F. Miller (Indianapolis, 1985), pp. 535–6.

22 See Habermas, *The Structural Transformation*, pp. 51–6. Habermas repeats the exclusion of women in his own account of the ideal public sphere as the community of liberal and literate men whose interests transcend the commercial and affective domains of the 'doubled private sphere'.

23 *LFF*, vol. 1, p. 197.

24 See Harriet Guest, 'Modern Love: Feminism and Sensibility in 1796', *New Formations: a Journal of Culture / Theory / Politics*, 'Conservative Modernity' 28 (Spring 1996), 3–20.

25 *LFF*, vol. 2, p. 20.

26 *Ibid.*, vol. 2, p. 65.
27 *Ibid.*, vol. 2, pp. 80–1.
28 *Ibid.*, vol. 2, p. 4.
29 *Ibid.*, vol. 2, p. 145.
30 *Ibid.*, vol. 4, p. 217.
31 *Ibid.*, vol. 4, pp. 269–70.
32 *Ibid.*, vol. 5, p. 117.
33 *Ibid.*, vol. 5, p. 12.
34 *Ibid.*, vol. 5, p. 25.
35 *Ibid.*, vol. 5, p. 258.
36 *Ibid.*, vol. 6, p. 86.
37 *Ibid.*, vol. 6, pp. 89–90.
38 *Ibid.*, vol. 5, pp. 174–5.
39 *Ibid.*, vol. 7, pp. 9–10.
40 *Ibid.*, vol. 1, pp. 192–3.
41 *Ibid.*, vol. 2, p. 157.
42 Robert D. Mayo, *The English Novel in the Magazines, 1740–1815* (Evanston: Illinois, 1962).
43 The following is a selection of the texts which Williams included in her letters or added in her appendices:

Vol. 5: Appendix
I. Protest from members of the national convention against an address from the committee of public safety (p. 83).
II. Manifesto – refuting accusations of conspiracy against the Gironde (p. 126).
III. Transcription of Madame Roland's defence, taken from her manuscript.

Vol. 6
Poem from a young man to his mistress the night before his execution (pp. 40–1).
The trial of Princess Elizabeth; the court accusations, her replies (pp. 52–63).
Letter from Brissot to Barrerre, deputy of the convention, from his prison (pp. 84–6).
Verse and prose letter from M. Maron (p. 118).
Appendix
I. Publication by Desmoulins, once a friend of Robespierre, expressing his indignation at the severity of the revolutionary laws against suspected conspirators (p. 25).
II. Letter from M Custine, son of a French general – to his wife on day of his execution (p. 49).
III. Madame Roland's secret history of the overthrow of monarchy and church in France (p. 172).

Vol. 7: Appendix
I. Memoir of M Custine, written from prison, on reading in the evening paper Robespierre's accusation against him.
II. Brissot's sketch of Marat (p. 59).
III. Article on the jailor Benoit, who was notable for his atrocities, received from a gentleman who translated Williams's letters into German (p. 163).

44 *LFF*, vol. 5, p. 198.

45 *Ibid.*, La Source, p. 42; Sillery, p. 45; Brissot, Gensonné, p. 163; Madame Roland, p. 195; St Étienne, p. 210; Dupré, p. 220; the Prussian, Bitauby, p. 234; Du Chatelet, p. 248; the Peruvian, Miranda, p. 243.

46 *Ibid.*, vol. 6, p. 78.

47 Helen Maria Williams, *Souvenirs de la Révolution Française*, trans. by Charles Coquerel (Paris, 1827). The main source of biographical information on Williams remains Lionel D. Woodward, *Une anglaise amie de la Révolution française: Hélène-Maria Williams et ses amis* (Paris: Librairie Ancienne Honore Champion, 1930), although Gary Kelly's account of Williams's life and works in *Women, Writing, and Revolution* extrapolates from Woodward's texts and updates the biography.

48 See Janet Gurkin Altman, 'The Letter Book as a Literary Institution 1539–1789: Toward a Cultural History of Published Correspondences in France', *Yale French Studies*, Special Issue, 'Men/Women of Letters', ed. by Charles A. Porter, 71 (1986), 17–62; Elizabeth C. Goldsmith, 'Authority, Authenticity, and the Publication of Letters by Women', in *Writing the Female Voice: Essays on Epistolary Literature*, ed. by Elizabeth C. Goldsmith, (Michigan: Northeastern University Press, 1989), pp. 46–59.

49 Goodman, *The Republic of Letters*, p. 138.

50 Dr. John Moore, *A Journal During a Residence in France from the Beginning of August to the Middle of December, 1792*, 2 vols. (1793–4); *A View of the Causes and Progress of the French Revolution*, 2 vols. (1795).

51 For instance, the letter which opens the fifth volume, written from Switzerland, dated (unusually) September 1794, and initiating a retrospective account of the scenes in Paris between 2 June and 28 July 1794, dramatically invokes an unnamed correspondent, rhetorically accounting for the passage of time between the publication of this and the last volume, and providing a rationale for the resumption of the narrative: 'After so long a suspension of our correspondence, after a silence like that of death, and a separation which for some time past seemed as final as if we had been divided by the limits of "that country from whose bourn no traveller returns," with what grateful pleasure did I recognize your hand-writing, with what eagerness did I break the seal of your welcome letter, and with what soothing emotions receive the tidings of your welfare, and the assurance of your affection! Your letter was a talisman that served to conjure up a thousand images of sorrows and of joys that are past, and which were obliterated by the turbulent sensations of dismay and of horror' (vol. 5, pp. 1–2).

52 Cited in Williams's entry in the *Dictionary of National Biography*.

53 *Ibid.*, vol. 7, p. 1; p. 10.

54 *LFF*, vol. 5, p. 257.

55 Walter Benjamin, *Illuminations* (1955; London: Fontana, 1973), pp. 263–4.

56 *LFF*, vol. 5, p. 203.

57 Cited in Mary Favret, 'Spectatrice as Spectacle', *Studies in Romanticism* 32 (Summer 1993), 273–295, esp. p. 295.

4 EXILES AND ÉMIGRÉS: THE WANDERINGS OF CHARLOTTE SMITH

1 Charlotte Smith, *Desmond*, ed. by Antje Blank and Janet Todd (1792; London: Pickering and Chatto, 1997), p. 50.
2 It also marked a turning point in her popularity as a writer, and in her critical reception. Her previous three novels: *Emmeline, or the Orphan of the Castle* (1788), *Ethelinde, or the Recluse of the Lake* (1789) and *Celestina* (1791) and her collection of *Elegiac Sonnets* (1784) had secured for Smith a healthy and 'polite' readership, and the favourable attentions of reviewers. *Desmond's* political stance, particularly Smith's portrait of French aristocrats, offended her own aristocratic acquaintances and the morality of the love-plot preoccupied some of the reviewers (see, for instance, reviews in *The European Magazine*, 20 (July, 1792), 22–5, *Analytical Review* 12 (August, 1792), 428–35 and *Critical Review* 6 (September, 1792), 100). Significantly, a similar adultery plot in *Ethelinde* escaped moral censure, so it was evidently the political persuasion of Smith's fourth novel that underlay the critical reception.
3 Lawyers were a particularly despised class of men for Smith. Having separated from her husband in 1787, to free herself from the devastating impact of his profligacy, she spent the 1790s engaged in a protracted and ultimately fruitless attempt to free up her children's legacy. She blamed the failure of her case on her husband's family's lawyers and took many opportunities to rail against their profession in her novels. This tendency provoked considerable criticism from her reviewers.
4 The male characters endlessly discover or imagine Geraldine in poses that signal her iconic status as a suffering mother. As well as Bethel's Burkean eulogy that is prompted by the sight of her with her children, Desmond dreams of her in a pose of maternal distress 'like a statue of Niobe' (p. 99), while Verney sardonically describes her 'looking for all the world like Charity and her three children over the door of an hospital' (p. 146).
5 The moral debate about *Desmond* was focused almost exclusively on the relationship between Desmond and Geraldine Verney, which is symptomatic of the extent to which Josephine is either so closely identified with Geraldine in the text as to escape reviewer's notice as a separate source of moral concern, or of the nationalist prejudice which sanctioned adultery with a French woman but could not condone it with an English one.
6 See Alison Conway, 'Nationalism, Revolution, and the Female Body: Charlotte Smith's *Desmond*', *Women's Studies*, 24 (1995), 395–409; Diana Bowstead, 'Charlotte Smith's *Desmond*: The Epistolary Novel as Ideological Argument', in *Fetter'd or Free?: British Women Novelists, 1670–1815* ed. by Mary Anne Schofield and Cecilia Macheski, Ohio University Press, 1986).
7 *Desmond*, p. 78.
8 *Ibid.*, p. 87.
9 'The Emigrants', *The Poems of Charlotte Smith*, ed. by Stuart Curran (Oxford University Press, 1993), pp. 131–63.
10 *Ibid.*, ll. pp. 332–7.

11 The *Critical Review* 9 (October 1793) complained that: 'Herself, and not the French emigrant, fills the foreground; begins and ends the piece; and the pity we should naturally feel for those overwhelming and uncommon distresses, is lessened by their being brought into parallel with the inconveniences of a narrow income or a protracted lawsuit' (p. 99). *The European Magazine* 24 (July 1793), suggested archly that blank verse is not the 'proper measure in which to complain – at least to do nothing else but complain' (p. 41).

12 Cited by Todd, notes to *Desmond*, p. 409.

13 *The Banished Man*, 4 vols. (London: Cadell, 1794).

14 *The European Magazine* 26 (October 1794), p. 273.

15 It recommends *The Banished Man* as 'a fulfilment of the requirements of a novel and for the pleasure it provides for those interested in the serious political issues of the day – not for those seeking love interest' (*ibid.*)

16 Koblenz was an important gathering place for emigrants.

17 The *Analytical Review* 20 (November 1794) complains that '[o]ne of the characters, that of Mrs Denzil, seems to be brought in for no other purpose than to give her an opportunity of representing her own misfortunes. Mrs Smith's fate may have been hard; her story may be proper to be laid before the public, but the case would certainly appear with more propriety, and with better effect in a distinct publication, than as an episode to a novel' (pp. 244–5). In a similar vein, the *Critical Review* 13 (March 1795) criticised Smith's taking the opportunity in the novel 'to give vent to her feelings, and claim the sympathy of the public for the distresses and perplexities of her private concerns... It is unjustifiable to make a novel the vehicle of accusations which ought only to be made in a court of justice ... and it is unwise to pour *herself* upon the public, instead of those fictitious distresses and diversified characters she so well knows how to describe (pp. 275–6). For a recent re-appraisal of Smith's tendency to 'market' her private problems see Jacqueline Labbe, 'Selling One's Sorrows: Charlotte Smith, Mary Robinson, and the Marketing of Poetry', *The Wordsworth Circle*, 5: 25 (1994), 68–71.

18 *The Banished Man*, vol. 4, p. 327.

19 *The Old Manor House*, ed. by Anne Henry Ehrenpreis, intro. by Judith Phillips Stanton, The World's Classics (1793; Oxford University Press, 1989).

20 Smith's racism and her imperialist tendencies are evident in her portraits of black servants and in her arguments against slavery, which, like much abolitionist rhetoric of the period, were founded on the assumption that colonialism would be better served by treating indigenous populations with less brutality.

21 Although *The Old Manor House* was generally received more favourably than *Desmond*, the trysts between Orlando and Monimia 'in *his* apartments' provoked the censure of the *Critical Review* 8 (May, 1793), 44–54.

22 *The Old Manor House*, p. 356.

23 Smith promised to provide an immediate sequel to *The Old Manor House*, which would trace the adventures of Warwick and Isabella. The single-volume novel, *The Wanderings of Warwick*, appeared in January 1794, with an irate advertisement from the publisher, blaming the delay and the brevity on the author.
24 *The Young Philosopher*, 4 vols. (London: Cadell, 1798).
25 She notes Wollstonecraft's influence in particular in the preface, paying tribute to the writer who had died shortly before *The Young Philosopher* was written.
26 *Critical Review* 24 (September 1798), 77–84.

5 MARY WOLLSTONECRAFT AND THE NATIONAL BODY

1 *The Works of Mary Wollstonecraft* (*WMW*), 7 vols., ed. by Janet Todd and Marilyn Butler (London: Pickering and Chatto, 1989), vol.1, pp. 183–4.
2 In this respect I want to raise questions about the critical tendency to indict Wollstonecraft for privileging the 'bourgeois mother' as the model of femininity. Cora Kaplan, for instance, arrived at this conclusion in her powerful analysis of Wollstonecraft's denial of the pleasured body, in particular the sexual body of the lower class woman, in her essay on Wollstonecraft in *Sea Changes: Essays on Culture and Feminism* (London: Verso, 1986) pp. 131–56. A more recent approach by Rajani Sudan comes to a similar conclusion via a different route, citing Wollstonecraft's investment in a patriotic discourse of maternal productivity as evidence of her implicit imperialism: 'Mothering and National Identity in the Works of Mary Wollstonecraft', in *Romanticism, Race, and Imperial Culture, 1780–1834*, ed. by Alan Richardson and Sonia Hofkosh (Bloomington: Indiana University Press, 1996). Although these essays provide valuable insights into the complicity of liberal feminism with discourses of class and racial oppression, they miss the ambivalence in Wollstonecraft's attitude towards the maternal body, not least her own maternal body, and its grounding in population discourse of the 1790s.
3 Michel Foucault, *The History of Sexuality: Volume One, an Introduction*, trans. by Robert Hurley (London: Allen Lane, 1978), p. 28.
4 See, for instance, Judith Butler, *Bodies that Matter: on the Discursive Limits of 'Sex'* (London: Routledge, 1993) and Elizabeth Grosz, *Volatile Bodies: Toward a Corporeal Feminism* (Bloomington and Indianapolis: Indiana University Press, 1994).
5 Jean-Antoine-Nicolas de Caritat, Marquis de Condorcet, *Sketch for a Historical Picture of the Progress of the Human Mind* (1795; London: Weidenfield and Nicolson, 1955) William Godwin, *Enquiry Concerning Political Justice and its Influence on Modern Morals and Happiness* (1793; Harmondsworth: Penguin, 1985).
6 Thomas Robert Matthus, *An Essay on the Principle of Population, as it Affects the*

Future Improvement of Society. With Remarks on the Speculations of Mr. Godwin, M. Condorcet, and Other Writers, The Works of Thomas Robert Malthus, ed. by E. A. Wrigley and D. Souden Pickering Masters Series, 8 vols., (London: Pickering and Chatto, 1986) vol. 1, p. 86.

7 See Frances Ferguson, *Solitude and the Sublime: Romanticism and the Aesthetics of Individuation* (London: Routledge, 1992); Catherine Gallagher, 'The Body Versus the Social Body in the Works of Thomas Malthus and Henry Mayhew', in *The Making of the Modern Body: Sexuality and Society in the Nineteenth Century*, ed. by Catherine Gallagher and Thomas Laqueur (Berkeley: University of California Press, 1987), pp. 83–106; Mary Jacobus, *First Things: the Maternal Imaginary in Literature, Art, and Psychoanalysis* (London: Routledge, 1995).

8 *WMW*, vol.5.

9 *Collected Letters of Mary Wollstonecraft*, ed. by Ralph M. Wardle (Ithaca: Cornell University Press, 1979), p. 218.

10 *A Vindication of the Rights of Men, WMW*, vol. 5.

11 *WMW*, vol. 6, pp. 441–6.

12 *Ibid.*, vol. 6.

13 *Ibid.*, pp. 146–7.

14 *Ibid.*, p. 141.

15 Adam Smith, *An Inquiry into the Nature and Causes of the Wealth of Nations, the Glasgow Edition of the Works and Correspondence of Adam Smith*, ed. by R. H. Campbell, A. S. Skinner and W. B. Todd (1776; Oxford: Clarendon Press, 1976) vol. 5, p. 51.

16 *WMW*, vol. 6. References to this publication will be abbreviated to *Scandinavian Letters*.

17 *Ibid.*,p. 127.

18 John Milton, *Paradise Lost*, 8, 11, 549–54. cited in *ibid.*, p. 129.

19 *WMW*, vol. 6, p. 128.

20 *Ibid.*, pp. 230–1.

21 *Ibid.*, p. 28.

22 Claire Tomalin, *The Life and Death of Mary Wollstonecraft* (1974; Harmondsworth: Penguin, 1985) suggests that Wollstonecraft conflates the October march with the violent turn of the *citoyennes* in 1793.

23 Vivien Jones, 'Women Writing Revolution: Narratives of History and Sexuality in Wollstonecraft and Williams', in *Beyond Romanticism: New Approaches to Texts and Contexts 1780–1832*, ed. by Stephen Copley and John Whale (London: Routledge, 1992), pp. 178–99, esp. p. 184.

24 *WMW*, vol.6, p. 207.

25 *Ibid.*, vol. 5, pp. 207–8.

26 *Ibid.*, vol. 6, pp. 233–4.

27 *Ibid.* p. 182.

28 Godwin, *Enquiry Concerning Political Justice*, p. 7.

29 Malthus, *Essay on Population*, pp. 115–6; p. 117.

30 Kathryn Sutherland, 'Adam Smith's master narrative: women and the Wealth of Nations', in *Adam Smith's Wealth of Nations: New Interdisciplinary Essays*, ed. by Stephen Copley and Kathryn Sutherland (Manchester University Press, 1995).

31 *WMW.*, vol. 6.

32 Imlay was one of many traders who broke the British embargo on French trade by importing in the name of neutral Scandinavian countries. Wollstonecraft agreed to act as Imlay's agent in Scandinavia after the disappearance of a ship in which he had invested.

33 *WMW*, vol. 6, p. 304.

34 *Ibid.*, p. 321.

35 *Ibid.*, p. 377.

36 *Ibid.*, vol. 5, pp. 117–8.

37 *Ibid.*, vol. 6, pp. 257–8.

38 *Ibid.*, pp. 294–5.

39 John Whale has addressed the discursive resonances of Wollstonecraft's representation of imagination in 'Preparations for Happiness: Mary Wollstonecraft and Imagination', in *Reviewing Romanticism*, ed. by Philip Martin and Robin Jarvis (London: Macmillan, 1992), pp. 170–89. His essay on the *Scandinavian Letters* provides another reading of her attitudes towards perfectibility: 'Death in the Face of Nature: Self and Society in Wollstonecraft's Letters from Sweden, Norway and Denmark', *Romanticism* 1:2 (1995), 177–92.

40 Vivien Jones, 'The death of Mary Wollstonecraft,' *British Journal for Eighteenth-Century Studies* 20: 2 (1997), 187–205.

41 *Collected Letters*, pp. 363–4.

6 PATRICIAN, POPULIST AND PATRIOT: HANNAH MORE'S
COUNTER-REVOLUTIONARY NATIONALISM

1 See Lucinda Cole, '(Anti) Feminist Sympathies: The Politics of Relationship in Smith, Wollstonecraft and More', *ELH* 58 (1991), 107–40; Donna Landry, *Muses of Resistance: Laboring-Class Women's Poetry in Britain, 1739–1796* (Cambridge University Press, 1990), pp. 254–73; Mitzi Myers, 'Reform or Ruin: "A Revolution in Female Manners"', *Studies in Eighteenth-Century Culture* 11 (1982), 199–216.

2 *The Yale Edition of Horace Walpole's Correspondence*, ed. by W. S. Lewis, Robert A. Smith and Charles H. Bennett (New Haven: Yale University Press, 1961), vol. 31, p. 320.

3 This is the caricature of More in Richard Polwhele's notorious misogynist poem 'The Unsex'd Females', which first appeared anonymously in *The Anti-Jacobin Review* in May 1799, and included derogatory sketches of, amongst others, More, Ann Yearsley, Charlotte Smith, Helen Maria Williams, Mary Hays and Mary Wollstonecraft.

4 *Walpole's Correspondence*, vol. 31, p. 319.

5 Hannah More, *Strictures on Female Education with a View of the Principles and Conduct Prevalent Among Women of Rank and Fortune*, *The Works of Hannah More*, 18 vols. (1799; London: Cadell, 1818), 7 and 8. References will be abbreviated to *Strictures* 1 and 2.

6 *Strictures*, 2, p. 220.

7 For an analysis of Burke's fear of 'the public', see Angela Keane, 'Reflections and Correspondences: The Unfamiliarity of Burke's Familiar Letter', in *Edmund Burke's Reflections on the Revolution in France: New Interdisciplinary Essays*, ed. by John Whale (Manchester University Press, 2000) pp. 193–218.

8 *Walpole's Correspondence*, vol. 31, pp. 376–7.

9 *Ibid.*, p. 370.

10 *Ibid.*, p. 373.

11 See David Simpson, *Romanticism, Nationalism and the Revolt Against Theory* (University of Chicago Press, 1993) for an account of the broader antipathy towards philosophical abstraction in British philosophical and literary traditions in the eighteenth and early nineteenth centuries.

12 This, of course, was part of Walpole's prefatory description of his Gothic romance, *The Castle of Otranto* (1765), defining his Gothic aesthetic against public, classical discourse and locating it in the wanton space of private fantasy.

13 *Walpole's Correspondence*, vol. 31, p. 341.

14 *Ibid.*, p. 372.

15 Hannah More, *Considerations on Religion and Public Education, with Remarks on the Speech of M. Dupont, Delivered in the National Convention of France, Together with an Address Ladies, etc. of Great Britain and Ireland* (1794), ed. Claudia L. Johnson, (Los Angeles: William Andrews Clark Memorial Library, University of California, 1990).

16 For an exploration of the 'anti-party' rhetoric of early nineteenth-century radicalism see Kevin Gilmartin, *Print Politics: The Press and Radical Opposition in Early Nineteenth-Century England* (Cambridge University Press, 1996).

17 *Remarks*, p. 381.

18 *Ibid.*, pp. 33–4.

19 *Walpole's Correspondence*, vol. 31, pp. 62–3.

20 *Strictures*, 1, pp. 6–7.

21 Kathryn Sutherland, 'Hannah More's Counter-Revolutionary Feminism', in *Revolution in Writing: British Literary Responses to the French Revolution*, ed. by Kelvin Everest (Buckingham: Open University Press, 1991), p. 55. See also Sutherland's analysis of More in 'Adam Smith's Master Narrative: Women and the Wealth of Nations', in *Adam Smith's Wealth of Nations: New Interdisciplinary Essays*, ed. by Stephen Copley and Kathryn Sutherland (Manchester University Press, 1995), pp. 97–121.

22 See Josiah Tucker, *A Brief Essay on the Advantages and Disadvantages which Respectively attend France and Great Britain, with Regard to Trade. With Some Proposals for Removing the Principal Disadvantages of Great Britain. In a New Method* (London, 1750).

23 *Strictures*, 1, pp. 261–2.
24 *Remarks*, pp. 22–3.
25 *Strictures*, 1, p. 46.
26 *Ibid.*, p. 33.
27 *Ibid.*, p. 51.
28 For analyses of the subversive social register of the evangelical movement in the 1790s see V. Kiernan, 'Evangelicalism and the French Revolution', *Past and Present: A Journal of Scientific History* 1 (1952), 44–56 and Gerald Newman, *The Rise of English Nationalism, A Cultural History 1740–1830* (London: Weidenfeld and Nicolson, 1987).
29 H. Thompson, *The Life of Hannah More* (London: Cadell, 1838), p. 222.
30 Mary Alden Hopkins, *Hannah More and Her Circle* (New York and Toronto: Longmans, 1947), p. 48.
31 First published in *Liberty and Property Preserved against Republicans and Levellers; a Collection of Tracts* (London, 1795). References are to 'Village Politics', *WHM*, vol. 1.
32 Olivia Smith, *The Politics of Language 1791–1819* (Oxford: Clarendon Press, 1984), p. 94.
33 'Village Politics,' *WHM*, vol. 1, p. 366.
34 The *Tracts* were reordered for the 1818 Cadell edition of More's Works as *Stories for the Middle Ranks*, *WHM*, vol. 4 and *Stories for the Common People*, *WHM*, vol. 5.
35 *Stories for the Middle Ranks*, *WHM*, vol. 4, pp. iii–iv.
36 In 1794, Coleridge, Southey and Hall collaborated on a play about the death of Robespierre. According to Hopkins, they dedicated it to More. The dedication is actually to H. Martin, but the fact that her biographer thought this possible is both a sign of the esteem with which she was held by these emerging literary lights, and of the reputation More had established as a counter-revolutionary figure. The 'young Romantics' did not carry this esteem into later life. 'Intellectually,' Hopkins argues, '[More] belonged to a generation already past, so that later on, when she came into contact with Southey, Coleridge, De Quincey, Cottle [the Bristol publisher] and others who sojourned in Bristol, she was prejudiced against their ideas. She carried the age of Johnson over into the time of Shelley and Byron' (p. 108).
37 Martha More, *The Mendip Annals: Or, the Narrative of the Charitable Labours of Hannah and Martha More in Their Neighbourhood. Being the Journal of Martha More*, ed. Arthur Roberts (London: James Nisbet, 1859), pp. 26–7.
38 The poem is reproduced as 'The Black Slave Trade', *WHM*, vol.1, pp. 369–90.
39 See, for instance, Moira Ferguson, *Subject to Others: British Women Writers and Colonial Slavery, 1670–1834* (London: Routledge, 1992).
40 *WHM*, vol. 1, pp. 372–3, lines 21–32.
41 *Mendip Annals*, pp. 16–17.
42 *Ibid.*, pp. 61–2.
43 For a full account of the status of the Sunday school movement in the

broader context of education reform in this period, see Alan Richardson, *Literature, Education and Romanticism: Reading as Social Practice 1780–1832* (Cambridge University Press, 1994).

44 References to 'the Blagdon controversy' can be found, for instance, in *The British Critic*, 17–19 and *The Anti-Jacobin Review*, 5, 9 and 11.

45 Edward Spencer, *Truths, Respecting Mrs Hannah More's Meeting-Houses, and the Conduct of her Followers; Addressed to the Curate of Blagdon* (London: W. Meyler, 1802). I am grateful to the Folger Shakespeare Library in Washington D. C. for allowing me to have access to this pamphlet.

46 Spencer is referring to More's association with the royal household and her advice on the education of Princess Charlotte, which was made public in 1805 in More's *Hints for Forming the Character of a Young Princess*.

47 Spencer, *Truths, Respecting Hannah More*, p. 71.

48 See Barbara Taylor, *Eve and the New Jerusalem: Socialism and Feminism in the Nineteenth Century* (New York: Pantheon Books, 1983) for an important account of the emergence of the relationship between the British reform and women's movements.

AFTERWORD

1 Anna Laetitia Barbauld, *The British Novelists*, 50 vols. (London, 1820), p. 59. *The British Novelists* was first published in 1810.

2 *Ibid.*, p. 1.

3 In the 1790s Barbauld produced a number of pamphlets on a range of public issues, including: *An Address to the Opposers of the Repeal on the Corporation and Test Acts* (London: Johnson, 1790); *Civic Sermons to the People*, Numbers I and II (London: Johnson, 1792); *Remarks on Gilbert Wakefield's Enquiry into the Expediency and Propriety of Public or Social Worship* (London: Johnson, 1792); *Sins of Government, Sins of the Nation; or, a Discourse on the Fast, Appointed on April 19* (London: Johnson, 1794).

4 In 1999, for instance, an industrial dispute led by the Association for University Teachers was prompted in part by the on-going discrepancies in pay and contractual arrangements between female and male academics in the so-called 'old' sector of British universities.

Bibliography

PRIMARY SOURCES

Barbauld, Anna Laetitia, *The British Novelists*, 50 vols. (London: Rivington; *et al*, 1820).

    An Address to the Opposers of the Repeal of the Corporation and Test Acts (London: Johnson, 1790).

    Civic Sermons to the People, Numbers I and II (London: Johnson, 1792).

    Remarks on Gilbert Wakefield's Enquiry into the Expediency and Propriety of Public or Social Worship (London: Johnson, 1792).

    Sins of Government, Sins of the Nation; or, a Discourse on the Fast, Appointed on April 19 (London: Johnson, 1794).

Beattie, James, 'On Fable and Romance', *Dissertations Moral and Critical* (London, 1783).

Burke, Edmund *Reflections on the Revolution in France is a Letter Intended to Have Been Sent to a Young Gentleman in Paris*, ed. by Conor Cruise O'Brien (1790; Harmondsworth: Penguin, 1989).

Clarke, James, *Survey of the Lakes* (1787).

Coleridge, Samuel Taylor, *Biographia Literaria*, ed. by George Watson (London: J. M. Dent, 1975; repr. 1984).

Condorcet, Jean-Antoine-Nicolas de Caritat, Marquis de, *Sketch for a Historical Picture of the Progress of the Human Mind* (1795; London: Weidenfield and Nicolson, 1955).

Gilpin, William, *Three Essays: on Picturesque Beauty; on Picturesque Travel; and on Sketching Landscape*, 2nd edn (London, 1794).

    Observations of the Western Parts of England (1786).

Godwin, William, *Enquiry Concerning Political Justice and its Influence on Modern Morals and Happiness* (1793; Harmondsworth: Penguin, 1985).

Hawkins, Laetitia Matilda, *Letters on the Female Mind, its Powers and Pursuits; Addressed to Miss H. M. Williams, with Particular Reference to her Letters from France*, 2 vols. (London, 1793).

Hume, David, *Essays Moral, Political, and Literary*, ed. by Eugene F. Miller (Indianapolis, 1985).

    A Treatise of Human Nature, ed. by L. A. Selby-Bigge (1739–40; Oxford: Clarendon Press, 1965).

Hurd, Richard, *Letters on Chivalry and Romance: Serving to Illustrate Some Passages in the Third Dialogue* (London, 1762).

Hutchinson, William, *Excursion to the Lakes in Westmoreland and Cumberland* (1774).

Liberty and Property Preserved against Republicans and Levellers; a Collection of Tracts (London, 1795).

Knight, Richard Payne, *The Landscape: A Didactic Poem in Three Books* (London, 1794).

Malthus, Thomas Robert, *An Essay on the Principle of Population, as it affects the Future Improvement of Society. With Remarks on the Speculations of Mr. Godwin, M. Condorcet, and Other Writers, The Works of Thomas Robert Malthus*, ed. by E. A. Wrigley and D. Souden, Pickering Masters Series, 8 vols., (London: Pickering and Chatto, 1986).

Montagu, Elizabeth, *An Essay on the Writings and Genius of Shakespear... To which are now First Added, Three Dialogues of the Dead* (London, 1777).

Moore, Dr. John, *A Journal During a Residence in France from the Beginning of August to the Middle of December, 1792*, 2 vols. (1793–4).

A View of the Causes and Progress of the French Revolution, 2 vols. (1795).

More, Hannah, *The Works of Hannah More*, 18 vols. (London: Cadell, 1818).

Considerations on Religion and Public Education, with Remarks on the Speech of M. Dupont, Delivered in the National Convention of France, Together with an Address Ladies, etc. of Great Britain and Ireland, ed. by Claudia L. Johnson, (1794; Los Angeles: William Andrews Clark Memorial Library, University of California, 1990).

More, Martha, *Mendip Annals: or, the Narrative of the Charitable Labours of Hannah and Martha More in Their Neighbourhood. Being the Journal of Martha More*, ed. by Arthur Roberts (London: James Nisbet, 1859).

Price, Uvedale, *An Essay on the Picturesque as Compared with the Sublime and the Beautiful; and, on the Use of Studying Pictures, for the Purpose of Improving Real Landscape* (London, 1796–8).

Essays on the Picturesque, vol. 3 (London, 1810).

Radcliffe, Ann, *The Italian, or the Confessional of the Black Penitents*, ed. by Frederick Garber, The World's Classics (1797; Oxford University Press, 1968).

A Journey Made in the Summer of 1794, Through Holland and the Western Frontier of Germany With a Return Down the Rhine: to which are Added Observations During a Tour of the Lakes of Lancashire, Westmoreland, and Cumberland (London, 1795).

The Mysteries of Udolpho, ed. by Bonamy Dobrée, The World's Classics (1794; Oxford University Press, 1966; repr. 1980).

The Romance of the Forest, ed. by Chloe Chard, The World's Classics (1791; Oxford University Press, 1986).

Reeve, Clara, *The Progress of Romance through Times, Countries and Manners* (Colchester, 1785).

Smith, Adam, *An Inquiry into the Nature and Causes of the Wealth of Nations, The Glasgow Edition of the Works and Correspondence of Adam Smith*, ed. by R. H. Campbell, A. S. Skinner and W. B. Todd (1776; Oxford: Clarendon Press, 1976).

The Theory of Moral Sentiments, ed. by D. D. Raphael and A. L. Macfie (1759; Oxford: Clarendon Press, 1976).

Smith, Charlotte, *The Banished Man*, 4 vols. (London: Cadell, 1794).

Celestina (1791).

Desmond, ed. by Antje Blank and Janet Todd (1792; London: Pickering and Chatto, 1997).

Emmeline, or the Orphan of the Castle (1788).

Ethelinde, or the Recluse of the Lake (1789).

Elegiac Sonnets (1784).

The Old Manor House, ed. by Anne Henry Ehrenpreis, The World's Classics (1793; Oxford University Press, 1989).

The Poems of Charlotte Smith, ed. by Stuart Curran (Oxford University Press, 1993).

The Young Philosopher, 4 vols. (London: Cadell, 1798).

Spencer, Edward, *Truths, Respecting Mrs Hannah More's Meeting-Houses, and the Conduct of her Followers; Addressed to the Curate of Blagdon* (London: W. Meyler, 1802).

Thompson, H., *The Life of Hannah More* (London: Cadell, 1838).

Tucker, Josiah, *A Brief Essay on the Advantages and Disadvantages which Respectively attend France and Great Britain, with Regard to Trade. With Some Proposals for Removing the Principal Disadvantages of Great Britain. In a New Method* (London, 1750).

Walpole, Horace, *The Yale Edition of Horace Walpole's Correspondence*, ed. by W. S. Lewis, Robert A. Smith and Charles H. Bennett (New Haven: Yale University Press, 1961).

Wardle, Ralph M., *Collected Letters of Mary Wollstonecraft* (Ithaca and London: Cornell University Press, 1979).

Warton, Thomas, *The History of English Poetry, from the Close of the Eleventh to the Commencement of the Eighteenth Century* (London, 1779–81).

West, Thomas, *Guide to the Lakes* (1778).

Williams, Helen Maria, *Edwin and Eltruda: a Legendary Tale* (London: Cadell, 1782).

A Farewell, for Two Years, to England: a Poem (London: Cadell, 1791).

Julia (London: Cadell, 1790).

Letters from France, ed. by Janet Todd, 8 vols. (Delmar, New York: Scholars Facsimiles and Reprints, 1975).

An Ode on the Peace (London: Cadell, 1784).

Peru: a Poem; in Six Cantos (London: Cadell, 1784).

Poems, 2 vols. (London: Cadell, 1786).

A Poem on the Bill Lately Passed for Regulating the Slave Trade (London: Cadell, 1788).

Poems on Various Subjects; with Introductory Remarks on the Present State of Science and Literature in France, 2 vols. (London: Whittaker, 1823).

Souvenirs de la Révolution française, trans. by Charles Coquerel (Paris, 1827).

A Tour in Switzerland, 2 vols. (London: Robinson, 1798).

Wollstonecraft, Mary, *The Works of Mary Wollstonecraft*, ed. by Janet Todd and Marilyn Butler, 7 vols. (London: Pickering and Chatto, 1989).

Wordsworth, William, *The Poetical Works of William Wordsworth*, ed. by Ernest De Selincourt (Oxford: Clarendon Press, 1940).

    Topographical Description of the Country of the Lakes in the North of England (1820); later revised as *A Guide Through the District of the Lakes* (1835).

    Lyrical Ballads, Selected Prose, ed. by John O. Hayden (Harmondsworth: Penguin, 1988).

The Letters of William and Dorothy Wordsworth, ed. by Chester L. Shaver, 2nd edn, vol. 1, 1787–1805 (Oxford: Clarendon Press, 1967).

The Letters of William and Dorothy Wordsworth, ed. by Alan G. Hill, 2nd edn, vol. 5, Part 2, 1821–8 (Oxford: Clarendon Press, 1978).

SECONDARY SOURCES

Adams, M. Ray, 'Helen Maria Williams and the French Revolution', in *Wordsworth and Coleridge, Studies in Honour of George McLean Harper*, ed. by Earl Leslie Griggs (Princeton University Press, 1939).

Altman, Janet Gurkin, 'The Letter Book as a Literary Institution 1539–1789: Toward a Cultural History of Published Correspondences in France', *Yale French Studies*, Special Issue, 'Men/Women of Letters', ed. by Charles A. Porter, 71 (1986), 17–62.

Anderson, Benedict, *Imagined Communities: Reflections on the Origin and Spread of Nationalism* (London: Verso, 1991).

Ariés, Phillipe, *The Hour of Our Death*, trans. by Helen Weaver (New York: Alfred A. Knopf, 1981).

Armstrong, J. *Nations Before Nationalism* (Chapel Hill: University of North Carolina Press, 1982).

Armstrong, Nancy, *Desire and Domestic Fiction: a Political History of the Novel* (Oxford University Press, 1987).

    Lennard Tennenhouse, *Imaginary Puritan: Literature, Intellectual Labor, and the Origins of Personal Life* (Berkeley: University of California Press, 1992).

Ashfield, Andrew (ed.), *Romantic Women Poets, 1770–1838: an Anthology* (Manchester University Press).

Ballaster, Ros, *Seductive Forms: Women's Amatory Fiction from 1684 to 1740* (Oxford: Clarendon Press, 1992).

Benjamin, Walter, *Illuminations* (1955; London: Fontana, 1973).

Bowstead, Diana, 'Charlotte Smith's *Desmond*: the Epistolary Novel as Ideological Argument', in *Fetter'd or Free?: British Women Novelists, 1670–1815*, ed. by Mary Anne Schofield and Cecilia Macheski (Ohio University Press, 1986), pp.237–63.

Breuilly, J., *Nationalism and the State* (Manchester University Press, 1982).

Butler, Judith, *Bodies that Matter: on the Discursive Limits of 'Sex'* (London: Routledge, 1993).

Castle, Terry, 'The Spectralization of the Other in *The Mysteries of Udolpho*', in

The New Eighteenth Century: Theory, Politics, English Literature, ed. by Felicity
   Nussbaum and Laura Brown (New York: Methuen, 1987), pp. 231–53.
Cole, Lucinda, '(Anti) Feminist Sympathies: The Politics of Relationship in
   Smith, Wollstonecraft and More', *ELH* 58 (1991), 107–40.
Colley, Linda, *Britons: Forging the Nation 1707–1837* (New Haven: Yale University
   Press, 1992).
Conway, Alison, 'Nationalism, Revolution, and the Female Body: Charlotte
   Smith's *Desmond*', *Women's Studies* 24 (1995), 395–409.
Copley, Stephen and Kathryn Sutherland (eds.), *Adam Smith's Wealth of Nations:
   New Interdisciplinary Essays* (Manchester University Press, 1995).
Copley, Stephen and John Whale (eds.), *Beyond Romanticism: New Approaches to
   Texts and Contexts, 1780–1832* (London: Routledge, 1992).
Cox, Philip, *Gender, Genre and the Romantic Poets* (Manchester University Press,
   1996).
Cunningham, Hugh, 'The Language of Patriotism', in *Patriotism: The Making and
   Unmaking of British National Identity*, ed. by Raphael Samuel, 3 vols. (London:
   Routledge, 1989), vol. 1, pp.57–89.
Davis, Lennard J., *Factual Fictions: the Origins of the English Novel* (New York:
   Columbia University Press, 1983).
Deane, Seamus, *The French Revolution and Enlightenment in England 1789–1831*
   (Cambridge, Mass.: Harvard University Press, 1988).
Duncan, Ian, *Modern Romance and Transformations of the Novel: the Gothic, Scott,
   Dickens* (Cambridge University Press, 1992).
During, Simon, 'Literature: Nationalism's Other? The Case for Revision', in
   Nation and Narration, ed. by Homi K. Bhabha (London: Routledge, 1990),
   pp.138–53.
Ellis, Kate Ferguson, *The Contested Castle: Gothic Novels and the Subversion of Domestic
   Ideology* (Urbana and Chicago: University of Illinois Press, 1989).
Favret, Mary, *Romantic Correspondence: Women, Politics and the Fiction of Letters*
   (Cambridge University Press, 1993).
   'Spectatrice as Spectacle', *Studies in Romanticism* 32 (Summer 1993), 273–95.
Felski, Rita, *Beyond Feminist Aesthetics: Feminist Literature and Social Change* (London:
   Hutchinson Radius, 1989).
Ferguson, Frances, *Solitude and the Sublime: Romanticism and the Aesthetics of Individ-
   uation* (London: Routledge, 1992).
Ferguson, Moira, *Subject to Others: British Women Writers and Colonial Slavery,
   1670–1834* (London: Routledge, 1992).
Fishman, J. (ed.), *Language Problems of Devoloping Nations* (New York: Wiley,
   1968).
Foucault, Michel, *The History of Sexuality: Volume One, an Introduction*, trans. by
   Robert Hurley (London: Allen Lane, 1978).
Fraser, Nancy, 'Heterosexism, Misrecognition and Capitalism: a Response to
   Judith Butler', *New Left Review* 228 (1998),141–9.
   Unruly Practices: Power, Discourse and Gender in Contemporary Social Theory (Cam-
   bridge: Polity Press, 1989).

'What's Critical about Critical Theory: the case of Habermas and Gender', in *Feminist Interpretations and Political Theory*, ed. by Mary Lyndon Shanley and Carole Pateman (Cambridge: Polity Press, 1991).

and Paul James (eds.), *Critical Politics: from the Personal to the Global* (Melbourne: Arena, 1994).

Freud, Sigmund, 'The Uncanny', in *The Standard Edition of the Complete Psychological Works*, ed. and trans. by James Strachey (1919; London: Hogarth Press, 1955), vol. 17, pp. 218–52.

Gallagher, Catherine, 'The Body Versus the Social Body in the Works of Thomas Malthus and Henry Mayhew,' in *The Making of the Modern Body: Sexuality and Society in the Nineteenth Century*, ed. by Catherine Gallagher and Thomas Laqueur (Berkeley, University of California Press, 1987), pp.83–106.

Nobody's Story: The Vanishing Acts of Women Writers in the Marketplace, 1670–1820 (Oxford: Clarendon Press, 1994).

Geertz, Clifford, *Old Societies and New States* (New York: Free Press, 1963).

Gellner, Ernest, *Nations and Nationalism* (Oxford: Blackwell Press, 1983).

Gilmartin, Kevin, *Print Politics: the Press and Radical Opposition in Early Nineteenth-Century England* (Cambridge University Press, 1996).

Goldsmith, Elizabeth C., 'Authority, Authenticity, and the Publication of Letters by Women', in *Writing the Female Voice: Essays on Epistolary Literature*, ed. by Elizabeth C. Goldsmith, (Michigan: Northeastern University Press, 1989), pp. 46–59.

Goodman, Dena, *The Republic of Letters: a Cultural History of the French Enlightenment* (Ithaca and London: Cornell University Press, 1994).

Grosz, Elizabeth, *Volatile Bodies: Toward a Corporeal Feminism* (Bloomington and Indianapolis: Indiana University Press, 1994).

Guest, Harriet, 'Modern Love: Feminism and Sensibility in 1796', *New Formations: A Journal of Culture/Theory/Politics*, 'Conservative Modernity', 28 (Spring 1996), 3–20.

'The Wanton Muse: Politics and Gender in Gothic Theory after 1760', in *Beyond Romanticism: New Approaches to Texts and Contexts 1780–1832*, ed. by Stephen Copley and John Whale (London: Routledge, 1992), pp. 118–39.

Habermas, Jürgen, *The Structural Transformation of the Public Sphere: an Inquiry into a Category of Bourgeois Society*, trans. by Thomas Burger with Frederick Lawrence (Cambridge: Polity Press, 1989).

Hargreaves-Mawdsley, W. N., *English Della Cruscans and Their Time, 1783–1828* (The Hague: Martinus Nijhoff, 1967).

Harper, George McLean, *William Wordsworth: His Life, Works, and Influence*, 2 vols. (London: Murray, 1916).

Helgerson, Richard, *Forms of Nationhood: the Elizabethan Writing of England* (Chicago and London: University of Chicago Press, 1992).

Hobsbawm, Eric, *Nations and Nationalism Since 1780: Programme, Myth, Reality* (Cambridge University Press, 1991).

and Terrence Ranger, *The Invention of Tradition* (Cambridge University Press, 1983).

Hopkins, Mary Alden, *Hannah More and Her Circle* (New York and Toronto: Longmans, 1947).

Howells, Carol Ann, 'The Pleasure of the Woman's Text: Ann Radcliffe's Subtle Transgressions', in *Gothic Fictions: Prohibition/Transgression*, ed. by Kenneth W. Graham (New York: AMS Press, 1989).

Jacobus, Mary, *First Things: the Maternal Imaginary in Literature, Art, and Psychoanalysis* (London, Routledge, 1995).

Janowitz, Ann, *England's Ruins: Poetic Purpose and the National Landscape* (Oxford: Blackwell Press, 1990).

Jones, Vivien, 'The Death of Mary Wollstonecraft,' *British Journal for Eighteenth-Century Studies*, 20: 2 (1997), 187–205.

'Women Writing Revolution: Narratives of History and Sexuality in Wollstonecraft and Williams', in *Beyond Romanticism*, ed. by Stephen Copley and John Whale, pp.178–99.

Kahane, Claire, 'The Gothic Mirror', in *The (M)other Tongue: Essays in Feminist Psychoanalytic Interpretation*, ed. by Shirley Nelson Garner, *et al.* (Ithaca and New York: Cornell University Press, 1985), pp. 334–52.

Kaplan, Cora, *Sea Changes: Essays on Culture and Feminism* (London: Verso, 1986).

Keane, Angela, 'Reflections and Correspondences: The Familiarity of Burke's Unfamiliar Letter', *Edmund Burke's Reflections on the Revolution in France: New Interdisciplinary Essays*, ed. by John Whale (Manchester University Press, 2000) pp. 193–218.

Kedourie, Elie, *Nationalism* (1960; Oxford: Blackwell Press, 1993).

Kiernan, V., 'Evangelicalism and the French Revolution', *Past and Present: A Journal of Scientific History* 1 (1952), 44–56.

Kelly, Gary, *Women, Writing, and Revolution, 1790–1827* (Oxford: Clarendon Press, 1993).

Labbe, Jacqueline,'Selling One's Sorrows: Charlotte Smith, Mary Robinson, and the Marketing of Poetry', *The Wordsworth Circle*, 5: 25 (1994), 68–71.

Landes, Joan, 'The Public and the Private Sphere: A Feminist Reconsideration', in *Feminists Read Habermas: Gendering the Subject of Discourse*, ed. by Johanna Meehan (London: Routledge, 1995).

Women and the Public Sphere in the Age of Revolution (Ithaca and London: Cornell University Press, 1988).

Landry, Donna, *Muses of Resistance: Laboring-Class Women's Poetry in Britain, 1739–1796* (Cambridge University Press, 1990).

Langbauer, Laurie, *Women and Romance: the Consolations of Gender in the English Novel* (Ithaca: Cornell University Press, 1990).

Laugero, Greg, 'Infrastructures of Enlightenment: Road-Making, the Public Sphere, and the Emergence of Literature', *Eighteenth-Century Studies*, Special Issue, 'The Public and the Nation' 29:1 (Fall 1995), 45–68.

Liu, Alan, *Wordsworth, the Sense of History* (Stanford University Press, 1989).

Mayo, Robert D., *The English Novel in the Magazines, 1740–1815* (Evanston,

Illionois, 1962).

McKeon, Michael, *The Origins of the English Novel 1600–1740* (Baltimore: Johns Hopkins University Press, 1987).

Miles, Robert, *Ann Radcliffe: the Great Enchantress* (Manchester University Press, 1995).

  Gothic Writing: a Genealogy (London: Routledge, 1993).

  'The Gothic Aesthetic: the Gothic as Discourse', *The Eighteenth Century* 32 (1991), 39–57.

Mullan, John, *Sentiment and Sociability: the Language of Feeling in the Eighteenth Century* (Oxford: Clarendon Press, 1988).

Myers, Mitzi, 'Reform or Ruin: "A Revolution in Female Manners"', *Studies in Eighteenth-Century Culture* 11 (1982), 199–216.

Nairn, Tom, *The Break-up of Britain* (London: Verso, 1981).

Newman, Gerald, *The Rise of English Nationalism, a Cultural History 1740–1830* (London: Weidenfeld and Nicolson, 1987).

Pateman, Carole, *The Sexual Contract* (Cambridge: Polity Press, 1988).

Phillipson, Nicholas, 'The Scottish Enlightenment', in *The Enlightenment in National Context*, ed. by Roy Porter and Mikulas Teich (Cambridge University Press, 1981), pp. 19–40.

Pocock, J. G. A., *Politics, Language and Time: Essays on Political Thought and History* (London: Methuen, 1971).

  Virtue, Commerce and History (Cambridge University Press, 1985).

Richardson, Alan, *Literature, Education and Romanticism: Reading as Social Practice 1780–1832* (Cambridge University Press, 1994).

  and Sonia Hofkosh (eds.), *Romanticism, Race, and Imperial Culture, 1780–1834* (Bloomington and Indianapolis: Indiana University Press, 1996).

Ross, Marlon B., 'Romancing the Nation-State: the Poetics of Romantic Nationalism', in *Macropolitics of Nineteenth-Century Literature: Nationalism, Exoticism, Imperialism*, ed. by Jonathan Arac and Harriet Ritvo (Philadelphia: University of Pennsylvania Press, 1991), pp.56–85.

  The Contours of Masculine Desire: Romanticism and the Rise of Women's Poetry (Oxford: Oxford University Press, 1989).

Said, Edward, *Culture and Imperialism* (London: Chatto and Windus, 1993).

Simpson, David, *Romanticism, Nationalism, and the Revolt Against Theory* (Chicago University Press, 1993).

Smith, Anthony, *The Ethnic Origin of Nations* (Oxford: Blackwell Press, 1986).

  Nations and Nationalism in a Global Era (Cambridge: Polity Press, 1995).

Smith, Olivia, *The Politics of Language 1791–1819* (Oxford: Clarendon Press, 1984).

Staves, Susan, *Married Women's Property in England, 1660–1833* (Cambridge, Mass.: Harvard University Press, 1990).

Sudan, Rajani, 'Mothering and National Identity in the Works of Mary Wollstonecraft', in *Romanticism, Race, and Imperial Culture, 1780–1834*, ed. by Alan Richardson and Sonia Hofkosh (Bloomington: Indiana University Press, 1996).

Sutherland, Kathryn, 'Adam Smith's Master Narrative: Women and the Wealth of Nations', in *Adam Smith's Wealth of Nations: New Interdisciplinary Essays*, ed. by Stephen Copley and Kathryn Sutherland (Manchester University Press, 1995), pp. 97–121.

'Hannah More's Counter-Revolutionary Feminism', in *Revolution in Writing: British Literary Responses to the French Revolution*, ed. by Kelvin Everest (Buckingham: Open University Press, 1991), pp. 27–63.

Taylor, Barbara, *Eve and the New Jerusalem: Socialism and Feminism in the Nineteenth Century* (New York: Pantheon Books, 1983).

Thompson, E. P., *The Making of the English Working Class* (1963; Harmondsworth: Penguin, 1968).

Todorov, Tzvetan *The Fantastic: a Structural Approach to a Literary Genre*, trans. by Richard Howard (Ithaca: Cornell University Press, 1975).

Tomalin, Claire, *The Life and Death of Mary Wollstonecraft* (1974; Harmondsworth: Penguin, 1985).

Trumpener, Katie, *Bardic Nationalism: the Romantic Novel and the British Empire* (Princeton University Press, 1997).

Whale, John, 'Preparations for Happiness: Mary Wollstonecraft and Imagination', in *Reviewing Romanticism*, ed. by Philip Martin and Robin Jarvis (London: Macmillan, 1992), pp. 170–89.

'Death in the Face of Nature: Self and Society in Wollstonecraft's Letters from Sweden, Norway and Denmark', *Romanticism* 1:2 (1995), 177–92.

Williams, Ioan (ed.), *Novel and Romance 1700–1800: a Documentary Record* (London: Routledge, 1970).

Wilson, Kathleen, 'Citizenship, Empire, and Modernity in the English Provinces, c. 1720–1790', *Eighteenth-Century Studies*, 'The Public and the Nation' 29: 1 (Fall 1995), 69–96.

Wolff, Cynthia Griffin, 'The Radcliffean Gothic Novel: a Form for Feminine Sexuality', *Modern Language Studies* 9 (1979), 98–113.

Woodward, Lionel D. *Une anglaise amie de la Révolution française: Hélène-Maria Williams et ses amis* (Paris: Librairie Ancienne Honore Champion, 1930).

Yuval-Davis, Nira, *Gender and Nation* (London: Sage, 1997).

Index

CAMBRIDGE STUDIES IN ROMANTICISM

General editors
MARILYN BUTLER *University of Oxford*
JAMES CHANDLER *University of Chicago*